The
PRS
GUITAR
BOOK

DAVE BURRLUCK

FOREWORD BY TOM WHEELER

THE PRS GUITAR BOOK

A Complete History Of Paul Reed Smith Guitars

BY DAVE BURRLUCK

A BACKBEAT BOOK

This new third edition 2007

First edition 1999; second edition 2002

Published by Backbeat Books (an imprint of Hal Leonard Corporation)

19 West 21st Street, New York, NY 10010, USA

www.backbeatbooks.com

Devised and produced for Backbeat Books by Outline Press Ltd

2A Union Court, 20-22 Union Road, London SW4 6JP, England

www.backbeatuk.com

ISBN: 978-0-87930-898-8

PRS SC 245 (2007)

CREATIVE DIRECTOR: NIGEL OSBORNE

EDITOR: TONY BACON, PETE CHRISP

DESIGN: SALLY STOCKWELL, PAUL COOPER

GUITAR PHOTOGRAPHY: MIKI SLINGSBY, MARC QUIGLEY

Origination and print by Colorprint (Hong Kong)

07 08 09 10 11 5 4 3 2 1

CONTENTS

FOREWORD BY TOM WHEELER

University of Oregon journalism professor Tom Wheeler is the former Editor-in-Chief of Guitar Player magazine, host of the American Guitar video series, and the author of The Guitar Book and American Guitars. He co-edited Richard Smith's Fender: The Sound Heard 'round The World, and contributed several chapters to Walter Carter's Gibson Guitars: 100 Years of an American Icon and to Balafon's Classic Guitars Of The Fifties and Classic Guitars Of The Sixties, as well as a dozen other books on guitar history.

Paul Reed Smith turned around and handed me a violin. "Hey, Tom," he said casually, "want to hold a Stradivarius?" Fellow participants at a guitar event at the Smithsonian in Washington DC, we were being given a private peek at some of the Institution's rarest instruments. It was revealing for me to examine the historic violin in the company of an acclaimed guitar builder. Although Paul treated the priceless treasure with all due reverence, I was struck by how matter-of-fact he was, looking through the soundholes and underneath the tailpiece, his gaze fixed as he commented on the ageing of the finish and the compound curve of the top. It might've sounded odd coming from someone less prone to questioning, but when Paul arched an eyebrow and observed that Stradivari "really knew what he was doing", I knew it reflected a depth of appreciation that could only come from a person who has spent his adult life working with his hands to make wood sing.

The Stradivarius wasn't the only masterpiece to have come under the fierce scrutiny of Paul Reed Smith, whom guitarist Howard Leese once called "the American Stradivari of the electric guitar". To this day Paul can remember the feel of the neck on a '57 Les Paul Junior he once held two decades ago, and the way the individual notes would ring when he strummed a chord through a particular P-90 pickup on a '53 Les Paul gold-top. For years before he gained worldwide esteem for his own guitars, discriminating players would entrust to him their prized instruments in need of repairs. "I spent a lot of time just holding those guitars," Paul says, "listening to what those players told me and, in a way, listening to what their guitars told me. I listened very deeply to the front pickup on a great old Strat. I played amazing Les Pauls from the 1950s - gold-tops, sunbursts, Juniors, Customs. Those were beloved instruments, holy grails. There was something very real about them, and I learned from every single one."

In fact, if you ask Paul about the key factor in his success, he'll acknowledge his own instincts and determination, but then he'll talk at length about his teachers. "My woodshop teachers, guitar players, builders – I spent hundreds of hours in the presence of these people, and in every case I was thinking, 'Teach me, teach me, teach me.'"

Chief among Paul's teachers is his mentor, Ted McCarty, the person to whom Gibson owes its modern golden age and the namesake of a whole series of popular PRS models. Paul has told me that Ted McCarty's life and wisdom provide lessons in being a man, in growing old with dignity and wit – and, to be sure, in building guitars. "There was nothing I didn't ask him," says Paul, "and he's been generous with his knowledge. No one had ever asked him this stuff. Everyone else wanted to know about the Moderne [a legendary prototype] or something, but I wanted to know about woods – which part of the tree? Which way do you saw it? I asked him about glues, jigs, fixtures, tooling, fret wire, injection machines, sanding – what grit did you use? Finishes, hardware, pickups – what gauge of wire? How many turns? He told me everything. He basically downloaded the hard drive."

Paul Smith learned his lessons well, if my inch-thick stack of PRS product reviews is any indication. They are written in several languages, but they all say the same thing: PRS guitars are among the best electrics the world has ever seen.

But why? Ted McCarty was indirectly or directly responsible for the various Les Pauls, The Flying V, the Explorer, the ES-335 and other classics, not to mention the humbucking pickup and Tune-o-matic bridge. Leo Fender, of course, designed the Telecaster and Stratocaster, to name only two Fender milestones. Didn't McCarty and Fender and their collaborators perfect the electric guitar four decades ago? Paul Smith might be the first person to say yes, because he still strives to produce a new guitar that equals the very best of the vintage classics.

And yet many observers think he's already there. No less seasoned a veteran than Hartley Peavey once told me, "Paul Reed Smith builds a better guitar than Gibson ever made on its best day." Although genuinely touched by the compliment, Paul wouldn't agree with it, not so much out of modesty but rather, I suspect, because he sees himself only midway along his journey of discovery and craft.

Still, he has already satisfied some of the guitar community's toughest customers, as evidenced a decade ago at one of the big expos in Texas. Guitar buffs had come from all over the world to buy, to sell, or simply to ogle the riches of America's guitar heritage. On display were thousands of treasures, from a pristine late-1930s Super 400 with its tag still dangling from a tuning key to a black-guard Tele that only recently had been pulled down from the attic in Georgia where its teenage owner had stashed it when he went off to war in Korea.

Some of the traders who'd come to Texas that summer had learned the game dealing out of their car trunks at parking-lot get-togethers long before founding music stores. To them, the golden era had withered in the mid 1960s, about the time Leo Fender sold out to CBS and Ted McCarty left Gibson. New guitars could hardly compare to the small-headstock Strats and TV-finish Les Paul Specials they'd grown up with. New guitars were pale ghosts of glories past, painful reminders that the great companies we all loved had long ago lost their way.

And yet judging by the displays at the Texas show, one brand of new guitars had been accepted even by flint-eyed vintage die-hards. In booth after booth, alongside vine-inlaid Epiphones from the Jazz Age and oven-knob Rickenbackers right out of A Hard Day's Night, I saw new solidbodies built not by any legendary figure but by a young man most of us hardly knew. What was so remarkable was not that these PRS guitars were beautiful – after all, I was in a vast arena gleaming with opulence in blonde and butterscotch and

Burgundy Mist. No, what struck me was how right these bird-marker newcomers looked among the mainstays of the guitar's storied past. They were unlike anything I'd ever seen, yet somehow... familiar.

Paul Reed Smith had first come to my attention when I was Editor-in-Chief of Guitar Player magazine. One of his customers called to rave about new guitars that supposedly combined the best of Fender and Gibson. "Oh great," I thought, "another Strat clone fitted with humbuckings." But when I saw the guitars, and held them, I understood that the new guy, whoever he was, was on to something much more profound. These were no mixed-feature platypuses suggested by some corporate committee but rather the handiwork of a deeply insightful craftsman who had absorbed to his very marrow the essence of the modern electric guitar and reinterpreted it for a new era.

As any player who reveres his or her instrument can tell you, there's something about a great guitar, some ineffable mojo, that lies beyond tone and feel and looks. Guitar Player said the PRS McCarty "may be the quintessential humbucker-equipped solidbody". After finding familiar definitions of "quintessential" in the dictionary (the most perfect manifestation; the essence in its highest and purest form), I found some extra words that may resonate with PRS owners: "of the substance composing the celestial bodies". If it's true, as Paul says, that sometimes when you build a guitar a little piece of God shows up, then I think it's fair to say that God must be on reasonably good terms with Paul and his builders at the PRS factory, for He seems to show up there with some regularity.

Paul Reed Smith still manages to introduce innovation after innovation while drawing deep from the well of American guitar aesthetics, not because he copies his heroes but because he is driven by the same passions that long ago motivated them to take what had been considered merely an amplified acoustic guitar and transfigure it into a new instrument of stunning range and impact.

Leo Fender, Ted McCarty, Paul Bigsby, Doc Kauffman, Paul Barth, George Beauchamp, Les Paul – some ran big companies and some worked in cramped shops, some played guitar and some didn't, but they were all screwdriver-and-blueprint guys, builders, doers. Each was driven by a fascination for how things work, a gnawing suspicion that guitars could perform a bit better (maybe a lot better), and a confidence that he himself had the imagination and the raw mechanical chops to pull it off. This same passion stoked the creative fire in the belly of Paul Smith when he and his lone assistant worked out of a tiny attic, and it motivates him today as one of the world's leading manufacturers.

Leo Fender once explained to me, "Many companies are run by people who are principally executives. Often, an executive is not adapted to the machinery end of the business. Maybe I came in through the back door." Paul

Smith came through that same door, the one that leads to the workbench with the fret files and the dovetail saws. Although he spends fewer days now with sawdust up to his elbows and is assisted by skilled collaborators, he is still the dominant creative force in PRS, and I think that's one reason why he has been able to succeed in the commercial mainstream while at the same time appealing to various elites such as vintage purists and rock stars.

People who know him far better than I can tell you more about what kind of person he is, but I can offer an observation or two. To quote Leo Fender again, "As far back as I can remember, I always had tools around. I like tools. Always have." That sounds like the Paul Smith I know.

People who work for him describe him with various adjectives, most of them synonyms for "intense". When necessary he can sharpen his focus into a laser beam of concentration. He's the kind of person who can dig into a project at midnight and never notice the sun coming up outside the window.

To say he has high standards only begins to explain the expectations he places upon everyone who works for him, most of all upon himself. A body design isn't good enough until it's "burnin' good!". A pickup's not good enough until it "sounds like God!". A neck doesn't play smoothly enough until it's... "forget about it!".

If PRS instruments have been celebrated by players the world over, Paul himself remains his own sternest critic. Surprisingly, he's not that impressed with past accomplishments. "They're not perfect," he says bluntly of existing PRS guitars. More than the satisfaction of reading positive product reviews or profit statements, it's the joy of learning that gets his juices flowing. Get him talking about what Dickey Betts' gold-top revealed about the effect of fret height on the way notes ring out on the treble strings, and you'll hear his voice accelerate through the gears like his beloved Corvette.

It's not the past that excites Paul Reed Smith. Get him talking about tomorrow, about the designs that exist in his patent drawings or in his imagination, and he revs up from sober practicality to the same breathless abandon that once inspired him to enrol in three high-school shop classes at the same time. The models in the current line are all well and good, but prototypes – that's where the action is.

"We're experimenting with new pickups," he gushes. "We're discovering things about finishes all the time. We're going to be substituting some different metals, and when we get the combination of all these things just right, forget about it! It's going to be such a leap forward! You won't be able to get near these guitars, they'll be so cool!"

When I point out the worldwide chorus of praise for the guitars his factory has been producing for a decade and a half, he explains patiently, "Yeah, but see, we're just starting to hit our stride."

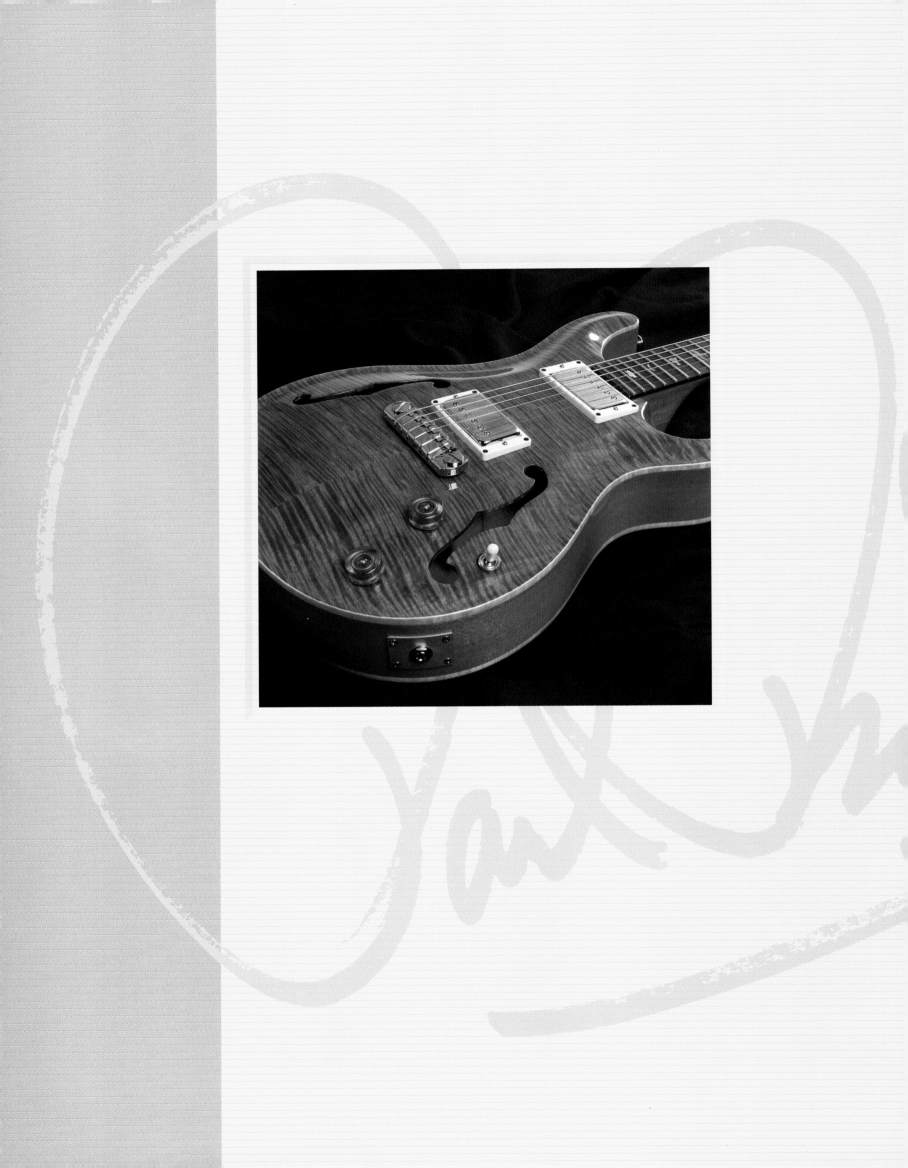

PART ONE: THE EARLY YEARS

Not many 24-year-old budding guitar-makers are commissioned to build a working instrument for their hero. Paul Reed Smith was to prove an exception. He had always dreamed of making a guitar for Carlos Santana, and was convinced that if he could just reach the great guitarist and build him an instrument, then he really would be able to make it as a guitar-maker. But Smith was not going to settle for a mere dream. He wanted something much more tangible.

His story started in 1956, February 18th to be precise. Paul Reed Smith was born in Bethesda, Maryland, on the outskirts of Washington DC, the son of Ernestine and Jack W Smith. He grew up with three brothers and a sister.

When Paul's father was young he was a big-band leader, though he gave it up to be a mathematician. "He loves music," maintains Paul today, "and he bought me a ukulele when I was four years old – I even knew a couple of chords. When The Beatles first came out my mother was one of the first people to buy their music. She used to play guitar and sing and my father encouraged us all. My mother had a Hi-Lo classical guitar and I remember trying to play 'Day Tripper' on it when I was about 12 or 13, in the seventh grade at junior high school. But the first thing I really played was bass. We used to play things like 'Proud Mary' during the eighth grade." Evidently Smith was keen on his music, and played bass then guitar in numerous short-lived bands during high school.

Like so many teenagers, Paul Reed Smith found that rock'n'roll and the electric guitar provided an escape and a way to gain confidence during those difficult years. "I decided to buy an electric guitar. I found out about a Telecaster for $140 at a local music store, Veneman Music, but when I got there it was gone. It broke my heart. I'd saved all my money washing cars and stuff – I guess I was in the ninth grade, 14 years old or something. So I found a three-quarter-size Gibson Melody Maker, the guy wanted 140 bucks and I bought it. I remember my mom asking was I happier now, and I said, 'Yeah, kind of.' I'd decided that guitar was my way out."

With the type of focused, almost obsessive dedication that would surprise many colleagues later, Smith set about improving his new-found voice. "I'd heard a guitar player in town, Rob Izzi. He had a beautiful vibrato and I decided that if I could get that it would be *the* sound. It took me about three weeks, but I got it. I couldn't play anything else but I could lay into a note. I still have that, it's in your wrist." Smith's interest in music and bands was growing. Now he had a direction.

Paul Reed Smith (above) in the summer of 1975 with one of his early "apprentice" pieces, an all-mahogany double-cutaway electric based on the style of Gibson's post-1958 Les Paul Special.

PAUL REED SMITH: THE EARLY YEARS

The teenage Paul Reed Smith quickly became absorbed in music. "I was in loads of bands, but I never had the intensity of guys like Clapton and Van Halen," he recalls. "Our first few gigs would stink before we'd get it together. But by the time I was 17 or 18 I used to go and sit in with bands in Washington DC at The Bayou club and guys would take me under their wing."

Smith's father once described him as "an enthusiastic kid, but it wasn't until he got into the guitar business that his creativity began to show up". Smith had started getting interested in building instruments in wood shop toward the end of senior high school, around 1972. "The first instrument I made was a bass," he remembers. "I bought a Japanese copy of a Hofner Beatle bass, took the neck off it and made a new body. I was around 16 at the time." What he now calls the "dyslexic Strat" body of this initial instrument hints little at Smith's future design skills, yet the first piece of the foundation was in place.

"I'd figured it out that I could work on guitars, and somehow I finagled a job at Washington Music Center as a

repairman," Smith continues. "I had repaired a three-quarter-size Les Paul Junior for a friend, and the guy at the store was interested in that when I showed him. He gave me a job. So I went back to school and said I've got enough credits that I want to be let off school half-days, and they agreed. I made all the arrangements.

"It was during the gas crisis of the early 1970s, and I remember sitting in the line all the previous day trying to get some gas for my car. Eventually I got some and headed to my first day. Someone stopped in front of me and I slammed into the back of them and had a car accident, the morning before I started my job. I called my parents – my father was not pleased – but I said I've got to get to this job, I'll deal with the car stuff later but I've got to get to the job. So they took me. I walked into Washington Music

Although a cursory glance might indicate that the guitar which Smith built for Peter Frampton in 1976 is largely in the style of a Les Paul double-cutaway instrument, there are in fact numerous significant differences. Primary among these is the use of a 24-fret fingerboard. The back view (right) also reveals that, despite the guitar's Badass wrapover-type bridge, the strings in fact pass through the body, with the anchor points clearly visible here.

This inscription on the back of Frampton's guitar is a rarity on Smith's pre-factory instruments. In fact, a friend wrote it. Smith's signature did eventually find its way onto his guitars though he admitted it took hundreds of attempts before he was happy with one from which the famous decal was made that adorned his production guitars from 1985.

▲ **PAUL REED SMITH**

GUITAR FOR PETER FRAMPTON

MADE IN: *1976*

The second guitar from West Street was this spectacular all-mahogany instrument, still in a Les Paul double-cutaway style, but with a carved top, recessed Badass bridge, master volume and tone with three-way pickup selector, and a 24-fret Brazilian rosewood fingerboard.

the headstock came from a different source. "I bought a shirt locally that had a picture of an eagle landing on it. I put the shirt on the Xerox machine: the bird that is on our headstock is literally that one. It came off that shirt. The one on the Frampton headstock is hand-drawn. It wasn't as good as it is now – I couldn't draw it very well by hand."

In May 1976 Smith went to a gig featuring Return To Forever and Santana at Capital Center where he hoped to show Carlos Santana the guitar he'd made for Frampton. He was beginning to develop a system. "I'd show the roadies the guitars. They'd spend half an hour with me checking 'em out and if they dug them and decided that I'm cool and I'm not going to kill their artist then they'd give me backstage passes. That's how I always get in."

An apparently affable roadie said he'd show Santana the guitar. But Return To Forever's roadies liked the guitar so much they insisted he show it personally to the band's guitarist, Al DiMeola. He was impressed, too – enough to immediately order an electric 12-string with a built-in phase shifter, a guitar DiMeola would later use on the title

cut of his 1977 solo album *Elegant Gypsy*. At the time, DiMeola said: "I personally feel that [Smith] has the ability to custom-make the guitar of anyone's dreams."

Eventually, Smith also got to show the Frampton guitar to Carlos Santana at that Capital Center gig, and the two jammed together backstage. "Santana said the guitar had a lot of love in it," Smith recalled, "but he decided not to buy one because he was ready to endorse another line of guitars." Not a bad night's work, however: Smith had a commission from Al DiMeola, and had played with his hero, Carlos Santana. Jane Armiger, Billy's sister, remembers that night well. "Paul came around and woke us up to tell us his news. It was 5am! He was really wired."

By mid 1977 Smith had built only 17 guitars, including basses and a double-neck, yet his client list boasted Ted Nugent (plus his guitarist Derek St Holmes), Peter Frampton (plus his bass player Stanley Sheldon), Al DiMeola, and Bruce Springsteen's bassist Gary Tallent. Smith had also made instruments for local bands Happy

Smith backstage (above) at a local concert venue in the mid 1970s with the solidbody Byrdland-style guitar he built for Ted Nugent. It was the first guitar he made at the West Street, Annapolis, workshop and is still owned today by Nugent.

The Man (Stan Whitaker's double-neck) and Artful Dodger. It was at this time that Smith formed a shortlived but productive partnership with Steve Hildebrand, a local craftsman. Bonni Lloyd then joined the pair. She had met Smith at St Mary's College. "Toward the end of 1976 Paul called me and asked if I could help out," Lloyd recalls. "I played guitar but knew nothing about making them. I thought I was going to help with admin, but I learned inlay and sanding. I became known as Sanderella. Steve Hildebrand was a very good cabinet-maker and boat-builder, a really fine woodworker. I learned a lot from Steve."

No doubt Smith learned from Hildebrand too – and very quickly. "Paul was like a sponge," Lloyd remembers. Smith and Hildebrand parted company after about a year together, leaving Lloyd as Smith's only assistant. "We'd do a ton of repair work – that was the bread and butter," she says. "But money was really tight. We used to sit and wait for someone to come in needing a set-up so we could get

lunch." Smith too recalled the hardships of this time, and how it proved almost impossible to survive as an independent luthier. The repair work took up more and more time. "I have to fight to get the money I need," Smith told a reporter in the late 1970s. "I haven't bought new clothes for a year."

Initially Smith worked and slept in an impossibly small attic at 33 West Street in Annapolis. Later he rented half and then all of an additional building at the back of West Street, and slept upstairs. "That shop out back was really small," remembers Lloyd. "It had one big long bench, one smaller, and a bandsaw at the back. It was really cold in winter and in summer it sweltered. But we had a stream of people coming in. One day [pickup-maker] Seymour Duncan came in and hung out. I'd often answer the phone: 'Hello, rock'n'roll rumour control.' We knew everything that was going on."

In May 1978 Smith completed an instrument for guitarist Roy Buchanan. "Paul and I talked to him about what he wanted," recalls Lloyd. "We asked if he wanted an

The view (below) into the rear cavity of a later guitar reveals a John Mann-made PRS vibrato – note the wording on the block.

Smith began to work with numerous collaborators as the workload at the West Street premises increased towards the end of the 1970s. John Mann (left) originally came to Smith needing a guitar repaired. An engineer by trade, he ended up helping with the design and manufacture of the PRS vibrato, as well as several other of the parts and hardware that would be needed by the fledgling guitar-making operation.

Smith's original partner was Steve Hildebrand, seen here (right) during a session at the guitar-making workshop in West Street, Annapolis. By all accounts, it seems that Hildebrand was a fine cabinet-maker who no doubt encouraged and helped Smith to hone his wood-working skills.

▲ **PAUL REED SMITH**

FIRST GUITAR WITH DRAGON INLAY

MADE IN: *c1979*

Here is another early all-mahogany guitar, with fabulously figured body. This example has much more pronounced arching to the body top, and is beginnning to move further toward the coming style of the production PRS guitars. Smith gigged this guitar

for many years. Along with the first-ever inlay of a dragon design on a Smith guitar, it has a retrofitted bridge humbucker that proved to be the prototype for PRS's later Deep Dish pickup. Also worthy of attention here is the instrument's simplified control layout that features two mini-switches for manipulation of the twin pickups – a set-up that would later prove attractive to Carlos Santana.

eagle inlay. He had that, but also asked if we could put his wife's name, Judy, on the headstock. I inlaid that. He was a sweet guy."

Not all custom-making and repair work was for professionals. John Mann first met Smith in late 1978. "I had been given an old Gibson SG and a Fender Princeton amp as a wedding gift," Mann remembers. "Someone had really trashed the SG. I tried to work on it. I re-finished it a couple of times but it just looked worse. My cousin who'd given me the guitar said there's this guy in Annapolis – you should meet him. Well, that guy was Paul, and he re-did the guitar. When I picked it up it looked just like it had come from the Gibson factory."

At the time Mann worked in the manufacturing shop at Westinghouse, a large engineering factory for the Navy on the outskirts of Annapolis near to the Chesapeake Bay Bridge. Smith thought that he and Mann might well be able to work on a few projects together – and he was right. Mann went on to help Smith design and machine the PRS vibrato bridge and make the majority of the hardware for

the production PRS guitars until the early 1990s. Despite his rising local reputation as a guitar-maker and repairman, Smith began to realise that his romantic vision of the craftsman in the workshop belied the reality. He couldn't make a living this way. So for about eight months at the end of 1978 and into 1979 he took a job as a repairman at Veneman Music in Rockville, to the north-west of Washington DC.

This marked the end of Bonni Lloyd's first stint with Smith – she would re-join PRS Guitars in 1986, staying until the mid 1990s. But Lloyd remembers the early days affectionately. "It was the best job I ever had. We would start around 11am. Paul was impossible to wake up – the opposite of now. I'd put on the coffee and bang on his room. He'd come down and we'd work till 10 or 11pm at night. We'd go to the pub or go to a gig – there were always musicians around." The job at Veneman Music was curtailed after Smith was dismissed for trying to sell his own hand-made guitars to the store's customers. So in 1979 he went back to Annapolis and started to crank up

Roy Buchanan was best known for his work using a Fender Telecaster, but the guitarist custom-ordered this guitar which

was completed by Smith in May 1978. As well as the usual headstock eagle, Buchanan's wife Judy's name is also inlaid there.

▼ **PAUL REED SMITH**

DOUBLE-NECK GUITAR

MADE IN: *c1980*

Along with regular six-string guitars, Smith had made double-neck instruments and basses almost from the beginning. This example was John Ingram's

"apprentice" piece, christened Big for obvious reasons. Note the new outline for the headstocks (see page 35). Reflecting the hard times facing Smith and Ingram, John sold the guitar to Journey's Neal Schon (seen with Big, right). Ex-Santana guitarist Schon had earlier ordered from Smith a maple-top six-string in the Santana style.

the guitar business again. During that brief "sabbatical" Smith had met up with John Ingram (aka Orkie) who was to become his new assistant. "I first heard about Paul around 1977 through a local band that I was infatuated with, Happy The Man," recalls Ingram, who today looks after orders and set-ups for artists at PRS. "Their guitarist Stan Whitaker had this double-neck, the first one Paul had made around 1976/77, and Rick Kennel had a bass. Their music was great and the guitars caught my attention. Stan gave me Paul's business card in 1978 so I went to see him at Veneman Music. There was this highly-strung, intense, nervous guy with big hair, working on a guitar. I just introduced myself and he showed me a guitar that he'd built. Paul was pretty unique, ahead of his time in terms of hand-making guitars, especially for major artists like Nugent and Frampton."

Certainly small custom-makers of electric guitars were rarer in late-1970s America than now. Some limited-production companies like Hamer in Wisconsin were by then offering a line of definite models while still emphasising hand-crafting. The industry relied primarily on the output of the Big Two, Fender and Gibson, although both had quality problems at the time. This had led some players to seek older "vintage" instruments, while numerous companies had sprung up selling new spare-parts as individual replacements or even for assembling at home into entire kit-style instruments.

Meanwhile, John Ingram's visits to Annapolis to hang out with Smith and soak up the local music scene became more frequent, even though he worked out of town. "Eventually," says Ingram, "in March 1980 Paul sat me down and said, 'You spend every weekend here. Why don't you move down, work in my shop, find an inexpensive place to live? I can't really pay, but I can use some help.' I knew I wasn't cut out to be a maintenance man at Gettysburg College for the rest of my days, so Paul moved me down in this godawful van he had – which eventually caught fire." Ingram found a place to live at 1207 Poplar Avenue. Smith also moved in there, at the same time as he

This (right) is where it all started. A familiar sight for struggling guitar builders, the cramped ground-floor workshop at West Street, Annapolis, is where Paul Reed Smith, Steve Hildebrand, Bonni Lloyd and later John Ingram hand-built all the original Smith instruments. It's ironic to note that, with the introduction of PRS's Private Stock guitars in the late 1990s, something of the flavour of these creative early days has been replicated in an attempt to offer

customers a real one-off service again. Back in the 1970s and early 1980s it would have been the workshop in Annapolis where local musicians visited to have their instruments serviced and repaired... and maybe even to order a custom instrument. If they did, it's interesting to speculate how many could have guessed that their original investment would have rocketed in value, as today these "pre-factory" guitars have become highly collectable items.

Smith is pictured (right) in the attic workshop at West Street that at one time doubled as his bedroom. He is holding the nearly-completed maple-top guitar that he was building for Carlos Santana (see pages 20/21 for the result). It was around this time that Smith began to investigate the sonic and constructional potential for instruments that featured maple tops on his customary mahogany bodies.

---

was renting the old attic in West Street as a workspace.

Just before Ingram became Smith's assistant, Smith had made his first guitar to feature an arched top made from curly maple. The use of this highly-patterned, attractive timber – also called figured or flame maple – was another distinct feature that would prove to be of fundamental importance when Smith launched PRS guitars in 1985. Up to that point Smith's guitars were made of mahogany, of sound construction and aimed at the working musician. But by making a maple-top guitar, Smith summoned visions of the hallowed Gibson Les Paul models made between 1958 and 1960. With their often extravagantly curly-maple sunburst arched tops, these instruments are felt by many to be the most beautiful and collectable electric guitars ever, both for their sound and appearance. By using maple tops, Smith would significantly widen the market for his guitars. Smith's friend Kevin Whisman had a particularly attractive

piece of furniture at this time, a wooden dresser that had curly maple drawer fronts. "I asked him if I could have the maple," remembers Smith, "and his mom said sure – she hated curly maple." No doubt seeing a flame-top Les Paul instead of a fancy drawer front, Smith replaced the figured wood with plainer cherry, stashed the curly maple and gave the dresser back.

The first guitar to use these dresser-drawer fronts was the first PRS maple-top guitar. It was made for Jeff Adams, who played in a local band called Face Dancer. "He ended up getting into money trouble," says Smith, "so he sold it back to me and I sold it to Howard Leese of Heart. Howard bought it from a Polaroid I sent him." The Golden Eagle, as Leese dubbed it, cost him $2,000 – a considerable amount for an electric guitar from an unknown maker – and became Leese's number-one guitar for some 15 years. "That guitar has been on records that have sold millions," says Leese, "so I guess it was

A quartet of early-1980s hand-made guitars by Smith is gathered together here (inset, left) for an impressive studio shot. The more expensive maple-top guitar and bass (far left and second right) are lined up alongside a plainer all-mahogany guitar and a fretless bass. This mix of mahogany-only and maple-top instruments continues at PRS to this day.

▼ PAUL REED SMITH

MAHOGANY GUITAR

MADE IN: *c1982*

This early-1980s all-mahogany guitar was one of the first from the West Street workshop to feature the new PRS Vibrato system (the arm is absent here), by now with *the addition of screw-down locking tuners. Note too the intentionally uncovered rear vibrato cavity (seen on the back, above). The instrument boasts spectacular figure on the one-piece mahogany body, and handsome decorative inlay around the join between the neck and the fingerboard (just behind the neck pickup).*

It is not only guitar tops that have been graced by the decorative qualities of curly maple, as much high-quality American furniture also benefits from the timber. It was from such a piece that the tops for the first of Smith's maple-top guitars were drawn.

worth what I paid." It's now a priceless piece. When offered a substantial amount for it in the mid 1990s, Leese refused to sell. "I still use the Golden Eagle, though now it's just for recording. It is, after all, the first curly-maple-top PRS guitar."

Heart's Nancy Wilson bought a 12-string from Smith while Leese waited for his second guitar – this one would have a single bridge-position humbucker. Smith still proudly displays in his scrapbook a photocopy of a cheque for $2,000 dated June 24th 1980 for that guitar and, although it's rarely been used by Leese and remains in pristine condition, it was the guitar that helped to hook Carlos Santana – of which more shortly.

Again, this sale to a prominent artist provided excellent PR. Heart were a hugely successful band during the 1980s, and in numerous magazine interviews Leese extolled the virtues of the instrument. He told one interviewer that Smith was a real perfectionist. "He's like one of those mad inventors who's always trying to figure out a new way," said Leese. "You wouldn't be surprised to

see him in a lab coat, with the [vacuum-testing] tesla coils going. He'd bring [me] a piece of wood – not a finished guitar – and a jar of acetone, because you can't really see the wood grain when it's dry. He'd say, 'What do you think of this for a top?' And he'd wipe it with the acetone to bring out the grain." Leese remains an ambassador for PRS to this day. "The thing that's never changed is the quality. To me Paul is the American Stradivari of the electric guitar."

Nancy Wilson's 12-string cost her $900. Larry Urie – then a local musician, today National Sales Manager at PRS Guitars – remembers the story. "We went to a Heart concert at Capital Center. Paul wanted to take some guitars and persuaded me to tag along. At this point Leese already had one guitar and I took an eight-string bass over that Paul had built for a friend, Rob Cherney, just to show to the band. And there was a neat 12-string that Paul had made. That 12-string is the one Nancy Wilson bought after we showed it to her. It didn't have the dragon on the body at the time – she said she'd buy it if Paul put a dragon on

Howard Leese, guitarist with Heart, is pictured (right, alongside the group's Nancy Wilson) with the very first curly-maple-top Smith guitar, which makes it a valuable guitar indeed. Leese called his new guitar the Golden Eagle, and has used it on countless Heart records and tours over the years. It was a photograph of this instrument in Smith's scrapbook that would later help to persuade Carlos Santana to order an instrument from the guitar-maker. The maple-top instrument didn't only impress other guitarists, however. Heart's highly experienced producer Keith Olsen, who also worked with Fleetwood Mac and the Grateful Dead, once remarked to Leese that it was probably the best-sounding guitar he'd ever heard.

it like the one on Paul's own guitar. So that was done." Just as with the bird inlays and arched curly-maple tops that became so important to the PRS image, the dragon theme – which Smith was to revisit spectacularly in the 1990s – was another product of this late-1970s/early-1980s period. But the idea went back further. "When I was a kid I had a sign on my wall that said Les Paul Custom Dragon," Smith recounted later, "and when I was 16 I knew I wanted to make a Dragon guitar, even though at that time I had no idea there'd be anything called a Paul Reed Smith Dragon."

While the 1980s brought Smith new high-profile customers, behind the scenes he was collecting people who were to become instrumental in his future success. "I met Eric Pritchard in 1980," says Smith, "and he began to teach me how to be a machinist. He showed me how to measure in thousandths of an inch, not 32nds. I still think in 32nds: the top on our guitars is still $^{26}\!/_{32}$" thick; I never thought $^{13}\!/_{16}$". But I was a good student and learned a lot. Eric still does engineering for us and he was responsible

for building the machinery to start the factory. And before the factory, he would create things like the dupli-carver [designed to carve body tops] and made a joiner, a planer and a few other machines."

Smith's apparent chance meetings with people, professionally or personally, often turned out to have profound effects on his destiny. Eric Pritchard, John Ingram and John Mann helped him to further his art. Ex-girlfriend Jude Van Dyke, with whom Smith also had a musical relationship in the late 1970s in bands like Kite and Jude, went on to design the Dragon I fingerboard inlay. More importantly, by late 1980 Smith had met his future wife Barbara who was to have a major impact on the impending success of PRS guitars.

Ever since Smith was 19 he had dreamed of crafting a guitar for Carlos Santana. "I figured if I could build Carlos a guitar I'd be made," he says. Although Smith had already met Santana and shown him the Frampton guitar, it was the dresser-drawer maple that eventually hooked the guitarist. But it so nearly didn't happen. In the fall of 1980

When Smith showed a one-pickup all-mahogany 12-string (below) to Heart guitarist Nancy Wilson, he happened to have his own dragon-inlaid guitar with him (see pages

14/15). Once she saw the dragon, Wilson insisted Smith took the 12-string back and sell it to her only when a dragon had been added.

Once Carlos Santana bought a guitar from Smith (the two are seen together, left) he was not short of praise for the instruments. "To me, the sound of guitars is like colours," Santana said once. "With some you get just green and yellow; this guitar is like the full rainbow."

Smith went to a Santana gig at the Merriweather Post Pavilion in Columbia, midway between Washington DC and Baltimore. "I go in and show a guitar to Carlos's roadie, John Gabrielli," Smith remembers. "He says that Carlos won't see me, but I show him my mahogany guitar with the dragon inlay and P-90 pickups. He takes it in. The guitar is going to do the talking for me, it's my only shot. About five minutes later the roadie comes out and beckons me in. There's Carlos sitting down and playing my guitar, and every note he's playing is feeding back – that's Carlos's thing. 'This is great,' Carlos says to me. 'Can I play it tonight?' Sure, I say.

"He starts to look through my scrapbook that I have with me. He comes across the curly-maple-top Howard Leese guitar and says, 'That's what I want.' Then, the crew almost grab me by the scruff of the neck to throw me out because it's time for Carlos to meditate. But Carlos says, 'No, let him stay.' So, he doesn't meditate but talks to me all the time, gives me his home phone number and we

agree on building him a guitar. As usual the deal is if he doesn't fall in love he doesn't have to buy it.

"So Carlos goes out and plays my dragon guitar... but it isn't happening. With the P-90s and his rig it just isn't working. He changes the guitar immediately. He comes off stage feeling bad. He's given me his number, he's made a deal. 'Carlos, it's the pickups,' I explain. 'I'll send you some pickups, it's not the guitar.' Eventually he agrees – and has the elegance not to ask for his phone number back."

Smith headed home to his workshop and called Howard Leese. Leese was due to send his single-pickup guitar back for some maintenance, so Smith persuaded him to send it via Santana, who at the time had started to record the *Zebop!* album. The guitar arrived at Santana's recording studio... in a locked and unopenable case.

"They called Howard but couldn't get to him," Smith continues. "The guitar sat there for two days and all Carlos knew was that whatever was in that case he wanted. John Gabrielli swears to this day that the combination for the case lock just came to him: he simply dialled it in and it

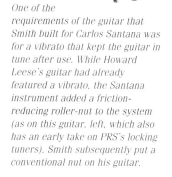

▼ **PAUL REED SMITH**

GUITAR FOR CARLOS SANTANA

MADE IN: *1980*

This is the first guitar that Smith built for Carlos Santana (right), and he used it on the road and in the studio for many years. It was only Smith's third maple-top guitar, virtually identical to that made for Howard Leese (page 19). The control layout with two mini-switches was designed for more flexible switching of two P-90 pickups, but Santana wanted them – even though a three-way toggle would have done the same job.

Unusually for a Smith-made instrument, the back of the guitar built for Carlos Santana (pictured above) has a backplate fitted over the vibrato cavity. The explanation is that the plate was added at the workshop to hide a small cosmetic mistake that Smith had made during the guitar's contruction.

One of the requirements of the guitar that Smith built for Carlos Santana was for a vibrato that kept the guitar in tune after use. While Howard Leese's guitar had already featured a vibrato, the Santana instrument added a friction-reducing roller-nut to the system (as on this guitar, left, which also has an early take on PRS's locking tuners). Smith subsequently put a conventional nut on his guitar.

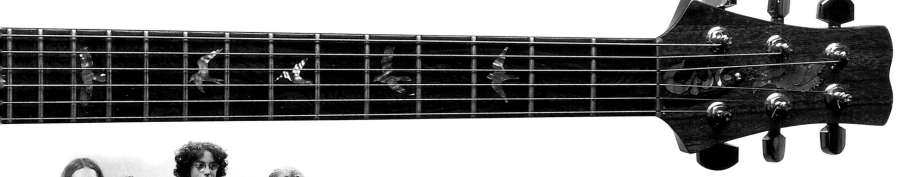

Although Smith was during the early 1980s becoming a highly respected maker of custom guitars and a noted guitar-repairer, he clung to an early aspiration to be a musician. He played in several bands, including Kite (pictured left). It wasn't until 1984 that

Smith decided to devote his professional time solely to guitars, although he still manages today to play in his group, The Dragons. It will probably come as no surprise to readers to learn that at the time of writing Smith uses his amber Dragon (page 71) for the purpose.

opened. He swears to god that's a true story. So John got Howard's guitar out. Carlos plugged it in and immediately started recording the album with it. They even opened the guitar up and because there was a capacitor on the volume control they figured the reason it sounded so good was because of that. I said, 'Er, no.'

"Anyway, they called me up and said I couldn't have Howard's guitar back. I said it's not my guitar. They said Carlos is having the guitar, forget about it, it's over. I said I'd call Howard to see if they could borrow the guitar and I'd build Carlos another." In the end, that's what happened. In discussing the specification of his new guitar Santana insisted on having a vibrato that stayed in tune. Smith remembers: "I said, 'How about a Floyd Rose?' He said no. I said OK, I'll put a vibrato on it that won't go out of tune, and he said great. I hung up the phone and said to myself, 'How the fuck am I going to do that?' Anyway, I went off to build him the guitar he used for a very, very long time." Aside from the fact that Smith was at last making a guitar for one of his major idols, the in-tune vibrato was yet

another challenge that would become a major selling point of the production PRS guitars. "Carlos's guitar took one month to make," Smith reported. He used all the methods he knew to make the vibrato stay in tune, including the installation of a roller-nut, locking tuners and a modified Stars Guitars brass bridge. "So... it's all done, and it really sounds magical."

"It fed back on every note – Seymour Duncan made me the pickups for it. We sent it off in the middle of November 1980... and I don't hear back for three days. Eventually I called John Gabrielli and asked if Carlos liked the guitar. He said, 'I'm not sure. He's willing to send the other one back, so that's a good sign. But I'm not sure.' I told them it was $2,000 either way, and I got a cheque."

Smith did get Leese's guitar back from Santana for repair (although Carlos borrowed it again in the mid 1990s when his treasured PRSs were stolen) and Santana's own PRS fulfilled the remaining recording commitment. Not long afterwards Carlos called again and ordered another, identical instrument but with a tone

Local musician Bill Holter (above) with the sister guitar to Carlos Santana's. It was Holter who drew the symbol of the sacred syllable "om" for the truss-rod cover that was subsequently added to Santana's instrument (as seen on the headstock in the main picture).

control in addition to the lone volume control of number one. "I made another and showed up at Constitution Hall with it," says Smith. "Carlos doesn't know I'm there, he doesn't know the new guitar is done. The crew give him the new guitar and he plays it. Carlos says, 'My guitar hasn't got any high-end!' The crew start cracking up. Carlos doesn't know it's his new guitar – it feels exactly the same, it looks the same but he doesn't realise there's a tone control. They say, 'Carlos, turn up the tone control.' He says, 'There is no... whoa!' He starts playing it. All the notes feed back, and he's happy."

Santana had told Smith that the first guitar had been "an accident of god" and that Smith would never be able to do it again. "He then said that the second guitar was an accident of god," laughs Smith. "I made him a third one, a prototype for the NAMM trade show of musical instruments – Seymour Duncan had started to make his

Firebird pickups and asked me to build a guitar to show off the new pickups. Afterwards, when I got it back, I took the Firebird pickups out, routed the guitar and put in two larger humbuckers – a Seymour Duncan Custom and Duncan '59. That became Carlos's third PRS. Then we made him a double-neck. When he got that he said, 'Well, I guess it's not an accident of god.' Finally he thought that maybe I was a guitar-maker."

Santana's high-profile use of his PRS guitars proved critical to the company's long-term success. "We couldn't have done it without his support," affirms Smith. "He gave my instruments instant credibility. Carlos, Howard Leese and Al DiMeola all said they didn't care what anyone else says, this is good. Without that... forget about it, it would never have happened. Their mark of approval was crucial. I guess I had it right. If I could build Carlos a guitar, I knew I had a shot."

Immediate short-term success was, however, a different matter. "Carlos played the second guitar I made him on Tom Snyder's late-night TV show. The whole show was

This fourth instrument for Carlos Santana finally convinced the guitarist that they were not "accidents of god". Smith said: "Finally, he thought that maybe I was a guitar-maker." These prototype wrapover bridges were patented in 1984 but have never been used on a production guitar.

nothing but close-ups of the guitar. My goal of making Carlos Santana a guitar had happened, and yet afterwards as I walked down the street nobody said anything different to me. I made that day happen, but nothing changed."

It may well have been this realisation that spurred Smith on to make the changes that would take his art from the attic to the outside world. Meanwhile, Smith and John Ingram continued to make guitars and sell 'em in order to maintain their hand-to-mouth existence. Journey's Neil Schon bought a guitar, and then later a double-neck. "That double-neck was my apprentice guitar," remembers Ingram. "We christened it 'Big'. I hadn't realised just how ungainly these things were. I was short of money and Paul said, 'Sell the double-neck.' We took it to a Journey concert and Neil Schon bought it in August 1981."

Behind the scenes, a new sophistication was gradually changing the guitars. Eric Pritchard and Smith worked on labour-saving machinery, including the dupli-carver that could shape arched maple tops in a fraction of the time Smith would take to hand-carve them. Although Smith favoured Seymour Duncan's PAF-like humbucking pickups, he and Ingram did their own research. First they looked at a humbucking version of the P-90 (later known as the Deep Dish), then a PAF-like humbucker. Ingram admits today that when it comes to pickup design, they're still learning.

By 1982 Smith's intentions and aspirations for guitar design were becoming more clear. "I designed something called the Sorcerer's Apprentice," he recalls, "a 27-fret guitar that Eric Pritchard and I drew. It has the headstock that we use now, and also the moon inlays." John Ingram was impressed by the guitar. He says: "Paul has such a keen sense of design. It cuts through all the bullshit and his mind works fast. It's frustrating sometimes because it's hard to keep up with him. When he turns into this powerhouse and decides to get something done, you know you either jump on and help or step aside, because he's going to get it done."

The intention was to get the Sorcerer's Apprentice into production, and to this end Smith made ultimately unsuccessful approaches to a number of existing guitar

Carlos Santana is seen (above) with an early Custom model from the factory era with a special finish in the Rastafarian colours of red, gold and green. But the guitarist still preferred the style of the pre-factory guitars, which led to the PRS Santana model, introduced in 1995 (see page 82).

manufacturers to try to interest them in building the model. Those he went to included the Japanese firm Yamaha, as well as US makers such as Guild and Kramer.

Yamaha had been making electric guitars since the 1960s, but during the mid 1970s had begun to impress players with distinctly improved quality and playability, exemplified by the fine SG-2000 model of 1976. (This was in fact that "other line" that Carlos Santana had endorsed.) "I went to Yamaha with our drawings," Smith remembers, "and they flew me to their HQ at Hamamatsu in Japan." They offered Smith $2,000 up front – "less than my hotel bill" – and one-and-a-half per cent of wholesale for the rights to his design. He wanted $80,000 up front and five per cent of wholesale. "I told them to forget it."

It was during 1984 that Paul Reed Smith and his custom-made guitar changed for good. Smith is pictured in an article in *Musician* magazine of July 1984 with a guitar that has the now-familiar PRS body shape. It was a fundamental change from the previous outline of Smith's

guitars which had been based on a double-cut Les Paul Junior. The new shape was the last component of what we now know as the modern PRS design. Smith explains its genesis: "You had your Gibson players and your Strat players. Fifty per cent played one, 50 per cent played the other. If you only made the Gibson guys happy, and if one out of two of those guys liked the guitar, you still only had 25 per cent of the market. I knew that if I didn't draw a line down the middle and combine the best features of the Fender and Gibson designs I was dead."

Smith had started to work on a new body shape with this in mind. "We took a Strat shape and a Junior shape," recalls Smith, "and drew them on top of each other and averaged the lines. That came out looking horrible. It was unusable. So I started on the new design, my baby. I worked very slowly, and it took about two years to draw. It was finalised late one night when we were living at Poplar Avenue. The sanding machine was in the garage out back.

"Me and my friend Cary Ziegler were sanding down a piece of mahogany shaped like the new body," he

▼ **PAUL REED SMITH**

"SORCERER'S APPRENTICE"

MADE IN: *1982*

Smith drew the design for this guitar with Eric Pritchard and took it to some of the big guitar-making companies of the time, such as Yamaha. The intention, which was never in fact realised, was to have one of these manufacturers

produce the model. Clearly, Smith was now looking for a way to reach a wider audience. The design marks the transition between instruments of the early-1980s Santana era and the later production Custom. Features on this guitar such as the headstock shape survived to the production PRS instruments, whereas others, like the radical 27-fret fingerboard and unusual pickup layout, did not.

PAUL REED SMITH'S
HIGH-CLASS HYBRID

Bridging the Age-old
Gap Between
Strat and Paul

The first published picture (left) of a guitar with the PRS-shape body and standard "moon" inlays. The non-standard Floyd Rose vibrato had been fitted in an attempt to sell the instrument to the Kramer guitar-making company. It wasn't only players who were promoting the guitars; J.D. Considine penned numerous early features extolling the virtues of Smith's guitars, this one in Musician magazine in 1984.

The time: somewhere in the early 1980s. The place: Annapolis, Maryland, about 50 miles east of Washington DC. The weather: sunny but evidently rather chilly. And here, in front of Barbara's camera, we find fledgling guitar-maker Paul Reed Smith and his trusty assistant John Ingram modelling, in one case at least, the as-yet unfashionable duffle coat, as well as a pair of what they called "Sorcerer's Apprentice" guitars. This was the instrument design that Smith tried to convince some big companies to produce.

continues. "I'd wake my wife Barbara and say, 'How's this?' She'd say, 'Nah, it's not right yet,' and go back to sleep. We sanded on, and we'd go back and wake her up. 'Is it good yet?' 'Nah.' Finally, about three in the morning, I woke her up, and she said, 'I'm tired. I don't want to look at it any more.' I knew it was done."

But no one recognised the potential of the finished article. "I tried to get many top guitar companies to do it," says Smith, "but it didn't work out. So... Barbara and I decided we'd do it ourselves."

J.D. Considine, a writer who'd given Smith valuable publicity during the early 1980s, remembers being invited to a key meeting with Smith, Barbara, Ingram, Pritchard, salesman Joe Blacker and others at the West Street shop. "We were trying to figure out how to raise money for a factory," says Considine. "I was asked to come down because Paul respected my opinion. Paul was worried about limiting his time from being a musician. He was like a kid at the end of the high dive." Smith also recalled the meeting: "They said to me to look at life honestly. What is

making remarkable headway? It's the guitar-making that's national news." And Ingram remembers the conclusion: "We'd decided we were going to do something mainstream, and the goal was to build prototypes, exhibit at the NAMM trade show and start the company."

In late 1984 Smith set off on a tour of East Coast retailers with Tim King to generate orders, armed with two of the prototypes. These were a vintage yellow Custom model with an eagle inlaid on the headstock, as pictured in the first PRS catalogue (and later stolen), and a pearl white Standard model (now in PRS's archive collection; pictured over the page). One of the dealers Smith met was Ralph Perucci, then head of the guitar department at a Sam Ash music store, this one in White Plains, New York.

"I'd read an article on up-and-coming luthiers in a magazine with a picture of Paul," Perucci remembers. "So when this tall, lanky guy comes in carrying two guitar cases I recognised him immediately. 'Are those PRSs?' I asked. He replied that they were. He said he was looking to get orders so that he could start his company. Paul had

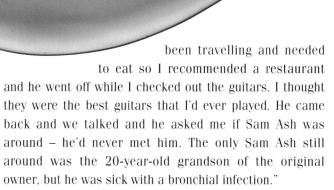

The chance to own a guitar handmade by Paul Reed Smith, luthier – as promoted in this late-1970s ad (left) – or even to send $3 for some information on such an instrument, was about to be consigned to the past.

been travelling and needed to eat so I recommended a restaurant and he went off while I checked out the guitars. I thought they were the best guitars that I'd ever played. He came back and we talked and he asked me if Sam Ash was around – he'd never met him. The only Sam Ash still around was the 20-year-old grandson of the original owner, but he was sick with a bronchial infection."

There was a large chain of Sam Ash stores, so Ash could be an important contact. Smith was intending to travel up to Connecticut and Maine, so Perucci suggested that Smith stop by on his way back when Ash would be better. Smith recalls coming back about five days later and calling Perucci to see if Ash was around. "Ralph said Sam was still sick, but gave me his number," Smith says. "So I called Sam from a phone booth in the middle of the Connecticut highway with all the cars whizzing by. Because he's sick he's got this slow and croaky New York drawl. 'Hey, Paul... Ralphy says you're doing it right.' He sounds like some Mafioso. 'I want you to go see my

brother on 48th Street. Go see Ritchie.'" Smith drove into the city to meet Ritchie Ash at the Sam Ash store on 48th Street, which for many years had been New York's centre for musical instrument shops.

"I walk in the store with two guitars and there's this guy on the floor opening a keyboard box with a knife, trying to make a sale. He turns his head around – just like in *The Exorcist* – and says, 'You didn't think you'd see me down here, did you?' He tells me to wait a minute, then takes me into a room and tries the guitars really loud. He loves 'em and gives me an order. 'I'll take 'em for this store, that store, all of 'em... and double it every month.' I was so shocked I couldn't find my car. I'd only parked it next door but I was in shock. I drove into the Holland Tunnel knowing that I was going underground for years. Because if I didn't fulfil that order I'd never, ever be able to go back to 48th Street."

The six Sam Ash stores ordered a total of 30 guitars with a value to the company of $20,950. Smith got further orders from ten more stores, bringing the grand total for

Gibson's Les Paul instruments had always been an influence on Smith, and back when Smith had worked at the Veneman Music store Les Paul had played one of Smith's instruments, apparently concluding that it was a "nice guitar". Smith also took the opportunity to have Les Paul sign his business card (inset here) as a memento of the meeting. In 1987 Smith saw Paul again, at the NAMM trade show that took place in Anaheim, and the two are pictured together there (left). Paul evidently again liked the guitars he saw and heard at the PRS booth

at the show; this must have seemed like a personal endorsement for the 30-year-old "upstart" Smith. He later wrote to Les Paul to thank him, and to invite him to visit the new PRS factory. "I cut my teeth on old Les Pauls," he wrote. "This factory would not exist without that inspiration." While PRS guitars started life as a hybrid of Fender and Gibson influences, as the years went by the Gibson influence, and notably that of the Les Paul models, would in fact dramatically increase.

▲ PAUL REED SMITH

"PRS GUITAR"

MADE IN: *1984*

This all-mahogany "PRS" model was later renamed the Standard. The instrument shown was one of the two guitars that Smith took on the road in late 1984 to attract orders to help attract finance and launch the PRS company. The idea was not just to win orders, but thereby to convince potential investors that there was a market

for Smith's instruments. Along with a maple-top Custom model that was subsequently stolen, this pearl white guitar was pictured in the first PRS catalogue, and today is the earliest surviving example of the modern PRS design. All the elements are in evidence: the 24-fret "moon"-inlaid fingerboard; the PRS Vibrato system; the new body and headstock shapes; and a control layout with (left to right here) a five-way rotary pickup selector, mini-toggle "sweet" switch tone filter, and volume.

PAUL REED SMITH
Fine Handcrafted Guitars
33 West Street
Annapolis, Maryland 21401

Fine Handmade Guitars — *Paul Reed Smith* — 33 West Street, Annapolis, Md. 21401 — 301/263-2701

It was not only the design of Smith's guitars that changed. The decision to start a production facility was one rarely taken by a small custom maker, and while catalogues, business cards and letter-heads (two examples, left) still bore the address in West Street, Annapolis, the search for factory premises for production of the PRS instruments had already begun. This would culminate in the move to the PRS factory in Virginia Avenue, Annapolis, during 1985.

the trip to $54,835. Working that forward for 12 months gave PRS an order projection totalling $296,925. To get investment to raise the capital necessary to actually start the company and make the guitars, Barbara prepared two prospectuses. One of them pointed out that this first set of orders had been taken in a ten-day period and thus constituted "a fraction of the market worldwide".

Orders were one thing. Raising the capital to start the factory was another. The original estimate of required capital in the first loan application was set at $425,000, and this rose to $500,000 in the second and successful formation of a limited partnership masterminded by investor Warren Esanu. In the meantime there was their exhibition at the February 1985 NAMM musical instruments trade show to think about, for which more guitars were obviously going to be needed. While on his sales trip, Smith had left Ingram behind to work on these.

"There were six new ones, plus the two prototypes that Paul had taken on the road," Ingram recalls. "We built those six in the old way, just me and Paul, John Mann

making the bridges, and Eric Pritchard as a constant consultant, coaching us from the sidelines and doing what he could engineering-wise. I credit Barbara with the push that got us to NAMM. She kicked Paul in the ass, and I tried to co-operate in every way I possibly could. She did the organisational stuff, called the NAMM people, got the booth, got the hotel reservations, arranged transportation. But we still hadn't raised the investment to start the company. We went to that NAMM '85 show on a wing and a prayer."

Smith reflects: "My wife worked really hard to get the company going. She was the one that pushed me to a place where we didn't have any money. When we sent the cheque off to the NAMM exhibition people we knew it was over – because we'd never be able to recover financially."

The dice were rolled; there was no going back. In fact, 1985 proved to be a year that Paul Reed Smith and his small team of co-workers and friends – and indeed the electric guitar industry – would never forget.

As the new PRS Guitars company moved into gear in 1985, the era of handwritten spec sheets (1982 example, above) was gone for good.

PART TWO: VIRGINIA AVENUE, 1985-95

Paul Reed Smith's professional life seems to run in ten-year cycles. In 1975 he made his first "real" guitar. In 1985, with a decade of experience as a custom-builder and repairer behind him, Smith and his small team moved into a factory in Virginia Avenue, Annapolis, that would become their home until the end of 1995. By that time, on the eve of their move to a new factory, they were virtually established in reputation if not production levels as number three behind the iconic electric guitar brands of Fender and Gibson.

But in 1985 such progress was little more than a pipe-dream. Yet Smith felt he had gone as far as he could as a custom-builder. "There was no doubt in my mind that I needed to change," he recalls. "My tax returns were all in the $8,000 range. I was also a semi-professional guitar player... but you'd earn maybe $75 to $100 a night. That's not a living."

It was in early 1985 that Smith and his team began their occupation of Virginia Avenue. It was before any capital had been raised to start the company proper, although the substantial orders raised by his late-1984 sales trip and the success of the first NAMM show gave hope that finance would be found. "We moved in on the understanding that when we raised the capital, we'd pay back-rent," remembers Smith. Mike Deely, one of Paul's original staff and now a sales representative for PRS, adds: "At the end of April 1985 we actually got in the place and started to set up. John Ingram and Paul had already started rough work on the 20 guitars for the summer NAMM show [known as the NAMM 20]. Between May and June we built and finished those 20. The first production serial-numbered instrument came off the line in August; there was now a crew of around 18. Guys like Geoff Jacobsen and Joe Knaggs, still with PRS today, had a ton to do with the finishing. It was acceptable on the first instruments, but really was nothing like what PRS is known for today."

It would be impossible here to document all the problems of the fledgling production-line – like the nightmare in the early days of having to re-fret and re-finish instruments, or the later pain of shelving innovative products such as the PRS amplifier, the PRS bass and the ill-fated acoustic guitar.

We'll let the guitars and the stories behind them do the talking. By the middle of October 1985, the 100th guitar had rolled off the production line. Then on June 27th 1986 came The Night Of The 1,000th Guitar party. The roller-coaster ride had begun.

Reflecting Smith's love of old Gibsons, the construction of the Custom (original body drawing and template, left) follows Gibson style closely. But the extra Fender influence created a guitar that might otherwise have been dismissed as a Les Paul with a different shape. Although Smith admits it's not just an amalgam of his earlier double-cut Les Paul outline and a Fender Stratocaster, the grace of the offset-double-cutaway Fender body is clearly evident in the new Custom.

CUSTOM, CUSTOM 22 AND 24 FRET, AND CUSTOM SOAPBAR MODELS

The PRS Custom was officially launched at the winter NAMM musical instrument trade show in February 1985 at a time when the guitar industry seemed gripped by hi-tech instruments and the virtuoso "metal" playing trend.

It's often said that the PRS Custom was evolutionary rather than revolutionary. At that '85 show, surrounded by so many odd-shaped electrics with guitar-to-synthesiser pickups, the old-school elegance of Paul Reed Smith's design looked substantially different. PRS's small mention and black-and-white photo in *Guitar Player* magazine's NAMM report, in an issue with Yngwie Malmsteen on the cover, stuck out like a sore thumb. In retrospect, the launch of the Custom couldn't have been better timed.

The guitar clearly drew from the past, but had many new and improved features. It had the basic constructional principles of Gibson's iconic 1950s Les Paul design. PRS's Custom had a one-piece mahogany neck, and this was glued into a one-piece mahogany body capped with a distinctly contoured curly-maple top, edged with what became known as "natural edge binding" or "non-binding". Instead of using the conventional separate and typically plastic material around the top edge of the body, Smith left the edge showing natural maple. "On an acoustic guitar the binding is to hide all the wood joints," he explains. "On a Gibson Les Paul it's used to stop the edge of the wood from getting dinged. I thought if you made the edge right and didn't stain it, you wouldn't have to bind it. I first did it in West Street on the very first curly-maple guitar."

Above all, the Custom wears Smith's influences boldly on its sleeve, with strong Gibson-meets-Fender flavours. This design "duality" extends further. The instrument uses a 25″ scale length (635mm) which is half way between Fender's longer 25½″ scale (648mm) and Gibson's 24⅝″ (625mm). Smith certainly wasn't the first to do that (Danelectro, for example, had used a 25″ scale from the 1950s). But along with the shaping, the five-way rotary pickup selector switch (which pulled Fender-like single-coil tones from the twin PRS humbuckers), not to mention

▼ **CUSTOM**

PRODUCTION PERIOD: *1985-CURRENT*

THIS EXAMPLE: *1985*

This vintage yellow Custom was PRS's second-ever production guitar. The guitar bears serial number 5 0002: the 5 indicates the year and the rest is the sequential number. It was manufactured after the company's second NAMM exhibition, when PRS began making guitars for the orders they had gathered at the trade show. Production actually began during August 1985, with a crew of 20 workers, and by October PRS had shipped their 100th instrument.

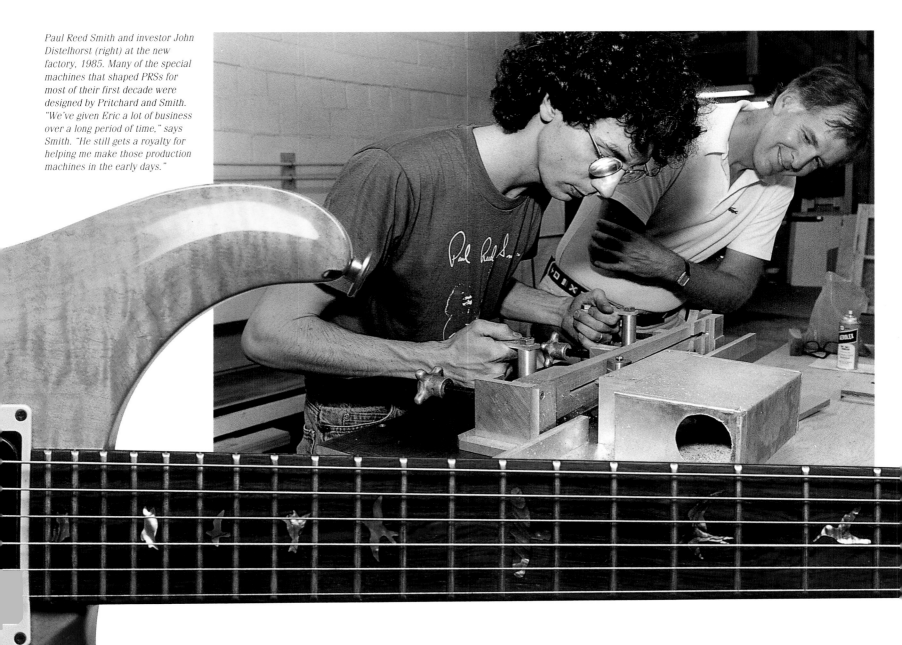

Paul Reed Smith and investor John Distelhorst (right) at the new factory, 1985. Many of the special machines that shaped PRSs for most of their first decade were designed by Pritchard and Smith. "We've given Eric a lot of business over a long period of time," says Smith. "He still gets a royalty for helping me make those production machines in the early days."

The cutaway chamfer (inset, right) is a crucial element of the PRS body design, aiding the player's left-hand comfort when working in the upper-fret area. You can also see in this picture the light-colour edge "binding" (not really binding at all) as well as the cherry-stained sides.

abandoned, a nut made from a nylon/Teflon compound (which Smith likes to refer to as "unobtainium") was installed to reduce friction, the headstock back-angle was made shallow (about seven degrees) and PRS/Schaller locking tuners were fitted as standard. Smith's original locking tuners, as used on the first Santana guitar, were customised standard tuners that were fitted with a small cap-screw to clamp the string within the post hole. "I called Eric Pritchard and said I needed a tuning peg where you can just put the string in, turn the peg and it's locked, just like a boat's rope-fastening cleat," Smith says. Pritchard suggested achieving this with a cam. The original version had a ring around the peg which did the job – but it was difficult to see its position, and Smith was afraid that if a string broke and a little piece got stuck in the peg it would jam up. "I said we should open it up so there's a slot and you can see what's going on," recalls Smith. "And I

suggested putting a little 'wing' on the locking collar to easily unlock it. Those cam-lock pegs were on the first guitars I took to NAMM in 1985."

In April 1986 *Guitar Player* magazine carried out a typically detailed review of the new PRS Custom. Rick Turner, a highly respected luthier in his own right, concluded: "Smith has put a lot of hard work and love into producing a guitar he believes in. I believe in it too; I have not played an electric guitar I liked better and very few I liked as much, including ones I have made myself. This is a wonderful, subtle instrument for discerning players who know the difference." Paul Reed Smith guitars were, at last, on the map.

As the 1980s progressed the Custom remained as *the* PRS guitar (as to a lesser extent did the Standard – see page 42), despite being joined in the line by the Studios, Specials, Signatures and CEs. In one of the increasingly frequent newspaper profiles of Smith – this one in *The*

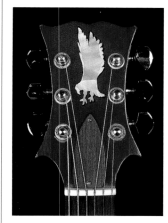

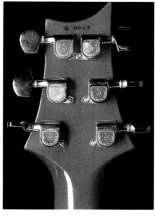

The first style of PRS headstock (above), this example from the 1976 guitar that was built for Peter Frampton (you can see the instrument in more detail on pages 11/12/13). The headstock is a three-tuners-a-side symmetrical design, but Smith later came to dislike the extremely ornate look. The early headstock also regularly featured an inlaid eagle – a PRS trademark today – that was originally copied from a T-shirt.

By 1980 Smith was using this "transitional" headstock design (above), seen here on a Santana instrument. The layout allowed for virtually straight string-pull over the nut – a desirable feature that aided efficient use of the vibrato. Note the early version here of PRS's locking tuners.

The "modern" PRS headstock (above), first used on the early "Sorcerer's Apprentice" guitar (pictured in its entirety on pages 24/25). It has a distinctive asymmetrical shape, and even straighter string-pull. It created the ideal platform for PRS's modern vibrato system with locking tuners. Note the now familiar "signature" logo which replaced the inlaid eagle on production guitars.

Two views of the headstock of the main guitar pictured on this page: from the back (above) and from the side (above right). The latter shows well PRS's locking tuners, a fundamental part of their in-tune vibrato system. They evolved directly from the adapted tuners

featured on the guitar made for Carlos Santana (see pages 20/21). The patent for PRS's locking tuners was granted on May 20th 1986, and cites Eric Pritchard as the inventor, Smith as the assignee. "It's Eric's patent that he's licensed to PRS," explains Smith.

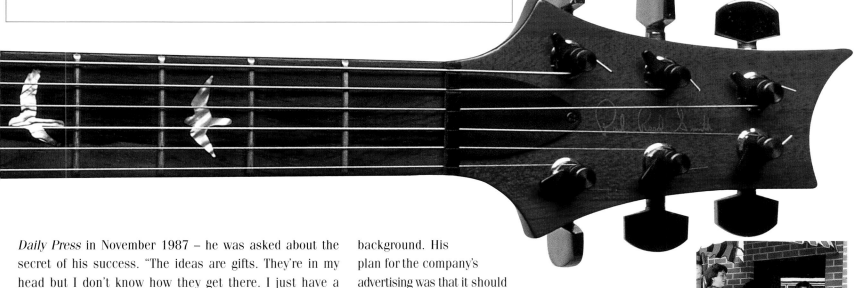

Daily Press in November 1987 – he was asked about the secret of his success. "The ideas are gifts. They're in my head but I don't know how they get there. I just have a strong vision about what a guitar can be, and I have people around me with strong visions. I've had a few brilliant ideas," he conceded. "But most of what you see is the result of hard work. It all comes down to baby steps. Look at a superior athlete: his body doesn't grow every time he works out. But he's spent his whole life working out, moving forward in baby steps." Asked what his most brilliant "baby step" was so far, Smith replied: "It's the bird inlays. People love those. I can't believe how many people have ordered that option."

Within a very short space of time, the Custom – and the whole ethos of PRS guitars – began to have a noticeable effect on the guitar industry. Even PRS's stylish advertising by Voss and Ward was carefully considered. Smith says that the early ads simply showed a beautiful instrument and the PRS name, using beautiful colours on a black

background. His plan for the company's advertising was that it should aim to be elegant and classy. It was frequently copied.

Of course, there was a major drawback to this quality quest. The price. Originally listing at $1,350, a Custom fully loaded with the optional birds and recommended Brazilian rosewood fingerboard would cost $1,550. That was a lot of money to pay for an electric guitar in 1985. At the same time a Fender US-made Vintage Strat listed at $750, and a Gibson Les Paul Standard was $999. PRS Customs were often called expensive, but many who began owning and playing them realised their value once they took account of the complex construction and timbers, the proprietary parts, the finishing and the hand-work.

The Customs were attracting the interest of numerous pro players, but it soon began to emerge that the guitars were selling predominantly to "weekend players or the semi-professionals" as Gary Waugh from the Gordon Miller

The original crew of six who helped set up the first PRS factory, photographed by Barbara in 1985. They are (left to right): David Witt (with moustache), behind him Jeff Lohmaugh, Paul Reed Smith (the man with glasses), John Ingram, Larry Melton (back) and Mike Deely (front, far right).

music store in Towson, Maryland, noted. "They have full-time jobs and can afford them." PRS said that 50 per cent of their instruments were sold to players aged between 25 and 35. "People who want them find a way," continued Waugh. "Younger players often say: That's the guitar I'll own some day." Waugh summed up the appeal: "You can't beat the sound, and that's the number one thing. It has the most popular sounds, plus a few unique ones of its own."

PRS certainly gave credence to the high-end "quality" sector of the guitar market. In the US, at least, the rising price of top Japanese-made electrics had put them closer in cost to high-end American-made product. But Robert Barratta of Rosewood Music in Ohio noted in summer 1986 that his sales of PRSs were increasing. He put this down to a growing demand over the previous 12 months for individual "custom" instruments from relatively small makers. "I went from zero to where I can now sell one custom guitar a week," said Barratta. PRS were no longer a custom operation. They made guitars on their new

factory production line, but their output was small compared to the big names like Fender and Gibson.

PRS aimed to offer consistent "custom shop" quality. Fender had in fact opened their Custom Shop in 1987, and the company's head of electric guitars, Dan Smith, observed later that year: "There's always been a demand for high-quality, custom instruments. Now that market is experiencing rapid growth. People are going back to the electric guitar, in part because of the influence of what they see on MTV. Those who started playing three or four years ago are simply making a natural progression up the price scale to very high-quality instruments."

PRS guitars were not only having an impact stateside. Britain and the rest of Europe slowly became an important market. "The first PRS I saw was in Gary Gand's store in Chicago in 1986," remembers Neville Marten, who went on to become editor of *Guitarist* magazine in the UK, and is a highly respected guitar player. "The pitch was: Forget your Gibsons and Fenders, this is the way to go. I didn't like the

▼ **CUSTOM**

PRODUCTION PERIOD: *1985-CURRENT*

THIS EXAMPLE: *1985*

This fine instrument is serial numbered 5 0005, making it the fifth guitar made by the new PRS operation, around August of 1985. It is essentially the same as the $1,370 guitar that luthier Rick Turner reviewed in the April 1986 issue of Guitar Player magazine, an article that would have a profound effect on the playing public's awareness of PRS

instruments and their potential. Turner seemed to be in no doubt about the importance of the PRS Custom before him, describing it as "a stunning success". He continued: "It had what good antiques, great cars and fine art objects have: an effortless sense of being just right for what they are." Later, Turner concluded by saying: "It may well become a new standard against which other guitars are compared." It's difficult to imagine the reaction to the review at PRS being anything other than total excitement.

Gradually, name players began to pick up on the PRS Custom, including guitarists such as Tom Johnston of The Doobie Brothers, pictured in this PRS ad (left). By 2002, there was no shortage of PRS users. Witness Chris Henderson (near right) of 3 Doors Down with his Custom 22 and Linkin Park's Brad Delson (far right) with his Custom 24.

▼ **CUSTOM 22**

PRODUCTION PERIOD: *1993-CURRENT*

THIS EXAMPLE: *1994*

The first major change to the Custom model came during 1993 with the new Custom 22, which was in effect a production version of PRS's up-

scale Dragon guitar. The new Custom 22 featured moon inlays and, like the 24-fret Custom of the time, listed for $2,180. No-cost options included a PRS vibrato and a "wide-thin" neck (the standard neck shape was not offered). An additional sum would be charged for options such as bird inlays, a premier 10-grade maple top, gold hardware, or a quilted maple top.

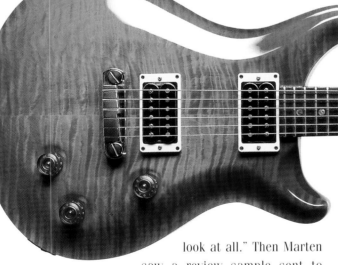

look at all." Then Marten saw a review sample sent to Guitarist. "My opinion hadn't changed on the looks, but I played this one and... well, I couldn't put it down. I wanted to buy it, despite being a real Gibson-and-Fender guy."

While the majority of guitar companies would have been more than happy with the Custom, a theme of constant change would soon emerge and would become crucial to the success of the guitars in particular and of PRS in general. The first changes to the Custom all concerned the pickups, electronics and switching.

The five-position switching underwent two changes before the system finally settled in 1989. The switch's middle position initially offered both humbuckers on, wired in parallel – like a Les Paul's middle switch position. In

October 1987 the centre position of PRS's five-way became the "Series Strat", which they describe as a warm version of the in-between treble and middle pickups of a Stratocaster. It did this by taking the two inside coils of the humbuckers and wiring them in series.

The next switch position to go was the "power out-of-phase", which was both humbuckers together out-of-phase. (According to PRS salesman Mike Deely, the company had to drop this switch setting because it infringed Gibson's wiring for their defunct L-6S model.) This was replaced by 1989 with the outer screw coils of the humbuckers combined in parallel for a "deep and clear" tone, like a Telecaster with both pickups on.

Apart from minor component changes, the five-position rotary "hybrid" pickup system remains the same today. It's important to point out that many of the subtle changes – which eventually became standard – were originally offered as options. The newer Fender-like setting in place of the "power out-of-phase" tone, for example, was being

This sales sheet (above) was issued in 1993 to promote the Custom 22 model.

▲ CUSTOM 22 / ARTIST PACKAGE

PRODUCTION PERIOD: *1993-CURRENT*

THIS EXAMPLE: *1998*

With the discontinuation of Artist series guitars in 1997, an Artist

Package is now available as a $1,200 option on Custom 22s and 24s, adding rosewood headstock veneer, paua bird inlays, Artist-grade flame or quilt maple top, "translucent toned back", gold hardware and leather case.

▲ CUSTOM 22 LEFT-HANDED

PRODUCTION PERIOD: *1999-CURRENT*

THIS EXAMPLE: *1999*

Although a handful of custom-ordered left-handed PRSs were made earlier. 1999 saw the

introduction of this first left-hand carved-top PRS, also available for the McCarty Model (vibrato or Stop-Tail). Bodies, necks, bridges, pot-tracks and even the numbers on the control knobs go the "wrong" way, and the bird inlays too fly southwards.

▲ CUSTOM 22 SOAPBAR

PRODUCTION PERIOD: *1998-CURRENT*

THIS EXAMPLE: *1999*

The first 1990s carved-top PRS with three pickups, maple set-neck and Fender-style lever switch.

offered as early as 1987. But despite the number of subtle changes to the Custom and the increasing variety of colour finishes offered, the first model addition didn't occur until the Custom 22 was launched in 1993.

The Custom 22 followed on from the first Dragon (see page 70) and the shorter, stiffer 22-fret neck had a major impact on its sound. The Custom 22 was in effect the production version of the Dragon guitar, without the expense of the decorative fingerboard inlay. Smith's dissatisfaction with the sound of the 24-fret guitars had grown over the years (detailed in the Dragon story, pages 70-76). By early 1994 there were 22-fret versions of the entire set-neck line of guitars. The still-listed EG II had, like the earlier EGs, always been a 22-fret guitar fitted with bolt-on-neck.

It wasn't only the length of the neck that changed. The standard neck shape became the "wide-fat" (or "Artist" profile as it's known in the UK) which combines the width of the "wide-thin" with the depth of the original "standard"

neck shape. A longer heel was introduced to further increase neck stiffness, and the Stop-Tail bridge (still with locking tuners) was the standard bridge – with, of course, a vibrato option. By 1998 the entire PRS line had been re-evaluated and the 24-fret guitars were suffixed with "24": the original Custom, for example, became the Custom 24 to differentiate it from the Custom 22.

The installation of computer-assisted machinery at PRS in the mid-1990s changed forever the way in which the guitars were made. Gone was the now-archaic dupli-carver and the old neck shaper, machines that had taken the PRS Custom from the attic into production. With these changes – not to mention the new purpose-built factory – the consistency of the product has today reached a level that few, if any, current production companies can match. The bird-inlaid Custom 24 remains at the heart of the line, but the Custom 22 and, more importantly, the McCarty Model created a different, fatter PRS tone that is taking the company into a new millennium.

Hold a Custom 24 (below) next to a Custom 22 (above) and the only obvious change is that the nut position on the 22-fret guitar (near right) sits about 18mm closer to the body than on the 24-fret guitar (far right). The scale length is the same: the space occupied by the last two frets has been removed.

▼ EMPLOYEE GUITAR

THIS EXAMPLE: *1992*

Apparently the last first-series bass made, dated February 20th 1992 and built for PRS employee Tom Bayster with custom features such as four pickups, Kahler bass vibrato and a translucent red finish – over the fingerboard too.

Bass 5

EARLY PRS BASS GUITAR MODELS

Like the Custom, the PRS Bass had its roots in Smith's West Street workshop, where four-, five- and eight-string basses were built as one-offs for a number of musicians. The PRS bass was originally launched at the summer 1986 NAMM show. Smith recalls that Mike Deely, a working bass player who'd joined up with Smith in 1984, "really pressed for it".

Appearing initially on an April 1986 pricelist, the four-string Bass-4 at $1,500 was priced slightly higher than the top-line Custom guitar, while the five-string Bass-5 went for $1,600. A fretless fingerboard (initially offered as rosewood, then ebony) was a no-cost option, and there was a $150 up-charge for a curly-maple top. Later in that year, the standard mahogany-body Bass-4 and Bass-5 held their prices, but the curly-maple option became the PRS Curly Bass-4 ($1,650) and the Curly Bass-5 ($1,750). The Signature Series Bass, introduced the following year, listed

Bass 4 TONE, BALANCE, POWER
Bass 5 RANGE, OPTIMUM STRING SPACING
The combination of woods, electronics and pickups give these basses tight powerful lows, punchy mids and clear highs without fret noise.
The BASS 4 and BASS 5 features
• Lightweight one-piece mahogany body
• Optional curly maple top
• "10" top and signature tops available
• 34 inch scale
• New slim hard maple necks
• Brazilian rosewood fingerboard (Ebony optional)
• Fretless ebony fingerboard available
• Moon inlays (Birds optional)
• Custom-built PRS single-coil bass pickups
• Hum-cancelling coil mounted in back
• Five-position rotary pickup selector
• Active electronic circuitry
• "Deep" and "clear" tone control functions
• Pre-amp bypass switch
• Rotosound Swing Bass Strings
• PRS cast brass bridge
• Electrostatic shielding
• Schaller tuners

Red, Tobacco Sunburst, Black Sunburst, Scarlet Sunburst, Emerald Green, Whale Blue, Tortoise Shell, Black Cherry, Gray-Black.

PRS's bass was offered in four- or five-string formats from the start. The idea was to have the same neck for both formats, but it *proved too big for a four-string and too narrow for a five. After around six months PRS changed to two separate neck specifications.*

▼ CURLY BASS-4

PRODUCTION PERIOD: *1986-92*

THIS EXAMPLE: *1987*

Note the faded blue finish and optional bird inlays of this early production bass. The "deep" and "clear" EQ controls were designed to *"restore the deep bass and high midrange that normally you'd get from an Ampeg SVT amp but wouldn't hear from a single-15 cab." A single-coil pickup system without hum was achieved by adding a hum-cancelling coil on the back (right), though PRS admit not enough research was done on coil-turns and magnet structure.*

▲ BASS-4

PRODUCTION PERIOD: *1986-92*

THIS PROTOTYPE: *c1986*

Standard moon inlays; Brazilian rosewood fingerboard. Under the opaque black finish is a mahogany body with glued-in maple neck.

at $2,800, the most expensive PRS at that time. The flat-fronted basses all featured a 34″ scale, one-piece glued-in maple neck, and Brazilian rosewood fingerboard with moon inlays (birds were optional).

Electronically, the instruments featured three PRS single-coil pickups plus a fourth, rear-mounted, hum-cancelling coil. These were controlled by a five-position rotary pickup selector switch, while an active pre-amp (with an active/passive switch for a 6dB boost) featured "deep" and "clear" EQ controls, plus master volume. The Signature Bass (available four- or five-string) was hand-signed by Smith, came with bird inlays as standard, and used an exceptional curly-maple top. The active circuit was designed to limit fret noise: the frequency response was rolled off at around 6kHz. "So anyone who wanted to sound like Marcus Miller couldn't do it," laughs Deely.

A proposed bolt-on-neck bass with passive electronics was suggested at the summer 1989 NAMM show, yet the CE Series basses which were in production by mid-1990 mirrored the electronics of the set-neck models – save for a bolt-on neck and alder back. The CE Bolt-On Bass-4 and Bass-5 listed for $1,200 and $1,300 respectively, with Maple versions at $1,450 and $1,550. They were popular but shortlived.

By the fall of 1991 the entire PRS bass programme had been officially curtailed, although examples were occasionally made into early 1992. A recession was beginning to affect everyone's business. Deely: "It became apparent that there'd have to be changes to the bass if sales were to pick up. There weren't enough orders to build basses every day, and changing the line to accommodate the production of basses disrupted cost-effectiveness. In fact it became a drag on production, a nuisance." Today, Smith considers that the basses contributed a number of neat ideas. "However, I didn't understand enough at the time to perfect them," he says. "They turned out to be the perfect basses for reggae players... but that was about it."

Mike Deely told Smith that carved-top basses, like his earlier pre-factory hand-made instruments, didn't really work unless they were played with a pick. "Paul needed some convincing to make a flat-fronted bass," Deely laughs.

PRS's first catalogue cover (proof copy, right) showed the Metal model. The odd angle was to hide this special order's non-standard star-of-David fingerboard inlays.

THE PRS GUITAR, STANDARD, SPECIAL AND STUDIO MODELS

On the early-1980s pricelists Smith was calling his all-mahogany instrument the Paul Reed Smith Guitar while his curly-maple-top guitar was listed as the Paul Reed Smith Custom. By the time the first official PRS list was issued in late 1984 Smith, still based at the West Street shop, called them the PRS Guitar and the PRS Custom, each instrument boasting the now-familiar features.

It wasn't until 1987 that the PRS Guitar became known officially as the Standard. But it could just as easily have been called the Original, because while it featured the new body shape and modern features, the all-mahogany neck and body construction harked back to the earliest of Paul's hand-made custom instruments.

"Well, there was a mahogany guitar and a curly-maple guitar, it was really that stupidly simple," laughs Smith. "You could say one was a twin-humbucking Junior, the other was a double-cutaway Les Paul. It was to do with price-points: a less expensive guitar for a working musician; and then one that had the beautiful top on it.

The PRS model, with the moon inlay, was supposed to be a workingman's guitar, for those who didn't have enough money to get the curly maple guitar. It just so happened that most people wanted the curly maple top." However, before the first guitar had rolled off the production line, there was another model introduction at the summer NAMM trade show of 1985: the PRS Metal.

Ritchie Ash of the Sam Ash music-store chain told Smith that PRS would need a guitar with a graphic design on the body to compete with similar instruments popular at the time. "He told me you need big inlays and a graphic like a Jackson," remembers Smith. "I wasn't so sure."

Trying to predict markets can be a tricky and an ultimately expensive risk. In this instance, however,

Originally listed as "the PRS Guitar", the early all-mahogany PRS model was renamed in 1987 as the Standard. This attractive example was finished in PRS's magenta pearl. Other colours available at the time for the model were pearl black, pearl white, fire red and mahogany sunburst.

▲ **METAL**

PRODUCTION PERIOD: *1985-86*

THIS EXAMPLE: *1985*

The Metal graphic design came from Bud Davis, a custom-car and motorcycle painter. PRS made some of the shortlived Metal

models with white (or, as here, black) bodies and blue stripes, while others (as on the cover of the first brochure, below left) had black bodies with purple-to-orange stripes. "You know what?" asks Smith. "We couldn't give them away! Now they're sought-after collectors items."

Despite the wild-man image enjoyed by Ted Nugent (left), his use of early production PRS guitars helped broaden their appeal. He is pictured (far left) in the mid 1980s with a Metal model finished in white with blue stripes. Nugent was Smith's first name customer after the guitar-maker moved to Annapolis in 1975, and continued to be a strumming ambassador when the PRS brand was established ten years late. More recently, Billy (left) of Good Charlotte plays a Standard 24.

Smith's reticence proved correct... but only after they'd actually made the guitar, a "heavy metal version of the PRS" as the first PRS brochure described the Metal. Ironically, the Metal shown on the cover of that brochure delayed PRS guitars reaching the small but influential market in Britain until a year after their launch. "I saw that first catalogue," remembers Doug Chandler, who was then running Chandler Guitars in London, one of the UK's foremost guitar stores specialising in quality instruments. Chandler is now Marketing Manager at PRS.

"You could see the bridge's saddle intonation screws were both slot-head and cross-head," he remembers of the Metal on the first brochure. "I thought it looked really cheesy, so I never called PRS. Then Paul called me, in 1986, and we ordered just two Customs. We had a store in Germany and started bringing them in there as well." What

▲ **STANDARD 24**

PRODUCTION PERIOD: *1998-CURRENT*

THIS EXAMPLE: *1998*

The Standard was a 24-fret guitar from its launch in 1987, and has mirrored the specification changes of the Custom in terms of pickups

and electronics. Four years after the 22-fret version of the Standard was added to the line in 1994 (see Standard 22 example below) the original 24-fret version was renamed the Standard 24 to avoid confusion. The 22-fret version now complements the original and still-current Standard 24.

▲ **STANDARD 22**

PRODUCTION: *1994-CURRENT*

THIS EXAMPLE: *1998*

A 22-fret Standard came along in 1994. For some time the Standard had also been offered at no extra

cost with a maple top and natural binding under various opaque colours (notably black and gold). So in 1998 the Standard 22 Maple Top and Standard 24 Maple Top were added, priced slightly more than a non-maple-top Standard but slightly less than a Custom.

▼ STANDARD

PRODUCTION PERIOD: *1987-CURRENT*

THIS EXAMPLE: *1987*

As David Grissom's well-played Standard proves, not all PRSs reside in collections! His gold-finish instrument has been heavily gigged – check out the careworn back, above – and

has also been upgraded at various times during its life. This has resulted in new pickups, new vibrato, new jackplate and new tuner buttons. Cosmetically inferior PRSs are marked "B" on the back of the headstock (left) and reserved as artist "loaners"; structurally inferior PRSs are bandsawed and never leave the factory.

PRS PAUL REED SMITH GUITARS

DAVID GRISSOM Austin, Texas

PRS Guitars 1812 Virginia Avenue, Annapolis, MD 2

David Grissom's gold-top Standard is featured in this PRS ad (above). The Texan guitarist is best known for his work with John Cougar

Mellencamp and Joe Ely. In recent years, the feedback he provided to PRS was fundamental to the evolution of the McCarty Model.

had changed Chandler's mind? "I talked to Paul on the phone after reading a *Guitar Player* article (see Materials, page 48). It was obvious that he cared passionately about what he was doing. Whether the product was good or bad, you knew it had to be special because of the effort he'd put into it. As it happened, when I got the first ones, all the things he thought made a great guitar I agreed with. It was never a cheap guitar, but we got some very influential reviews, and all the right people spotted the quality. You can always spot something that's made by a company that cares."

While the PRS Metal made a swift exit, the Standard remains today the most affordable set-neck PRS. But a further attempt was made after the Metal's demise to satisfy the shred-crazed rock fraternity. This came with the introduction in 1987 of the Special model. "Developed for

the hard rock/metal player, the Special is fast, loud and powerful," said the product flyer. "It has a great wide-thin neck, a clean clear rhythm sound, kick-butt lead tone, tremolo up-routing and tone control to please the most demanding musician." According to PRS's October 1987 pricelist the Special was pitched at $1,640; this was $150 more than a Standard, $40 less than a Custom.

However, while the Special was really a Standard with upgrades, it introduced the wide-thin neck and the HFS humbucker, features that would outlast the model itself. And it was the first PRS guitar to come as standard with a tone control instead of the "sweet switch".

The Special also featured a back-routed vibrato to allow more upbend. "Boy, was that a craze," smiles Smith, a little uncomfortably. "[PRS salesman] Ralph Perucci started the wide-thin neck idea. He said you gotta make this... so we did. It needed a new neck jig because the truss rod wasn't as deep, and at first I carved them by hand." Now another PRS staple, the often-ordered wide-

▼ STUDIO MAPLE TOP

PRODUCTION PERIOD: *1988-90*

THIS EXAMPLE: *1990*

The Studio was the first and only set-neck PRS with a humbucker at

the bridge and two single-coils at the neck and middle positions. But PRS's implementation of this "hot and sweet" pickup combination, prompted by LA studio musicians in the late 1980s, proved shortlived on the Studio.

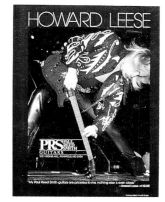

Heart's Howard Leese (left) remembers Smith loaning him this Special model with experimental red-and-black "crackle" finish. "I told my roadie to bung it in the truck, so they couldn't have it back. By the time they arrived to collect it, it was 200 miles away."

The Special (below) first had a neck pickup that looked like a humbucker, but was a single-coil. By 1989 it had a proper Vintage Bass humbucker. The Special's new bridge humbucker was the HFS. Officially, the letters stand for "hot, fat and screams".

THE **PAUL REED SMITH** SPECIAL

PRS **PAUL REED SMITH** GUITARS ®

thin neck is an option on all the CE, Standard and Custom models except the new Custom Soapbar.

In 1988 the Studio was added, a further model that built on the basic recipe of the Standard. At first it listed for $1,640, rising to $1,730 by 1990. While the Special – a "kick-ass rock'n'roll guitar" according to the 1989 colour brochure – brought in more than just a pickup change, the Studio was initially a Standard with three different pickups. And with an optional "Special Package" of wide-thin neck, tremolo up-routing and tone control, the Studio could be ordered nearly identical to a Special, just with different pickups. Even a Custom-like version was offered, too: by 1989 a curly maple top was optional ($250 extra) and by 1990 this had turned into a proper model, the Studio Maple Top (which listed at $2,000, alongside the Custom now at $1,820). Not surprisingly, although the Studio was dropped along with the Special in 1990, the Studio's legacy to the PRS line was a pickup package which was offered as an option until 1996.

▲ **SIGNATURE**

PRODUCTION PERIOD: *1987-91*

THIS PROTOTYPE: *1986*

The first ultra up-scale PRS was the Signature model – and this is prototype number one. Outwardly, it's identical to a Custom but for the hand-signed logo and the outrageous maple top. At the time, this was the best you could get.

▶ **UNKNOWN ONE-OFF**

THIS EXAMPLE: *1996*

This unusual one-off has the cedar top and semi-hollow body of a Limited Edition, but a small eagle on the headstock, a sweet switch and a vibrato. It also has multi-tap pickups, an option at the time.

THE SIGNATURE AND LIMITED EDITION MODELS

It may have seemed a strange move when PRS, in only their second year of production, introduced a guitar that had a suggested list price that was nearly $1,000 more than the company's existing flagship model, the Custom. This was especially so when one considered that words like "high-end" and "expensive" had already been used alongside the fledgling company's name.

Paul Reed Smith explains matter-of-factly how this came about. "I showed a guitar to William Compton, a psychologist and teacher, and he said, 'You don't charge enough.' My mind just reeled," says Smith. "So we thought: let's take absolutely the best maple tops, put them on the guitars, and I'll sign 'em. And it worked."

The Signature, introduced at Summer NAMM 1986 along with the PRS bass, was the first "ultimate" PRS guitar and its success paved the way for a number of limited edition collectors' guitars. However, unlike some of those later editions, the Signature model simply employed the very best quality timbers available to PRS, and did not add any specific decorative embellishments. With its "exceptional curly maple top" as the promotion for the new model put it, along with the hand-signed headstock and the fingerboard's bird inlays as standard, the Signature was otherwise identical to the Custom.

"We just made 1,000 of the Signature. And do you know why it was that we quit?" asks Smith. "I used to go on long sales tours and while I was away there would be these guitars sitting in the finish room at the factory, and the guys couldn't do their jobs unless I signed 'em. So they had me sign model decals and they put those under the finish a

At first the Signature model was planned to have an unlimited life, but the apparently good idea of having Smith hand-sign each logo (close-up, right) turned into a production nightmare. The busy Smith could not always guarantee being available at the right time. So it was that the Signature was halted after 1,000 had been made.

PRS
GUITARS

SOLID ELECTRICS

Paul Reed Smith
(301) 263-2701

1812 Virginia Ave., Annapolis, MD 21401

Smith's signature, as seen on this Voss designed business card (above), has become a prime PRS logo.

▲ LIMITED EDITION

PRODUCTION PERIOD: *1989*

THIS EXAMPLE: *1989*

Here is a standard-specification Limited Edition, equipped with a five-way rotary control and a tone control, Tune-o-matic-style bridge and stud tailpiece. Only 300 were made, more than justifying the

name of this particular PRS model. Perhaps the most striking aspect of the Limited Edition, apart from its semi-hollow body, was the use of highly unusual figured cedar for the top. Both the examples of the Limited Edition shown on these pages demonstrate the visual appeal of the timber, with dramatic enmeshing of figure and contrasting grain patterns.

couple of times. They even threatened to sign 'em themselves. So that was the end of that."

While the Signature was originally planned as an open-ended model in terms of proposed production numbers, the Limited Edition has to be one of the rarest and least-known PRS models. It was announced in 1989 and was the first PRS guitar to feature as standard a non-vibrato Tune-o-matic bridge and stud tailpiece (gold-plated only). The body of the Limited Edition had hollow tone chambers, but was without any f-holes. Although of Signature quality and price, the guitar introduced timbers for tops that were new to PRS, primarily cedar and redwood (although some even rarer examples are known in curly maple, and possibly even lacewood). The Limited Edition was intended as a limited run of 300 guitars. Smith explains: "We were trying to change up all the time, right? The tops for the

Limited Edition were something brought in by Michael Reid [PRS's long-term wood supplier]. He'd found a log of redwood that had been in salt water for 15 years, and the curls in the figure were as large as my thumb. Then there was curly cedar and curly maple. We hollowed the bodies out and glued a quarter-inch back on to them." The redwood-top guitars, however, proved problematic. "The wood had long grain lines that were once full of resin," says Smith. "Because the wood had soaked in salt water all that time the resin had gone, leaving these slots that we had to fill in with polyester finish." Both the Signature and the Limited Edition proved that there was a lucrative market for ultimate-quality limited-production guitars. It was a lesson well learned. "In reality," says Smith, "we'd made enough. We wanted to keep them exclusive and we wanted to move on."

The Signature model was one of the instruments featured (inset, centre) in PRS's full-colour catalogue issued during 1989.

MATERIALS: WOOD AND METAL

"The whole idea is to understand why those old Les Paul guitars – the Standards, the Customs, TV models, cherry sunbursts and gold-tops – were great guitars," Smith told *Guitar Player* magazine in 1982. In an article titled "Alternative Solidbodies" by Stanley Hall, Smith outlined his philosophy as a guitar builder. Most of what he said remains true to this day. "I owned a '53 gold-top and a '57 Junior with a single-piece mahogany body," Smith said. "The gold-top felt good, so I used that as a model for how a guitar should feel when you play it. I used the Les Paul Junior as a guide to the sound. My ambition was to make a guitar that felt as good as the gold-top – or better – and that would sound better than the Junior."

Smith told *Guitar Player* that the difference between a solidbody electric and an acoustic guitar is mainly one of volume. The magazine concluded: "He believes that each type of guitar must have a rich singing voice. If an electric lacks this quality, no amount of electronic or electric sleight-of-hand doctoring will make up for it. As far as he's concerned, the sound is inherent in the acoustic properties of the wood." Back in 1982, the idea that a solidbody electric was primarily an acoustic instrument was relatively new, certainly in mainstream guitar-building circles. Sustain was the primary objective, often created by un-resonant, dense and exotic woods, heavy, chunky hardware and a myriad of electronics.

Smith remembers sitting in his shop around 1976 wondering whether he should trust that the old guys had done their homework on musical-instrument woods... or spend tens of years re-doing it by experimenting with all the woods in the world. He concluded that he should trust them. Spruce, ebony, mahogany, maple, East Indian rosewood, Brazilian rosewood – always the same main woods – have been used for guitar-making and violin-making for years. There must be a reason for that, Smith figured. "These old guys, at Gibson and Fender for example, listened to everything. To my ears, old Juniors, Specials, Les Pauls sounded good, so did old Strats with

Bodies using spruce (far left), swamp ash (centre) and mahogany (left; plus back, above). Mahogany is PRS's key raw material. Of the solidbody models, the Standard and CE use full mahogany bodies; Santana, CE Maple Top, McCarty, Custom and Artist use mahogany backs plus maple tops.

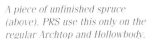

A piece of unfinished spruce (above). PRS use this only on the regular Archtop and Hollowbody.

Ash (above) is used for the Swamp Ash Special to bring a Fender-like tonality to this bolt-on-neck guitar.

The bolt-on CE guitars and basses had bodies of alder (above), as will the new bass scheduled for 2000.

Unlike many manufacturers, PRS use one-piece mahogany (raw block, above) for bodies and necks.

Maple's natural colour (above) is rarely seen on a PRS: it's usually covered by a translucent finish.

Brazilian rosewood 'boards. Sometimes the maple-board ones sounded really good too, and the basses sounded great – those old Tele basses sounded real good acoustically, even if the pickup was unusable."

Although curly maple would later become synonymous with PRS, the core materials of the majority of the guitars are mahogany and rosewood. This is exactly the same recipe used by Gibson for those Juniors and Specials that Paul loved so much. But the young luthier's homework didn't stop at a common name. Mahogany is a varied wood, and much depends on the exact species and origin.

Gibson had used Honduras mahogany, a now general term for South American mahogany – Swietenia macrophylla – which typically comes from central and northern South America. "That term 'Honduras mahogany' was used until about ten years ago," says Smith. "You just don't see the wood any more. I've never seen a piece of wood that says 'Honduras'. It really comes from Peru, Bolivia, Brazil. It rings like a bell, it's strong, easy to work,

easy to sand. We grade mahogany: for example, the hardest, straightest, crispest stuff went on Artist guitars. We still take a plane to every plank for necks before we buy it."

Brazilian rosewood was also crucial to the Gibson recipe of the 1950s. Unfortunately, although PRS used this type of rosewood for fingerboards on all their standard production models until 1991, the scarce wood is now banned from international trade. "Brazilian rosewood rings like a bell," says Smith. "It has a long sustain time and a beautiful note to it. When you hit it there are two notes an octave apart and it just rings." Smith's "Private Stash" of woods includes some Brazilian rosewood neck blanks and fingerboards which will end up only on extra-special-order guitars, but generally PRS now use East Indian rosewood, primarily for fingerboards and to a lesser extent for necks.

Saying that a certain wood sounds a particular way can be highly misleading, and many top luthiers – Smith included – shy away from such classification because they

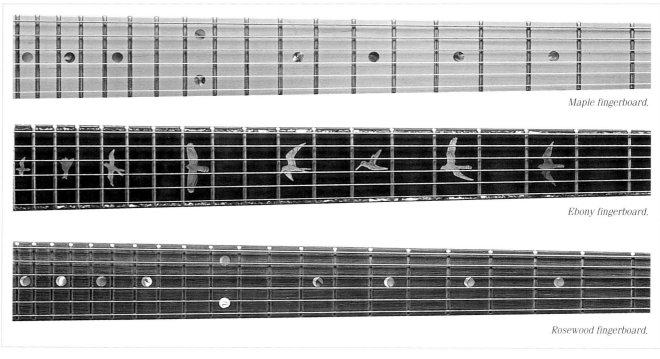

Maple fingerboard.

Ebony fingerboard.

Rosewood fingerboard.

Harder rock maple (above) is for necks, but unusually for a guitar-maker PRS use it quarter-sawn.

The 10th Anniversary had a fingerboard of ebony (above), but this traditional wood is rare on PRSs.

Brazilian rosewood (above) is hard to get now and is reserved for PRS limited runs and Private Stock.

East Indian rosewood (above) is the standard fingerboard material for PRS now; also used for some necks.

know too well that the performance of the raw material can be so variable. Apart from species and weight, the condition of the wood – specifically, how well it is dried – is crucial to the final performance, resonance and longevity of the resulting guitar. PRS use a hot-room system to further dry down the bought-in wood to their precise specification. "We used the hot room from day one at the first factory," explains Smith. "This place is real important. Neck wood, top wood, body wood, back wood and fingerboards are dried there, and the fingerboards have their own special drying oven. Our wood does not become a guitar unless it's dried down to at least six per cent moisture content. Kiln-dried wood is usually eight to ten per cent. We dry our fingerboards even more because we don't want the fret-ends to pop out, a problem caused by fingerboard shrinkage."

It's not just dry wood that PRS crave. All their necks come from the stiffest quarter-sawn wood (as opposed to slab-sawn). Imagine looking at a section through a neck. With quarter-sawn wood, the grain is at 90 degrees to the fingerboard; slab-sawn, it's parallel to the fingerboard. Softer mahogany is usually quarter-sawn by most high-end makers, whereas maple is typically slab-sawn. This selection of stiffer quarter-sawn maple brings another quality bonus to PRS's most cost-effective guitars. Another feature that sets PRS apart from the majority of guitar manufacturers is their use of one-piece wood wherever possible, especially for necks and bodies. Smith thinks that, quite simply, it sounds better.

As well as mahogany for bodies and necks, PRS use maple for their bolt-on CE necks and for the Swamp Ash Special. The CEs have rosewood fingerboards; the Swamp Ash has a figured-maple board. The Custom Soapbar is a set-neck guitar but with a maple neck and fingerboard.

There is much debate about the relative sound of set-neck (glued-in-neck) guitars and bolt-on-neck guitars. PRS

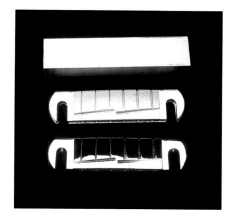
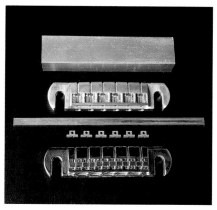
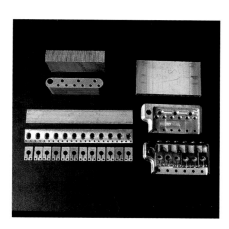

Excel Machine & Fabrication Inc are based in a state-of-the art machine shop in Baltimore, Maryland. Headed by Joe Johnson and Randy Perry, Excel make the Stop-Tail and vibrato bridges and the majority of hardware parts for PRS Guitars. Johnson met up with Smith in the late 1980s and, in an attempt to impress him, made some neckplates – the design of which you now see on the bolt-on guitars. "Paul's exact words were, 'You guys are first class.' It certainly helped to open the door," laughs Perry. Using production-efficient CNC machinery, Excel began making parts for PRS in the early 1990s. They started on the Stop-Tail bridge in 1991 (and later the adjustable version), and around the same time produced the vibrato. This changed from the previous single-piece brass casting to a two-piece brass design. For a short period in 1992-93, Excel experimented with a stainless-steel-topped bridge – initially with a brass block, and then aluminium. Unhappy with the sound, PRS reinstated the two-piece brass design in 1993. Picture 1 (left) shows the aircraft-grade extruded solid aluminium stock of the Stop-Tail (top), the machined bridge (centre) and the finished, plated item (below). Picture 2 shows the component parts of the Adjustable Stop-Tail which adds brass saddles (made from square-rod stock) on to the aluminium base. Picture 3 illustrates the component parts of the vibrato. Picture 4 shows the vibrato's brass top-plate being machined, and picture 5 is a view of the Stop-Tail being machined.

say there is little difference in sustain but that each has its own characteristic tone: glued-in mahogany necks make for a typically warm and woody tone with a richly-defined midrange; bolt-on maple necks are typically livelier with more presence and definition.

East Indian rosewood has been used for PRS fingerboards since the introduction of the CE line, and on the set-neck guitars from 1991. But making the neck itself from the same hardwood is a relatively new option – and apparently unique. "It's all about stiffness," explains Smith. By reducing the length of the neck (from 24-fret to 22-fret), increasing the thickness (the wide-fat neck) and using a very strong wood like rosewood, Smith knew that the physics implied he would have a very stiff neck.

The rosewood necks are available as a $600 option on the McCarty guitar. That might seem expensive, he says, but it's a rare and valuable option. "If you had the only gold in the world, what would you charge for it?" The wood that causes more problems than any other for PRS is

swamp ash. It's difficult to work and is unpopular in the factory, reports Smith. "But anything that sounds good and sells is worth sticking with."

Some woods are becoming scarce and some, primarily certain rosewoods and mahoganies, are surrounded by environmental issues, overseen by the Conference on International Trade in Endangered Species (CITES). The result could be a number of changes to the woods used by PRS as we enter the 21st century.

"I expect mahogany will go on CITES within four or five years," says Smith. Such a move could at best limit the available stock and at worst ban it from international trade, as has happened with Brazilian rosewood. Smith says that this will not be a problem for PRS... so long as they find other woods that sound good. "It will be cut down whether I'm here or not," he says. "I don't think we're doing anything immoral by making beautiful instruments out of it. But if it stops, it stops. Like Brazilian rosewood: OK, cool, no problem. We found an alternative."

MATERIALS: THE FIGURED MAPLE TOP

Curly maple is a highly figured, or patterned, wood. Under the vibrant, stained and coloured finishes used by PRS, it helps to create a guitar that for many is as much a work of art as a working musical tool. Conversely, the opulent appearance of a PRS curly maple top has drawn many a derogatory phrase, from "over-pretty" to "furniture guitar" and worse.

In the fall of 1980 Paul Reed Smith made a fortuitous contact, with one Michael Reid. "Somehow he'd got my name from a lumber dealer nearby who said I had some curly maple," remembers Reid, "so I sold him a little bit.

"When you meet Paul you rarely forget him. He was nothing like anyone I'd ever met before. I don't say that in a disparaging way: he's just an unusual guy. He was so intense and direct. He knew exactly what he wanted and didn't mince his words. He was laying all these lines on me about guitars he had to make and who he'd made guitars for. This was very shortly after he'd used a friend's dresser drawer-fronts for curly-maple tops. I think that the maple I

initially supplied him was for the first Santana guitar." At that time Reid was making reproduction furniture. Now he buys the majority of PRS's wood for the company. "I started as 'the maple guy'. But now I'm responsible for getting hold of all the wood Paul needs."

Although curly maple has been synonymous with guitars such as the Gibson Les Paul since the late 1950s, PRS refuelled the demand almost as soon as their instruments came to market in the mid 1980s. Reid says that when PRS picked up steam, all the other manufacturers took notice and there was much more competition to get hold of figured maple – also called curly or flame maple. Another figured variant is "quilted" maple. (See the various finished examples on pages 55 to 57.)

"We would pay almost whatever it took, within reason, and we actually drove the price up ourselves," Reid continues. "We said we wanted the top stuff – don't even send us the low-grade maple. And if you want that quality, you have to pay for it. Quilted maple can be even more

On these pages we show some extreme examples of the stunning tops that PRS can achieve at the high-end of the line. This 1998 Santana custom (left), a special order for Hollies guitarist Tony Hicks, has a fine "fiddleback" curl.

A beautifully quilted McCarty Hollowbody II produced in 1999 (left). Note the prominently wavy grain lines running at 90 degrees to the quilt. This example is graded as a "double 10-top", meaning top quality flamed maple has been used for both top and back.

This close-up (above) of a fabulous quilted-maple 10-top (a PRS grade that denotes high quality at the top of a 1-to-10 scale) demonstrates the sheer beauty of one of the rarest varieties of curly maple.

top has been used. The "10-plus" tops find a home on the Artist-level instruments and, of course, on the Private Stock models. If you're lucky, important or rich enough, you may get a top from Paul's Private Stash. This seems to contain some of the most extravagantly curly maple anywhere on our planet.

Predicting which tree will bear curly wood is an inexact science. "I understand that the figuring comes from stress, not from genetics," offers Smith. "What the loggers think is that if you have a canopy of trees very high and a baby tree down lower, and daddy tree falls over, all of a sudden there's all this light that comes through the canopy. Baby tree grows really fast... and curly. So if you can hold back the light, then give a tree a lot more than it's ever had, the chances are it will be curly."

Michael Reid says that the University of Washington did a long-term study on the subject, taking seeds from trees that were figured and crossing them with seeds from un-figured trees in an attempt to reproduce figured wood in a

laboratory. "Nothing they did worked, from what I understand. I do know for sure that bird's-eye figure occurs in trees that grow below a certain latitude, and only in slow-growing sugar maple. But as for the rest of it... I really don't know."

Once a curly log is discovered, it needs to be correctly processed before it gets close to being part of a PRS guitar. Imagine a rectangular block of maple. Along the sides run "wave" shapes. By slicing the blank in two – as you would to cut a bun before buttering it – you slice through the wave, and open the blank like a book. You then see the curl, like lines across a page. The type of wave, and the extremes of width and distance between its "peaks" and "troughs", will influence the look of the curl.

A slightly curved wave will result in a mild curl; a triangular wave will be more spectacular; and a square wave will be the strongest. "The stronger the waveform and the contrast between the peak and the trough, the better the top," explains Smith. "Collectors seem to look

An attractively tight curl is seen on this 1998 prototype for the top-of-the-line McCarty Archtop Artist (left). The curl is bookmatched at a rising angle, often referred to as "chevron" curl for its shape.

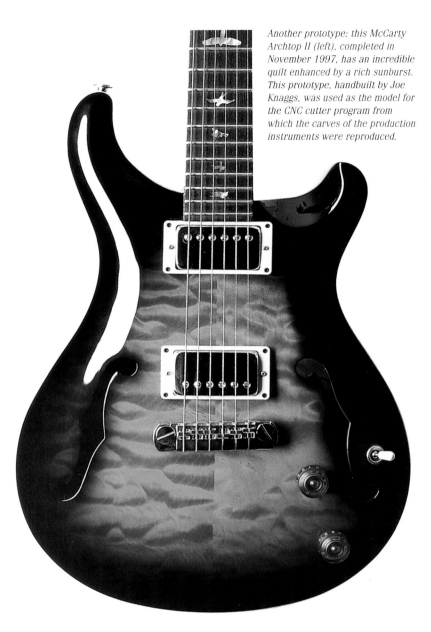

Another prototype: this McCarty Archtop II (left), completed in November 1997, has an incredible quilt enhanced by a rich sunburst. This prototype, handbuilt by Joe Knaggs, was used as the model for the CNC cutter program from which the carves of the production instruments were reproduced.

This translucent purple finish on a quilted 10-top (above) creates a magnificent visual effect.

for wider, real deep curl with very strong contrast, as wide or wider than your little finger. The look of the curl will change in the light, too. A real bland piece of wood can suddenly 'leap' if you move it in the light." Because the relative hardness between the peaks and the troughs of the curl differs, certain types of colour-staining and sanding techniques can emphasise the curl.

The way in which a log is cut will also affect the final look of the curl. A quarter-sawn rectangular blank (with grain running parallel to the long sides) creates a pronounced and symmetrical curl. If the blank is slab-sawn (with grain running parallel to the shorter top face of a rectangular blank) the curl twists and looks more diverse – and, unlike the curl, the grain will *not* be symmetrical across the halves of the bookmatched. top. Smith says, simply, that the curl of a slab-sawn piece will be "less curly and more wiggly".

The look of a curly-maple top will be further altered by the type of maple used. PRS use two main types of maple

for guitar tops: West Coast and East Coast. Smith says that East Coast maple, also known as red maple, is what PRS started with. Later they added West Coast maple, also known as big-leaf maple, which comes from British Columbia, Washington state, Oregon and Southern California. "And then there's sugar maple," adds Smith. "It's also known as hard or rock maple, and it comes in bird's-eye. It's mostly for necks, though we have used some sugar maple for tops."

In its raw state red maple is, confusingly, a little whiter; it's actually big-leaf maple that has a slightly salmon-like hue, explains Michael Reid. "Red maple is so-called because it has very bright red buds and bright red leaves in the fall, and a red sub-bark. In fact in the north, red maple is called white maple."

When it's quarter-sawn, red maple is often distinguished by small dark-brown streaks running with the grain (parallel to the centre join on the guitar's top). When it's slab-sawn, the dark-brown streaks are less obvious and

This 1997 Artist IV (left) is finished in indigo, bringing an almost velvet-like quality to its already impressive quilted maple. Or perhaps it's a little like gazing into the Caribbean Sea?

A further example of colour enhancing the natural beauty of wood, the 10-top of this staggering 1998 Custom 22 (left) is finished in a luscious dark cherry sunburst.

more wavy. Big-leaf maple, a much faster-growing wood, can be cleaner in appearance, without the brown streaks, and often has a very fine curl (sometimes called "pinstripe" or "fiddleback"). While it's dangerous to generalise, Reid points out that quilted maple is almost exclusively big-leaf. "It's very rare in red or sugar maple. And it will be slab-sawn to maximise the figure."

Over the years Reid has of course seen a great deal of maple. "I've seen a lot so far this month! But I still remember specific logs from 20 years ago. They have personalities, they're all a little bit different. The average log is hard to get excited about now, but when I get a good log there's nothing like it. The fellow that cuts the East Coast maple with me treats a good log like a diamond. And he really knows how to cut it. He gets really charged up, too, when we get a good one."

Describing the sound of a maple-top/mahogany-back guitar compared to an all-mahogany-body instrument is necessarily full of generalisations. PRS's *Sales Guide* puts it like this: "The maple top on a mahogany body adds a little more definition to the natural warmth of the mahogany. An all-mahogany body is warmer-sounding and great for straight-ahead rock guitar (or any music for that matter)." Few would disagree.

Then there are the more subtle tonal differences between the different types of maple used by PRS. "The truth is that big-leaf is a little softer than red maple, and it has a little softer tone," says Smith. "The hardest classified maple of the four that grow in the US is rock maple, then red, silver and big-leaf. But if you made a bat out of big-leaf you could still hit a baseball with it. It's still pretty hard."

And, of course, just because a piece of maple has a spectacular curl, it won't necessarily sound as good as it looks. "I've heard Les Pauls with really curly maple tops that sounded great, and really curly Les Pauls that didn't," says Smith. "What makes a great-sounding piece of wood? The better it rings."

The Artist series gave PRS the opportunity to use some astonishing curly-maple stock, as seen on this 1991 guitar (above).

THE CLASSIC ELECTRIC, CE AND EG MODELS

Looking back over the history of PRS, the introduction of the bolt-on-neck Classic Electric (later simply called CE) proved to be a masterstroke. When it was launched in June 1988 at the summer NAMM trade show in Atlanta, Georgia, the Classic Electric at $1,099 became the first "affordable" PRS guitar.

But with its bolt-on maple neck, maple fingerboard with abalone dot inlays, and two-piece alder body – and despite its standard PRS shape, 24-fret fingerboard and twin humbuckers – the Classic seemed to bring more of a Fender vibe to PRS. As a 1989 brochure said: "Maple and Alder: bolt-on traditional feel with a sound all of its own."

Initially the market was confused. Was the Classic supposed to be a PRS update of a Fender, in the same way that the Custom was an update of the Gibson Les Paul? Or was it supposed to be simply a PRS guitar at a lower price-point? Whatever the precise intention, the latter path proved to be the way forward. "The Classic Electric reflected an obvious need for us to reach a lower price-

point," remembers Mike Deely, who started in the woodshop at PRS and is now a sales representative for the company. "People simply said of our high-line guitars, 'Hey, they're really nice guitars. And I can't afford one.' We were looking for the same feel but at a lower price-point. However, the very first Classics didn't work. They had that big metal switch and opaque colours – no translucent finishes, no maple tops, no bird inlays. So they weren't really a less expensive guitar with all the finer points. The Classic later became what it is now. It's not that much less expensive, but a different guitar. That evolution happened over a year and a half."

By 1989 the Classic had also undergone a change of name. Smith explains: "Hartley Peavey called us and said, 'I own the word Classic. You can't use it, I have a common law trademark on it.' So we went to the abbreviation." The CE was born. Six years later the CE's body changed to

▼ CE 24 MAPLE TOP

PRODUCTION PERIOD: *1998-CURRENT*

THIS EXAMPLE: *1998*

When the Classic Electric (later called the CE) was launched in the late 1980s it was criticised for not

having the up-scale features that players had come to expect from a PRS instrument. However, once maple tops were added (as below), and with the exception of the guitar's black-faced headstock, it's doubtful that anyone would have known from the front that a Classic

owner was playing a bolt-on-neck guitar. And with the change of the model's body wood from alder to mahogany, specs narrowed even further. The CE Maple Top is available with either 22 or 24 frets (such as this emerald green CE 24), offered with PRS Vibrato or Stop-Tail.

▼ CLASSIC ELECTRIC

PRODUCTION PERIOD: *1988-89*

THIS EXAMPLE: *1988*

The Classic Electric (flyer, right) would simply change its name to CE in 1989. The Classic's original natural maple

headstock face with large PRS Electric logo was swiftly changed "by popular demand" to a black-faced headstock with the standard "signature" logo. Options of a rosewood fingerboard and a wide-thin neck were quickly added. The original electronics consisted of two Vintage humbuckers with a

metal-tipped three-position toggle switch, as here, voicing both humbuckers independently plus the two inside coils in series. This was soon replaced with an HFS bridge humbucker and Vintage Bass pickup controlled by the standard PRS five-way rotary. A tone control was always standard.

one-piece mahogany from alder, likewise the back of the CE Maple Top's body. This fundamental change was in fact never officially announced. PRS's internal "Engineering Change Notification" sheets (ECNs) allow any proposed change to be discussed by key staff. Each designated employee must sign the ECN document, approving the change for production efficiency.

The ECN for the CE's move to a mahogany body is dated August 16th 1994 and gives six reasons: "To stop CE reject due to (finish) checking and sinking glue-lines; reduced labour; higher yield of stock; better availability of stock; CE and Custom stock could be interchangeable; better price of stock." No comments on any tonal changes were given, nor any date of actual implementation. But this final change supports the supposition that although the CE was

originally introduced to bring a more bolt-on "Fender" vibe to the company, it has developed into a "cost-effective" alternative to the Custom and Standard – albeit with a slightly different tone when compared to the mahogany set-neck versions. This leaves the Swamp Ash Special (see page 88) to create a Fender vibe for PRS.

So PRS's first bolt-on-neck guitar, the CE, had been a cost-effective addition to the line as far as the company were concerned, but only went part way to satisfying the demand from the lower end of the market. PRS's answer was the EG (as in Electric Guitar), and although two series were offered in the first half of the 1990s, neither lasted. Smith says this was because PRS were losing money on every EG model they made.

The EG series introduced a new shape to the PRS line and also provided the company's first 22-fret production guitars. The first-series EG originally listed for $860, alongside the CE at $1,210. It had a flat-front alder body. The lower part of the body's outline suggested a contoured

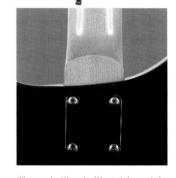

The early Classic Electric's serial number was placed on the back of the headstock, and did not appear on the neckplate (above), unlike subsequent examples.

▼ **CE 22 MAPLE TOP**

PRODUCTION PERIOD: *1994-CURRENT*

THIS EXAMPLE: *1998*

Rumours that the Classic Electric had been introduced after a major US dealer challenged PRS to make a cheaper guitar – and said that if PRS didn't, then he'd just get a copy made overseas – are denied by Smith. This is supported by the swift introduction of the CE Maple Top, which appeared in 1989. "The introduction of the Classic Electric was about all these fingerboards and tops that we were throwing away," explains Smith. "It was a disgrace. The tops weren't between our 7 to 10 rating – they were 6s or 5s. We needed a guitar at a more affordable price-point; we thought this would do it. It's worked for a long time." The CE also followed the general additions to the PRS line in 1994 of shorter 22-fret neck versions. At first the new CE 22 and CE 22 Maple Top featured Dragon Treble and Bass pickups, in line with the Custom model.*

With the CE models, PRS widened the net of players choosing their guitars, evidenced by these ads from the 1990s featuring players such as Alex Lifeson of Rush (right), and Brian 'Damage' Forsythe of Kix (far right) opting for a vintage sunburst CE.

Stratocaster, while the more familiar PRS-shape offset horns had chamfers almost like a Gibson SG's. There was a bolt-on maple neck with an East Indian rosewood fingerboard and abalone dot markers, plus the standard PRS vibrato – but non-locking Schaller tuners.

There were two models, differing only in pickup specification. The EG 3 featured three slanted Seymour Duncan single-coils, while the EG 4 had a Duncan single-coil at the neck and middle positions, plus initially an HFS II humbucker at the bridge, quickly superseded by an HFS. With the exception of the side-mounted output jack, all the pickups and electronics were mounted on a pickguard and controlled by a Fender-style five-way lever – the first PRS guitar to use this switch – along with a master volume and two master tone controls. This unusual tone system was quickly replaced by separate tone knobs for the neck and middle pickups, like a Strat's.

"The first EG was shoved down Paul's throat," remembers PRS salesman Mike Deely. "It was something that Joe Knaggs and Jack Higginbotham at PRS were a big part of. A management consultant, Rene Al, who was working for the company was pushing for a lower-price guitar, another step down, and I was in favour of that too. We built a guitar and showed it to Paul. He played with it a little bit, approved it, and that one went out for about a year, then disappeared. The second-series EG came much more from Paul and [PRS R&D man] Winn Krozak."

The second-series EG was launched in 1991. Looking more like the PRS Bass, the alder-body EG II ($1,070) had a flat body front. There was in addition a three-piece-maple-top version, the EG II Maple Top ($1,320), plus a "10-top" option (a PRS term indicating use of the most attractively figured maple top available).

Again, a bolt-on maple neck with 22-fret dot-inlaid rosewood fingerboard was used, similar in profile to the previous EG's neck with a shape that was, says Smith, "bigger in section than our wide-thin option but basically very similar". This time there were locking tuners, and the

PRS received a number of "complaints" about the first-series EG models, mostly in the form of feedback from customers and dealers, and primarily in the US. The most common reaction was that people didn't like the way it looked – even though sales were respectable in the UK and in Germany. The result was the new EG II series (left) of 1991 which appeared to revisit the style of PRS's flat-topped bass models.

▲ EG 4

PRODUCTION PERIOD: 1990-91

THIS EXAMPLE: 1991

The first-series EG models, the EG 3 and EG 4, were PRS's original attempt at providing an "affordable" instrument.

▲ EG 3

PRODUCTION PERIOD: 1990-91

THIS EXAMPLE: 1991

First-series EGs came with two pickup layouts: three single-coils (EG 3, here), or two single-coils and a humbucker (EG 4, above).

▼ EG II

PRODUCTION PERIOD: 1991-95

THIS EXAMPLE: 1992

EG II pickup layouts were: HFS humbucker at bridge and neck plus central single-coil, like this lefty; three Fralin "domino" pickups; and HFS at bridge plus two "dominos".

► EG II

PRODUCTION PERIOD: 1991-95

THIS PROTOTYPE: c1991

This experimental EG model featured the traditional PRS set-neck, unlike the regular EG bolt-on structure, as well as three non-standard single-coil pickups.

pickguard-mounted electronics were re-designed. Lindy Fralin, a noted pickup guru from Richmond, Virginia, had a lot to do with the Zero Noise "domino" pickup used on some EG IIs. Smith felt the pickup was lacking in gain. "But ultimately I think the basic problem with the EG II was its 'acoustic' sound. I wish we'd had our Upgrade Kits [see Electrics, page 81] back then," says Smith today of the second EG. The EG II was eventually discontinued during 1995, just before the company moved from the old Annapolis factory to its brand new plant in nearby Stevensville.

The EG was the first PRS production model offered in left-hand form, added to the line in 1993 in both maple-top and non-maple-top formats. And the EG II was the first PRS guitar to be made using computer-assisted machinery. The bodies were cut outside the factory by Baltimore-based engineers Excel (see page 51) who went on to take over the majority of PRS's hardware manufacturing during the 1990s.

▲ EG II

PRODUCTION PERIOD: 1991-95

THIS EXAMPLE: 1991

This sunburst EG II shows one of the three types of pickup layout offered on the model: three Lindy Fralin Zero Noise 'domino' pickups. All production EGs have a 'bolt-on' neck joint, secured with screws through a neckplate (left).

THE ARTIST I, ARTIST II AND ARTIST LIMITED MODELS

By the start of the 1990s PRS Guitars were considered a force to be reckoned with. Andy Ellis, associate editor of *Guitar Player*, noted that both PRS and Hamer (another smaller US guitar company which had built its reputation on quality) were "run by visionary builders, not a corporate mentality". Ellis continued: "Generally people who own PRS guitars are super-enthusiastic. [PRS's] status in the guitar world is very exclusive." The early-1990s article contextualised the company's growth: PRS, said Ellis, had sold around 15,000 guitars since 1985; the Virginia Avenue factory now employed 70 people who made around 400 guitars a month; and in 1990 the company had grossed $4 million.

But the successful public face of the company disguised a worrying development. Many top professional guitar players weren't totally happy with the sound of PRS guitars. It wasn't that the guitars sounded bad, it was simply that the sort of players who were attracted to the quality and look of the instruments wanted a bigger sound

with more low-end. After the hi-tech and virtuoso flash of the 1980s, players were also looking for more traditional sounds. While Fender's growth had mushroomed since the mid 1980s and included a high-line Custom Shop, Gibson still couldn't compete with the luxuriant, detailed quality of PRS. For many, a PRS Custom looked like an evolution of the Gibson Les Paul – yet it didn't capture that guitar's notorious big, fat tone.

So with the Signature Series and Limited Edition guitars reaching the end of their natural lives, and with the criticisms of major artists ringing in his ears, Paul Reed Smith set about the next "ultimate" PRS line: the Artist Series. Smith describes it as "the beginning of trying to make Dickey Betts happy". The Allman Brothers' guitarist was a renowned lover of the Gibson Les Paul sound and feel. "He didn't like the sound of our guitars," recalls

▼ **ARTIST I**

PRODUCTION PERIOD: *1991-94*

THIS EXAMPLE: *1991*

As the replacement for the earlier Signature model (see pages 46/47), the first PRS Artist continued the idea of using exclusive woods and top-grade materials that were deemed almost "too good" for the regular production PRS instruments. The high-line Artist guitars were more significant, however, in that they marked the beginnings of a series of fundamental changes to Smith's original design. These modifications would ultimately manifest themselves on the later Dragon and McCarty Model launched during the 1990s.

Models might change, but PRS's well designed promo material (Artist I flyer, right) is as important today as when the company started.

▼ **ARTIST I**

PRODUCTION PERIOD: *1991-94*

THIS PROTOTYPE: *1991*

This is the first of a handful of production prototypes made for the Artist Series. Outwardly, with the exception of the headstock logo (see below), this guitar looked identical to a 24-fret Custom model. But virtually every facet of its construction, along with the pickups, are different from a contemporary Custom. These differences include the selection by PRS of high-grade timbers, the glues that were used in the construction, the special Artist Series pickups, as well as a different design of neck and the associated heel.

Smith. "I figured that we had to make the neck wood stronger, and bigger. It was the beginning of trying to change the design, the beginning of where we were eventually to go with the whole 22-fret thing." Paul's original assistant, John Ingram, looked after artist guitars and set-ups and was in a unique position to hear grass-root comments. "We got a lot of complaints from artists that the stock production guitars had a funny, irritating, high-midrange sound that didn't sit comfortably in a mix anywhere," says Ingram. "That's why the guys in Aerosmith told me they stopped using our guitars."

Smith continues: "I'd made promises to a lot of people that we'd make improvements as to the way the guitars sounded, and the only way to do that was to change the way they were made." Smith agrees that PRS were trying to chase a fatter, Gibson-like tone. "The old PRSs didn't sound bad, but they had a thinner tone. The whole idea

was that I wanted a better acoustic sound. We began to experiment by gluing the necks in with epoxy, gluing the tops with epoxy, gluing the frets with different glues. We experimented with all kinds of things: bigger necks, longer heels. We found out that making the necks a little bigger, the bodies a little bigger and the necks a little shorter got closer to where we wanted to be." Much of these early-1990s experiments ended up on the Dragon and McCarty models, but Smith says that the beginnings were with the Artist. "I was trying to find a stronger neck," he says.

However, the first Artist Series guitar appeared simply to be a continuation of the Signature line. Released in 1991, the Artist I listed for $3,780 (plus $330 for its leather hardshell case). "Occasionally a mahogany board comes into our shop that is extra dense and resonant," ran the promotional blurb. "Sometimes the figure and curl in a particular block of curly maple is absolutely exceptional. These rare pieces become the Artist Series. My favorite stains, violin glues, abalone inlays, vintage tones... Our

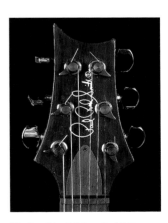

The headstock (above) of this earliest Artist prototype was the first to feature the now familiar "signature" logo intricately inlaid in abalone. It was only possible thanks to Larry Sifel's Pearl Works operation and their computer-assisted inlay techniques. These would become a major feature of later limited-edition PRS guitars.

▶ **ARTIST II**

PRODUCTION PERIOD: *1993-95*

THIS EXAMPLE: *1995*

When the Artist II was launched in 1993 at $3,780 the first Dragon with 22-fret neck and non-vibrato bridge was already out. Launched with the Artist II were the Dragon II and Custom 22. The 22-fret non-vibrato Artist II thus bridged the gap between the standard Custom 22 and the limited Dragons. Inlay and purfling included an abalone-inlaid "signature" headstock logo again by Pearl Works. This II has non-standard covered pickups.

▲ **ARTIST LIMITED**

PRODUCTION PERIOD: *1994-95*

THIS EXAMPLE: *1994*

A year after the Artist II, along came the Artist Limited, a model intended as a limited edition of just 200 pieces. The instrument, which listed for $7,000, upped the specification of the Artist II and entered the territory of the collector who likes to hunt for ultimate guitars. The Artist

Limited also added 14-carat gold bird inlays and abalone purfling around the fingerboard, the truss-rod cover and the headstock. Timbers include South American mahogany for neck and body and a big-leaf maple top. Coincidentally, both this Artist Limited and the Artist II above are in PRS's amber finish. Also, both were ordered with optional quilted maple tops, lifting them even more into the realms of extraordinary examples of PRS's finest work.

This ad for the Artist II (left) dates from 1993 and is one of a series of single-sheet flyers issued by PRS during the 1990s.

The flyer for the Artist Limited (left) had Smith saying: "The first time I held the finished prototype I was struck by the exceptional beauty of this instrument."

▼ CUSTOM

PRODUCTION PERIOD: *1985-CURRENT*

THIS EXAMPLE: *1992*

This guitar, custom-built for Jesse Toliver Urie, has a non-standard fingerboard which was in effect the prototype for the maple-purfled style of the Artist II board.

The Artist Limited saw the return of the original eagle logo to the headstock (above), first seen back on Smith's pre-PRS work and today used to indicate an instrument from the Private Stock scheme but without the outside binding.

very best." The Artist I was still a 24-fret guitar, but by using a longer heel and carefully chosen mahogany neck-blanks, some of the stiffness that Smith needed was created. "The stiffer the neck is, a more traditional ringing sound is achieved – more Les Paul, less Strat or Les Paul Junior double-cutaway," said Smith. Of course, the Artist I also featured the wide-fat neck profile, Brazilian rosewood fingerboard with abalone bird inlays, and the usual PRS hardware. It also employed the typically hide or horse glue used in violin making for all its wood-to-wood joints, except the neck to fingerboard which was epoxy. These "violin glues" were used in the belief that, together with a thin acrylic urethane finish, they would help to achieve the maximum possible resonance in the instrument.

A tone control, not a sweet switch, was standard on the guitar, along with two new Artist 90 humbuckers (as they were originally called) wired to the standard five-position rotary switch. "We're using different magnets – but I'm not telling anyone what sort," Paul said enigmatically. "We

wind the pickups differently. Basically, it's a mechanised version of a hand-wind. We put different pickups in different guitars. If we think the guitar sounds a little thin we'll put in a fatter pickup, and vice versa. It's the first time we've done this on individual instruments."

However, along with the desire to change the tone of the guitar, one feature hinted at future, more decorative possibilities. The headstock's Brazilian rosewood face had a "signature" logo of inlaid abalone. This would not have been possible without Larry Sifel and his computerised inlay facility Pearl Works, based in Mechanicsville, Maryland. Sifel had already been cutting the bird inlays (as well as the fingerboard cavities for them), and supplied the headstock logo immaculately inlaid into a thin veneer ready to be glued to the headstock. It was the start of a relationship that would create some of the finest inlaid guitars ever. Four further Artist Series guitars appeared: the Artist II (in 1993); the Artist Limited (1994); and the Artist III and Artist IV (both 1996; see pages 92/93).

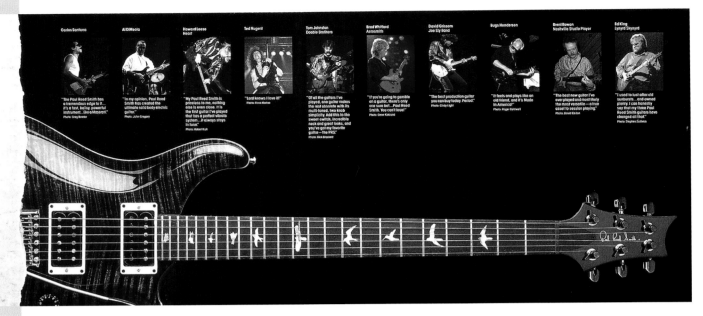

MARKETING, COLLECTABILITY, AMPLIFIERS AND ACOUSTIC GUITARS

What is the most collectable PRS guitar? According to Rick Hogue of Garrett Park Guitars in Annapolis, Maryland, a leading PRS dealer, there are quite a few that will attract immense interest. "The maple-topped pre-production instruments, such as the Santana-style guitars, will easily fetch five figures and up," he maintains. "Some have sold for two or three times that amount."

That's quite a return for owners of these guitars and basses who put faith in the then unknown Paul Reed Smith – and paid around $2,000. It also raises the question of the additional value that might be attached to the pieces owned by name players such as Carlos Santana and Howard Leese. "Then there's the early 1985 and '86 PRS guitars like the Custom," says Hogue. "They're pretty desirable too, and are some of the most collectable."

In terms of value, as well as collectability, the limited-edition PRSs have a distinct appeal to collectors. Among this type of guitar, the Dragon I is the top draw, closely followed by the Dragon II and III. "The Dragon I started it

all," says the UK's Garry Malone, one of the major collector of PRSs in the world. "There were only 50 made, and everyone thought, 'I've got to have one.'" Demand outstripped supply. Malone believes that a Dragon I is currently worth $25,000 – over three times its original full list price. "Even the Dragon product flyers are now collectable," he laughs.

"Paul has always marketed himself really well," says Hogue. "He's a genius guitar-builder, but also skilled at knowing how much the market will bear. I told him that I thought calling the latest Dragon the 'Dragon IV' would be a big mistake. People assumed that the Dragon had been a limited edition of 250 pieces and was finished. He was careful to take advice, and called the new one the Dragon 2000. This in my opinion did nothing to hurt the collectability of the original guitars."

Any of the limited-edition guitars from the Signature, Artist and Dragon series, up to and including the latest Dragon 2000, seem to hold tremendous investment

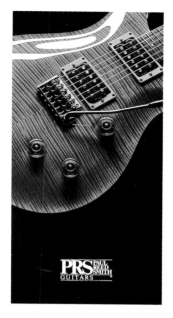

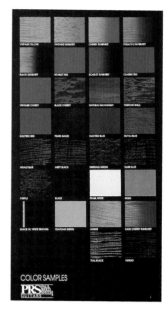

potential. Hogue also points out that early-number McCartys and Santanas are highly collectable, and that the first and last numbers of any limited run are even more desirable. High-end collectability is not only about rarity but also appearance. Attention centres on the inlay detail and the look of the maple top. "The quality of the top is always a primary consideration in terms of collectability," says PRS's Doug Chandler, who before he relocated to the US ran one of the most highly respected UK stores, specialising in high-line product – including, of course, PRS guitars.

It might surprise some readers to learn of the apparent value of "employee guitars" (see pages 84/85), the custom instruments built for PRS staff. It seems that the employees themselves have got wise. "Some of them get advice as to what is the best thing to have and what they can get the most money for. It's become a business," says Hogue. "Some of the real early employee guitars are quite unusual. In value, they will be right there above a

Signature, but below what a new Private Stock would cost." The discontinued basses and amps also hold appeal to some collectors. "The basses are slower," reckons Hogue, "but every PRS collector wants an amp." One of the handful of PRS acoustics would be a prize find, as Hogue says: "Any prototype or unusual piece will command a great deal of interest."

Jim Jannard, a major California-based collector of PRS instruments, owns what Hogue rates as the ultimate PRS: a Dragon I with solid-gold inlay. "The number one best piece in the world!" Hogue exclaims.

"I think the Rosewood Limited is their finest piece," counters collector Garry Malone. "Paul took a step back into tradition with the exquisite tree-of-life inlay but added, for the first time on a production guitar, a rosewood neck. Out of all the PRS guitars built, it has the most ornate headstock, and the sound too is spectacular. I may be a collector, but if a guitar doesn't sound good, I'm rarely interested." Malone also believes that the Private

Over these pages we show a selection of some of the stylish and well-produced catalogues and promotional material that PRS have issued through the years in support of their marketing efforts. Some of these have since become collectable as the popularity of PRS has increased among collectors as well as players. The inside spread from the 1989 catalogue (opposite, top) features a number of players using PRS guitars for the purpose that their creators intended. Ten years later, the McCarty Hollowbody makes an appearance in the 1999 catalogue (opposite, below). On this page, the fold-out "pocket" catalogue of 1992 is shown (top, centre) with its illustration of a Dragon I fingerboard. Alongside and below are some of the individual sheets issued during the 1990s, including that for the Dragon III and for the Artist III and IV.

Stock guitars are now of major interest and value. "They should be better than the Dragons, because they're one-offs. The wood quality is better and you can actually choose the type of curl, the inlay and specification."

Major collectors seem to have ignored other discontinued lines such as the cost-effective EG guitars. "I've never had anyone going crazy over those," smiles Hogue, "though the second series with the Fralin pickups seem to hold their value." It seems the early Classic Electrics, with their alder bodies, are also beginning to attract some interest.

The quality of PRS guitars has had its own effect on the second-hand and collectors' market. "The trouble is people don't give them up," says Hogue. "They are costly guitars that hold their value. In many cases there's only ten or 15 per cent difference between the price of a new model and a good second-hand example." He believes it's the style and quality of PRS instruments that attracts collectors and dealers like himself who

previously only dealt with the old vintage classics from established makers such as Fender and Gibson. "PRS have moved into the slot behind Fender and Gibson," Hogue suggests. "We've converted a lot of guys who previously would only consider old guitars. They now realise that PRS instruments play well, stay in tune, sound great and look great. So they leave their old guitars at home."

AMPLIFIERS AND ACOUSTIC GUITARS

Not all of PRS's projects have had the same success as their electric guitars. "We thought we could make an amplifier that sounded like a tube amp but didn't have any tubes [valves] in it," says Smith of the unsuccessful venture by PRS into amplifier production.

"I thought the American tube manufacturers were going to go out of business, that there'd be no tubes. I was right about that part, though I had no idea the Iron Curtain would fall and that the East Europeans were suddenly making enough tubes to last a lifetime." The original

Over the years many PRS pickups have been available after-market though in limited quantities. For more info see the Model Key.

The PRS guitar that never was. This black and white flyer can only hint at the instrument's potential. PRS acoustics may return, but...

The PRS amp "preliminary product info" folder (above) outlined the specs of the HG-70 head and 412 cabinet plus the HG-212 combo.

concept was sound enough: to produce an amp that was reliable. "Tube amps are heavy," says Smith. "They break all the time, the tubes go bad. I thought Marshall 4-by-12 cabinets were too big. I also thought an amplifier would be a good accompaniment to our guitars."

The circuitry for the PRS amps included a "Harmonic Generator", from which the HG-70 head and HG-212 combo took their prefixes. "It added harmonics to the clean tone as well as the distorted tone," explains Smith. The circuitry was developed by Eric Pritchard. "I bet him he couldn't do it," laughs Smith, "but he did a pretty good job." Indeed, Pritchard is still working on his "tube emulator" for his own company, Deja Vu Audio.

The PRS amps were not well received but Brad Tolinski in Guitar World magazine concluded his review of the HG-70 head and 412 cabinet thus: "All in all, this is probably the most impressive product I've reviewed all year." But later, the realisation hit that the industry didn't want anything to do with solid-state amps, not to mention the

relatively high list-price of the amps. There was also the time and money they drew from the company. It all meant that, after some 350 units had been shipped, PRS's amp project was stopped. "The project died in my arms. It was very difficult," concludes Smith.

The acoustic project, co-developed with noted acoustic guitar maker Dana Bourgeois, followed in the early 1990s. It was again seen by Smith as a natural adjunct to the business. "We made a prototype which I thought sounded remarkable," he recalls, "and we started sending it to people all over the country. To this day I think it sounds remarkable... but nobody else did. Dana went off and formed his own company, making essentially that design, so clearly there was a market.

"I just thought that if we could make acoustics of the quality Dana was making, then we'd be home," says Smith. "He's a very gifted guitar-maker, and it was a good guitar. In total there were 11 prototypes made, that's all. Number 11 was recently stolen, so if anyone finds it..."

More of the striking promotional material produced by PRS is shown on these two pages. The fold-out catalogue issued in 1995 (opposite) was in the same style as some of the earlier individual sheets (see previous pages), but had the bonus of folding out to reveal on the back a poster-size image of Carlos Santana playing one of his PRS guitars. The guitar side also featured the Santana model, as well as the current line of colour options. On this page is the front and back of PRS's very first catalogue, from 1985 (top, left and centre), next to a page from the 1989 brochure.

Until the Dragon I, PRS's vibrato bridge was used on the majority of their guitars. But the Dragon's new Stop-Tail bridge/tailpiece became equally important as the 1990s progressed and musical styles changed. Smith always liked the sound of Gibson's old "wrapover" bridges, and the Stop-Tail went back to that design but, typically, addressed its shortcomings without changing tone. The old bridge offered only partial intonation adjustment, but Smith with the help of Winn Krozack created a pre-intonated "ridge" allowing near-perfect intonation for .009" and .010" strings. An adjustable version appeared in 1998 on McCarty Archtops.

▲ **DRAGON I**

PRODUCTION PERIOD: *1992*

THIS PROTOTYPE: *1992*

The lmited run of just 50 examples and the fantastic fingerboard inlay

make the Dragon I a very desirable item today. But it was also the first set-neck PRS to introduce a 22-fret fingerboard – later applied to many other models in the line – as well as the company's new Stop-Tail combined bridge and tailpiece.

THE DRAGON MODELS

"When I was 16 I had a dream about a guitar with a dragon inlaid down the neck. Twenty years later, the technology became available to inlay such a complicated design with precision. This year's Dragon has 201 pieces of abalone, turquoise and mother-of-pearl. In addition to the inlay, these instruments have some fundamental design changes: 22 frets, a new PRS Stop-Tail, increased headstock angle, Dragon pickups, a wide-fat neck and gold hardware." With that brief statement, the first PRS Dragon guitar was launched in 1992, with a list price of $8,000.

Outwardly, the Dragon I was the most extreme example to date from PRS of an ultra high-end "collector" guitar. It pushed into the shade previous flagship models such as the Signature and the Artist. While this collector-appeal of the instrument alone had a great deal of value, the first Dragon guitar would have a more lasting and important role: it started to re-write the specification of the PRS

guitar. Whereas the Artist I had already begun the quest for a bigger-sounding PRS, the Dragon went further. It was the first production PRS instrument (aside from the bolt-on-neck EG) to feature a shorter 22-fret neck.

"Ralph [Perucci] and I designed it on my kitchen table at Christmas," remembers Smith. "We talked about the changes, and I knew we had to change the neck." Smith says he was aware that, mathematically, the stiffness of a neck goes up by the cube of the reduction of its length. He knew, too, that the unsupported length of a Les Paul neck is 14 frets, as is that of an old Strat. "Any time I'd found an old guitar with a short, fat neck it sounded better," Smith recalls. "I really believe that a big neck makes a big sound and a thin neck makes a thin sound."

PRS's wide-fat neck was already on offer, but here it came into its own. For the first time the profile was featured on the shorter 22-fret neck. The neck was made

▶ **DRAGON I**

PRODUCTION PERIOD: *1982*

THIS EXAMPLE: *1982*

"Paul took two prototypes of the Dragon to the '92 NAMM show and got orders for 36," says Larry Sifel, boss of inlay artists Pearl Works. "I was really thrilled. Within a couple of months he called and said we've got to do more. We ended up doing 50." This is number 31.

This first prototype of the most collectable PRS model (headstock inset below) was made for Paul Reed Smith and now resides in the

company archive. Add that to the fact that Dragon Is are now worth in excess of $20,000, and one wonders what the value of this particular guitar might be.

The eagle (right) on the "PRS Original" is actually glued to the face of the headstock, as opposed to the usual method of inlaying into the veneer facing. "The guitar sounded so good," says owner Paul Reed Smith, "that I was kind of in a hurry to get it finished." Hence the production short-cut by the boss.

stiffer still by a longer heel that protruded nearly two inches out from the body – almost twice as far as the regular neck's heel. Smith has said that if the PRS wide-fat neck was any bigger "it wouldn't be a guitar any more" and admitted that it was inspired by an example of the so-called "baseball" Stratocaster neck from the early-1960s period, as well as a '58 Les Paul neck. "Our wide-fat neck is still way smaller than an old Les Paul neck," Smith reminds us.

"But 'wide-fat' is really a misnomer," he says. "If you want a really wide fat neck, then pick up a [Fender] Jeff Beck Signature Strat. Now that's fat. Our 'wide-fat' means that it's a well-carved old-Les-Paul type neck – and it's not even as deep as those. I should never have called them that, I guess," he laughs. "It's not really that wide, and it's

▲ **"PRS ORIGINAL"**

THIS PROTOTYPE: *1994*

"PRS Original" was a proposed name before "Private Stock" was settled on to distinguish the company's special one-off and prototype instruments from the regular production lines. This amber coloured guitar with its Dragon I fingerboard inlay was the first prototype for the Guitars Of The Month series (see page 85) which in turn foreshadowed the Private Stock scheme. It was also the first PRS instrument to use a rosewood neck.

Paul Reed Smith (left) with the "PRS Original" pictured above. "I'm pretty much a one-guitar guy once I find one that sounds good," he says. This one clearly does: it's been Smith's main guitar for gigs and clinic tours since 1994.

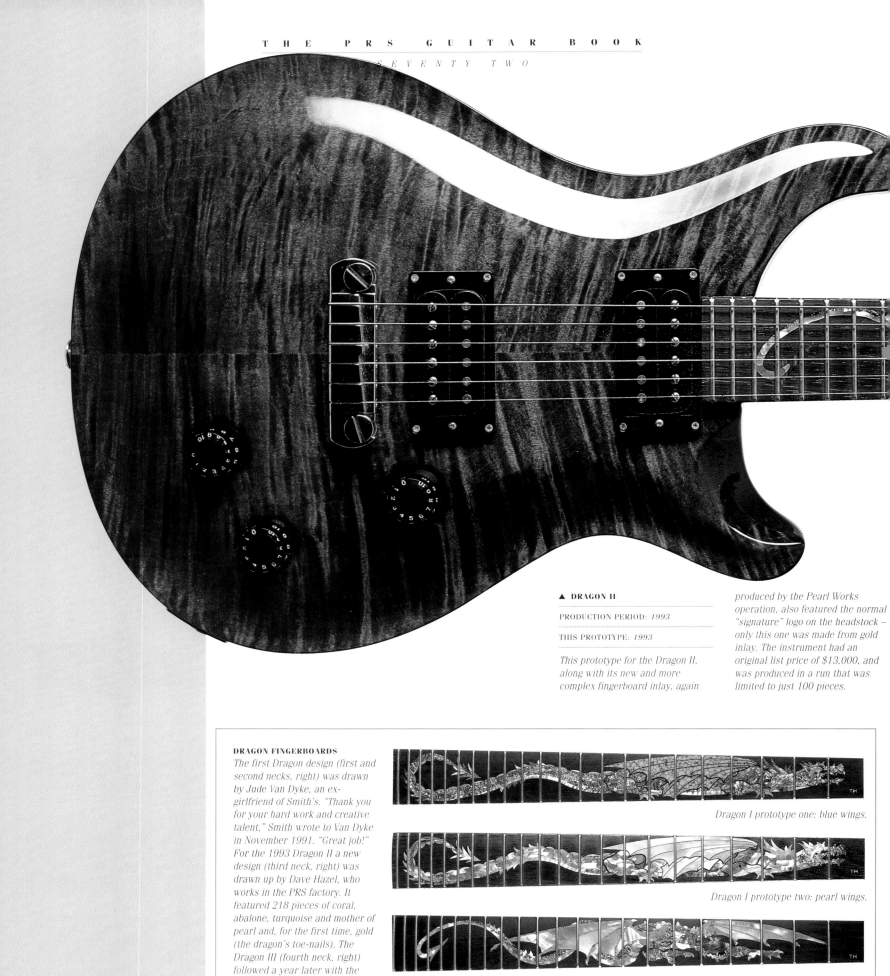

▲ DRAGON II

PRODUCTION PERIOD: *1993*

THIS PROTOTYPE: *1993*

This prototype for the Dragon II, along with its new and more complex fingerboard inlay, again

produced by the Pearl Works operation, also featured the normal "signature" logo on the headstock – only this one was made from gold inlay. The instrument had an original list price of $13,000, and was produced in a run that was limited to just 100 pieces.

DRAGON FINGERBOARDS
The first Dragon design (first and second necks, right) was drawn by Jude Van Dyke, an ex-girlfriend of Smith's. "Thank you for your hard work and creative talent," Smith wrote to Van Dyke in November 1991. "Great job!" For the 1993 Dragon II a new design (third neck, right) was drawn up by Dave Hazel, who works in the PRS factory. It featured 218 pieces of coral, abalone, turquoise and mother of pearl and, for the first time, gold (the dragon's toe-nails). The Dragon III (fourth neck, right) followed a year later with the most complex inlay yet, designed by Jeff Easely, a top Dungeons And Dragons artist. The intricate Dragon III featured a 438-piece dragon inlay of gold, red and green abalone, mother of pearl, mammoth ivory and stone.

Dragon I prototype one: blue wings.

Dragon I prototype two: pearl wings.

Dragon II prototype one.

Dragon III prototype one.

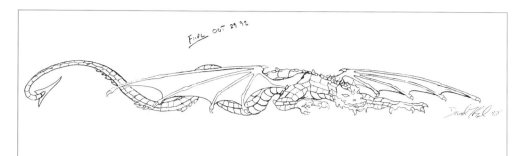

The final drawing (left) of Dave Hazel's design for the Dragon II fingerboard inlay, dated October 1992. Hazel works with Joe Knaggs at PRS on the company's high-line Private Stock and prototype projects. All the Dragon motifs are trademarked: the Dragon II's "fanciful representation of a design of a dragon" was registered during 1993.

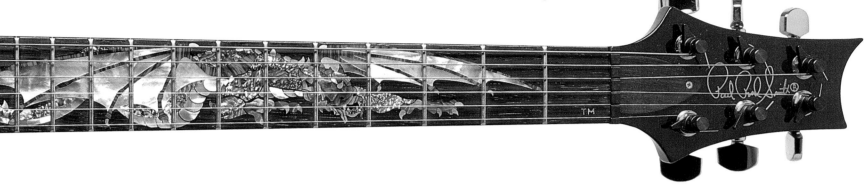

Once the line drawing of each of the Dragon designs is finalised, a detailed colour key is made (for the Dragon III, right) identifying individual materials.

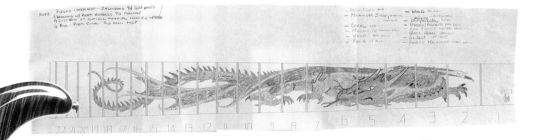

not really that fat! The Dragon I was all about bigger necks, 22 frets and the Brazilian rosewood fretboard. The Dragon II and III are identical, just different fingerboard inlay." (Brazilian rosewood was abandoned for fingerboards on the standard PRS production instruments because it simply wasn't available in suitable quantities.)

The Dragon I was also the first guitar to be designed without the company's vibrato system in mind (although a very small number have been specially ordered with vibrato). This allowed the headstock angle to be increased to approximately 11 degrees, which is flatter than the vintage Les Paul of around 17 degrees, but steeper than a standard PRS back-angle of about seven degrees. Smith says the extra angle puts a little more tension on the nut, that "every little facet makes a small difference". The new

angle was subsequently applied to all 22-fret guitars except the EG.

But it wasn't just the acoustic sound of the instrument that was changed, because the Dragon introduced a pair of namesake humbucking pickups. The Dragon Treble pickup, conceived by John Ingram, was apparently Smith's personal favourite. "Fat with zero loss of clarity," went the description. "Sounds great clean or high-gain. The Dragon Treble has a powerful ceramic magnet combined with our highest number of turns." As for the Dragon Bass: "This lower-output pickup has a great combination of rich, warm bass and 'angelic' high-end. Beautiful for solos and rhythm. Vintage alnico and vintage winding."

Smith said at the time that he found the neck pickup exactly like a Gibson PAF humbucker, while the bridge pickup "gives you all the power you need". He was evidently pleased with the new pickups, and while they featured nothing especially new in their construction, the treble was, he said, "really powerful but retains a pretty

▲ DRAGON III

PRODUCTION PERIOD: 1994

THIS PROTOTYPE: 1994

The Dragon III also featured a headstock with the "signature" logo inlaid in gold, not abalone, and the model name was inlaid in red abalone on its truss-rod cover. The Dragon III had a list price of $16,000, again limited to 100 pieces. "The Dragon III fingerboard inlay is composed of incredibly tiny pieces, some the size of a pin-head," remembers Larry Sifel of Pearl Works. "There's a lot of gold too. We had a truck that would come by every Thursday for months on end to deliver $4,000-worth of gold each time. They'd ask, 'What are you guys doing?'"

Close-up of the dragon's head on the Dragon 2000.

high end that you don't normally hear". Smith also revealed to me at the time what he meant by "fat", a term that would creep into PRS-speak more and more as the decade progressed. If it has bass and midrange and no top, I'd call it 'dark'. But 'fat' means a really nice bass, the midrange is very solid and there's enough high-end for definition but it's not shrill. That sounds 'fat'."

Further tonal change occurred due to the Dragon I's shorter neck. As the scale length didn't change, the neck humbucker sits further from the bridge than on the 24-fret guitars. "It adds a little extra bass to the neck pickup," said Smith. "It's moved about ¾" but the main tonal change I hear comes from the guitar itself. I actually think the treble pickup position is more critical. A ¼" change in position either way and you'll really hear it. Move the bass pickup the same distance and you don't really hear that much difference." Of course, the wood choice for the Dragon I was second to none. The neck and

back were South American mahogany, the top curly maple with a slightly deeper "Dragon carve" arch, and the fingerboard Brazilian rosewood. The hardware was all gold-plated and the "signature" headstock logo was inlaid abalone.

But for most the Dragon was not about tonal improvements. It was simply about the amazingly intricate inlay that stretched along the fingerboard, a fabulous work-of-art that adorns what has to be one of the most striking electric guitars ever made, translated into reality by Larry Sifel's Pearl Works company. "This dragon changed our life and probably changed Paul's life a bit too," smiles Sifel. More fabulously-inlaid Dragons followed: the Dragon II (1993) and Dragon III (1994). However, the most outrageous design was devised for the Dragon 2000, launched at the NAMM trade show in 1999 with a potential list price of $20,000. This time the inlay was wrapped over the lower bouts of the arched-top

THE McCarty Model

There is no better example of Paul Reed Smith's approach to the development of the solidbody electric guitar than the McCarty Model, launched in 1994. It may have looked like a slightly plainer version of the company's Custom 22 model, but it was the embodiment of all the changes that Smith had been experimenting with during the early 1990s. And yet, importantly, it looked back to the golden age of the instrument.

The model's name was a tribute to Theodore "Ted" McCarty (see feature opposite), who up to that point at least was a rather overlooked pioneer of the electric guitar. This was probably because no instrument nor company had previously borne his name. Yet McCarty had joined Gibson in 1948 and was its president between 1950 and 1966. As such he was directly responsible for running this most prestigious of American guitar companies during the period that produced the Les Paul, ES-335, Flying V, Explorer, Firebird, SG, Byrdland, the Tune-o-matic bridge, the humbucking pickup and a lot more. When McCarty

started his tenure at Gibson, he recalls. "We had 150 employees and 60,000 square feet. When I left in 1966 we had 1,200 employees and the factory covered two city blocks, 250,000 square feet."

But the McCarty Model wasn't just about Smith's interest in Gibson's classic Les Paul. It was a combination of factors. Guitarist David Grissom had called Smith in late 1992 saying he wanted a guitar that sounded like Duane Allman on The Allman Brothers' *Live At Fillmore East* album. "Basically, all the things Ted had been talking about, all the things we were aiming for, and all the things that David Grissom wanted were the same things," says Smith. "The McCarty Model was essentially a Dragon with a thicker body, thinner headstock, lighter tuners and different pickups. We'd already been toying with many of the guitar's features, and some were already in production, like the steeper headstock angle, the wide-fat necks, longer heels, 22 frets and thicker bodies. David's request helped put that combination together." Like the Artist and

▼ McCARTY MODEL

PRODUCTION PERIOD: *1994-CURRENT*

THIS EXAMPLE: *1994*

This model was the first to bear Ted McCarty's name, which has since been applied to the Archtop and Hollowbody instruments, and at the time of writing was planned for the forthcoming single-cutaway solidbody PRS model (see page 102). The launch of the PRS McCarty Model in January 1994 presented a guitar that listed for

$2,900, some $720 more than the Custom 22 which was the highest-priced PRS outside of the limited-edition Artist and Dragon. Note the non-locking tuners and three-way toggle here. The McCarty Model came in two colours: McCarty Sunburst (Smith's favourite, and the finish of this guitar) plus McCarty Tobacco Burst (McCarty's preferred hue). The first 100 McCarty Models were signed and numbered on the backplate (see below, right). This example is number 47 of that first run.

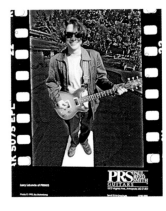

The McCarty Model quickly became the preferred choice of many artists, including the two guitarists on these mid-1990s PRS ads: Larry LaLonde of Primus (far left) and Ross Childress of Collective Soul (near left).

do know is that the combination works. I think the McCarty Models sound like old Les Pauls: really wonderful guitars. Consistently, they sound good." The headstock itself changed too, being slighter thinner at $^{19}/_{32}$" (15mm) instead of $^{21}/_{32}$" (16.5mm), like an old Les Paul. And the guitar featured non-locking tuners of lighter weight, replicas of the keystone-buttoned Klusons that graced the old Les Pauls.

The McCarty was the first PRS to advertise what they called Michigan maple, better known as red maple. "We dubbed it Michigan maple," said Smith, "to let people know it's the same kind of maple as Gibson used in the 1950s. There are several kinds of maple, and a lot of our guitars use either big leaf maple or red maple. The McCarty guitars specifically use red maple."

Another first for PRS was the use here of covered humbuckers: a seemingly retrograde step, but one that as

Dragon before it, the McCarty Model brought more changes to the PRS recipe. While features such as the 22-fret wide-fat neck with its longer heel and steeper headstock back-angle were retained, the thickness of the mahogany back was slightly increased, creating an overall body thickness of two inches. In 1994 Smith had seemed unsure exactly what effect that feature had. "The body thickness is just one factor," he said then. "We're playing with a lot of factors: the pickups, the bridge, the kind of wood the tops are made of, and the head angle. It contributes, but to what percentage I don't know. What I

▲ McCARTY MODEL

PRODUCTION PERIOD: *1994-CURRENT*

THIS PROTOTYPE: *1994*

Just as well this is a prototype: note the position of the headstock logo. This would never pass PRS's stringent quality control checks.

The first 100 McCarty Models were signed on the backplate (above) by Ted McCarty, and numbered accordingly.

TED McCARTY

Paul Reed Smith found out about Ted McCarty during an early-1980s visit to the patent office, when he kept noticing McCarty's

name appearing on Gibson patents. "I thought: who's Ted McCarty? Then I realised he was the one who did the Gibson thing. I've always sought teachers, whether it be in business or whatever. So I wanted to meet Ted and talk about the art."

They first met in 1986 (Smith and McCarty are pictured in the factory, right). "I wanted to know about what glues he used, what he glued the frets in with, how he levelled the fretboards, how he dried them, how he bound them, and how he glued the necks on,"

recalls Smith. "Ted said: Nobody's asked me these questions in 20 years! People only wanted to know where they could they find a Moderne or a Flying V. They didn't want to know about the art. Unbelievable. So we hired him as a consultant and he downloaded the hard disk."

Smith spent a week with McCarty at the ex-Gibson president's residence in Maui, Hawaii, soaking up information, especially about PAF pickups and the Les Paul model (McCarty, with dark tie, is pictured with Les Paul at Gibson in the 1950s, left). "I asked Ted why the early Les Pauls had a gold top. He said, 'So we could hide from Leo [Fender] the fact that they had a maple top.' But Ted, I said, you could see the maple top inside the horn. And he said, 'Yeah, but Leo never looked!'"

Smith and McCarty gradually became friends. "When I started PRS," says Smith, "we'd never made guitars before on a production level. When Ted joined Gibson, they'd been making guitars for 50 years. I had no experience, and that's why I needed help." Sadly for the guitar world, McCarty died in 2001.

The McCarty Model

The biggest McCarty Model in the world sits atop the building housing the Hard Rock Café in Baltimore, Maryland (pictured left, and in ad far left), very visible evidence of the ever-rising reputation of PRS instruments.

---

the 1990s progressed became de rigueur for many other guitar-makers. Under the brass covers were two PRS Dragon Bass pickups, both alnico-powered and the closest PRS made, at the time, to Gibson's classic PAF. "The covers affect the pickups a lot," said Smith of these first covered 'buckers. "Take 'em off and you'll get more high-end and bass."

Another seemingly backwards step was the use, again for the first time on a PRS, of a Gibson-style three-way toggle pickup selector switch, replacing the more versatile five-way rotary switch of earlier models. The toggle offered the classic Gibson-style selections of either humbucker on its own, or both in parallel.

The brass pickup-covers were changed in late 1995 to nickel-silver covers, initially unplated and just buffed. PRS's internal ECN sheet revealed the reasons: "Less midrange loss; more authentic looking; easier to solder; cheaper in long run: no plating." But by April of the following year it was decided to plate the covers with

nickel or gold, to prevent tarnishing and enhance quality. By January 1995 these covered humbuckers were referred to as "new McCarty" pickups, and by February 1996 a pull/push switch was added on the tone control to coil-split the pickups for three additional single-coil tones.

While the McCarty Model clearly pays homage to the late-1950s Gibson Les Paul, did McCarty himself have any design input? "I didn't contribute any specific designs," he says. "By that time my sight was so poor I couldn't do it. Anyway, Paul was perfectly capable of doing that: the PRS McCarty is his design."

"It's kind of like the way they did it at Gibson," suggests Smith. "They designed the Les Paul, and put Les Paul's name on it. The reason we called it the McCarty Model is because everything Ted was teaching me is incorporated. He taught us how to make PAFs. I said they were made like this, he said no. All the ways people think they were made, Ted told me different. Our Dragon Bass pickup is the result. So yes, Ted did have a part in the design."

PICKUPS AND ELECTRICS

PRS PICKUPS: FROM STANDARD TO SOAPBAR

The Standard Treble and Standard Bass humbuckers were the first PRS pickups, used from 1985 on the Custom and Standard, and the Signature. Like regular humbuckers, both had a "feeder" magnet under the two coils, but unlike most humbuckers they had actual magnetic slugs in the non-adjustable inner coil (not the usual non-magnetic polepieces). This meant they achieved a more accurate "narrow-aperture" (or Strat-like) pickup sound when split.

"The idea was to have a Fender coil and a Gibson coil – and it worked," says Smith. "You could get a really clear rhythm tone, then you'd kick the sweet switch in to get darker lead tones. The problem was those pickups were bright. But if you put in a simulated tone control and a lower-value pot, and changed the output wire, they sound wonderful. Then, because the high E and B sounded too bright, we changed those slugs to stainless steel. For a long time there were four magnetic polepieces and two non-magnetic stainless steel ones, on the Treble only."

By 1987 PRS were making six pickups – Standard Treble and Standard Bass, HFS, Vintage Treble and Vintage Bass, and Single-Coil Bass. All were sold separately at a list price of $90 each, albeit in limited numbers. At the same time a "pickup-change" charge of $50 was made if you ordered a guitar but required different pickups.

The PRS Studio of 1988 had two PRS single-coils in neck and middle positions and a new humbucker, the Hot Vintage Treble. The single-coils were similar to the Single-Coil Bass: just the slug-magnet bobbin of the Standard pickup. The following year two more humbuckers, the Chainsaw and the Deep Dish, had appeared on the pricelist, and the Single-Coil Bass was dropped.

By 1990 the pickup complement had changed yet again. With the exception of the Studio and Studio Maple Top (both with the same Hot Vintage Treble and two single-coils), the EGs (see right) and the Limited Edition (with a pair of Vintage humbuckers), the entire PRS line of Signature, Custom, Standard, Special, CE and CE Maple Top had switched to an HFS at bridge and Vintage Bass at neck. Meanwhile, in the list of optional pickups, two more humbuckers were added: the HFS II and the Deep Dish II.

In 1991 the line of optional pickups was trimmed to include just the HFS, HFS II, Deep Dish II, Vintage Bass and the Multi-Tap pickup system. The Artist model had replaced the Signature and with it came a pair of new Artist humbuckers. With the 1992 Dragon Series and the subsequent Custom 22 came the important Dragon Treble and Bass pickups. Two new but shortlived signature pickups also came out: the DH Treble and David Grissom.

During 1994 the Standard 22, CE 22 and CE 22 Maple Top were all outfitted with Dragon Treble and Bass pickups, matching the existing Custom 22, and "zebra"-bobbin pickups (one black, one cream) were offered along with the standard double-black-bobbin types (both by now $100). These were joined by the "gold" pickup, at $110, with gold-plated poles to suit a guitar with gold hardware.

The McCarty Model of 1994 saw the first covered humbuckers on a production PRS guitar, at first a pair of Dragon Basses under brass covers, but by January 1995 these became the McCarty Treble and Bass, with nickel-silver covers (un-plated; later nickel- or gold-plated). These "new McCarty" pickups were on most of 1995's Guitars Of The Month; gold-plated ones were on the '95 10th Anniversary and '96 Rosewood Limited and Artist IV.

The new Santana guitar of 1995 introduced "zebra" Santana pickups, replicas of the Seymour Duncan '59 (neck) and Custom (bridge) of Carlos's original. The Swamp Ash Special of 1996 was the first PRS since the EG and Studio with three pickups: a McCarty Treble and Bass plus Duncan Vintage Rails in middle position.

By 1998 new versions of the covered McCartys, the "specially voiced" McCarty Archtop pickups, were made for the McCarty Archtops and Hollowbodys. Also new were Dragon II covered humbuckers, replacing the previous uncovered Dragon pickups on all 22-fret CEs, Customs and Standards. The 24-fret CEs, Customs and Standards still had the now-classic pairing of HFS and Vintage Bass.

Bringing the pickup story full circle, the recent two-pickup McCarty Soapbar and three-pickup Custom Soapbar saw the return of the P-90-style pickup that nearly lost Smith the deal with Santana back in the late 1970s. PRS use single-coil P-90-style soap-bar pickups "specially built and voiced by Seymour Duncan".

EG PICKUPS & ELECTRONICS

First-series EG models came in two variants. The EG 3 sported three Duncan single-coil pickups; the EG 4 opted for an HFS at bridge with two Duncan single-coils. Originally, both EGs featured a master volume, five-way lever pickup selector (like a Strat's) and an unusual tone system with two controls (with different-value capacitors) working on all pickups. Later, the first tone knob operated on the neck pickup and the second on the middle pickup (like a Strat), but examples exist where the first tone operates on the neck and middle pickups, the second on the bridge humbucker.

The second-series EGs offered three pickup formats: HFS at bridge, Fralin single-coil in middle and HFS at neck; HFS at bridge and two Fralin "domino" Zero-Noise hum-cancellers; or three Fralin Zero-Noise hum-cancellers. The Zero-Noise hum-cancellers used two coils, arranged like a Precision bass pickup but in a smaller cover, offering single-coil-like tonality with hum-cancelling properties. Controls were a five-way lever selector, master volume and master tone. The tone control had a pull-push switch to split the HFS humbuckers or, on the type with three Zero-Noise pickups, to offer a dual-tone effect that shifted "from a Fender sound to a Gibson sound".

FIVE-WAY ROTARY SWITCHING

"Some love the five-way," says Smith, "but a whole lot don't. It's dead between Fender-land and Gibson-land." PRS's five-way selector runs counter-clockwise from position 10 to 6 (coinciding with the 10 to 1 numbers on the control knob). The original five-way selections from around 1985 to 1987 are:

Treble Pickup (10) Volume up: PAF-like with extra bite; volume down: similar to a Strat in treble position.

Power Out-of-phase (9) Volume up: great "fat rock" tone similar to wah-wah pedal cocked half-way back; volume down: good funk tone.

Both Pickups (8) Like a Les Paul in "middle", but clearer.

"Strat" (7) Identical tone to in-between the treble and middle pickups on a Strat.

Bass Pickup (6) Volume down: classic clear rhythm tone; volume up: like an old PAF pickup's bass tone.

In 1987, position 8 was changed to give the two inner (slug) coils of each humbucker, in series, for a fat Strat-like tone. In 1989, position 9 was changed to provide the two outer (screw) coils of each humbucker in parallel.

MULTI-TAP PICKUP SYSTEM

This first appeared in 1989 and uses two humbuckers and the five-way rotary switch. Additional "tap wires" taken from each coil of the bridge pickup and from a certain point on one coil of the neck pickup allow for extra voicings that are lower in output than the full coil. "I don't think it worked that well," says Smith. Multi-Tap pickup system selections on the five-way rotary were:

Deep Dish II Bridge Humbucker (10) "Great for solos," said PRS.

Tapped Bridge Humbucker (9) Produced a sound akin to the Vintage Treble: this was "good for rhythm".

Thick Coils (8) Two inside (untapped) coils in parallel.

Thin Coils (7) Inside coils (tapped) in parallel: a thinner version of a Strat-like tone.

Vintage Bass Pickup (6)

A lesser-known variant of the Multi-Tap system was the "Ed King rig" which added a PRS single-coil between the two humbuckers of the Multi-Tap:

Deep Dish II Bridge Humbucker (10)

Tapped Bridge Humbucker (9) Produced a sound akin to the Vintage Treble.

Treble and Middle Single-coils (8)

Bass and Middle Single-coils (7)

Vintage Bass Pickup (6)

FROM SWEET SWITCH TO UPGRADE KIT

The only tone control on early PRS set-neck guitars was a small mini-toggle "sweet switch". In an early-1980s *Musician* magazine, writer JD Considine said it "can transform the angry aggression of [a] PAF tone, virtually identical to Edward Van Halen's signature snarl, into the muted dignity and jazzy smokiness of a '59 Les Paul".

A normal tone control was offered as an (unlisted) option, and first came as standard on the '87 Special, then on the Studio, Classic Electric and Limited Edition. By late 1991 the sweet switch was replaced by a tone control on Customs and Standards and all subsequent models.

PRS's five-way rotary switch was a key original feature, but not everyone found it easy to use. The first break came with the 1988 Classic Electric, which originally had a chrome-tipped three-position mini-toggle giving: bridge humbucker; inside coils in series; neck humbucker. By June 1990 this changed to the standard five-way rotary.

Aside from the EGs, the next model without the five-way was the 1994 McCarty Model. This originally used a three-way Gibson-type toggle switch: just bridge; both pickups (in parallel); neck humbucker. Later this was changed to include a coil-split (voicing the inside slug-coils of both pickups simultaneously) working from a pull-push on the tone control. The three-way toggle and coil-split switch became known as "McCarty electronics", appearing as standard on the 10th Anniversary and Artist IV, and from 1998 as an option on CE, Standard and Custom models.

The single-coil McCarty Soapbar uses just a three-way toggle, obviously without the coil-split function, while the Swamp Ash Special uses a three-way toggle to switch its two McCarty humbuckers. It also has a pull-push on the tone control that splits the neck pickup only and activates the middle-placed Seymour Duncan Vintage Rails.

At first the Santana "reissue" used two mini-toggle switches, as on Carlos's original handmade PRSs. With both switches down, the bridge pickup is selected; both up, and the neck pickup is voiced. With the forward switch down and rear switch up, both pickups are voiced (in parallel); with the forward switch up and rear switch down, the guitar's output is muted. From the 1998 re-launch of the Santana guitar as a special-order-only item, a three-way toggle replaced the two mini-toggles, resulting in a name-change to Santana II for the 1999 catalogue.

New in summer 1998, the Upgrade Kit was designed to improve the "fatness" and midrange definition of pre-1993 PRSs. The kit includes lighter tuner buttons and locking-tuner thumb-screws, to improve the acoustic response, and some nickel-plated-brass bridge screws to improve midrange response. Also provided is a simulated tone-control kit for sweet-switch guitars, and some "vintage" high-capacitance hook-up wire to warm up the tone.

▼ SANTANA

PRODUCTION PERIOD: *1995-98*

THIS PROTOTYPE: *1995*

Fifteen years after first making a guitar for Carlos Santana, PRS made a "re-issue" of their most influential artist's guitar. It matched the original as closely as possible, keeping the distinctive "early" shape and body purfling.

Pre-factory guitars made for Carlos Santana and others such as Neal Schon (his guitar, right) were hand-carved. Ironically, the 1995 Santana model was one of the first made with PRS's new CNC machines.

THE SANTANA AND 10TH ANNIVERSARY MODELS

Nineteen-ninety-five was a landmark year for PRS. It was their tenth anniversary: the company had evolved from upstarts into highly respected manufacturers, constantly pushing forward on quality, technology and tone.

Importantly, 1995 was also the year that two Fadal CNC routing machines were installed at PRS after Smith was encouraged and advised to buy them by Bob Taylor (of Taylor Guitars) and Sterling Ball (of Music Man). These machines would slowly take over the entire cutting and shaping of PRS bodies and necks, finally retiring the long-serving dupli-carver and neck-profiling copy lathe.

PRS were also busy promoting new 22-fret guitars, especially the Custom 22 and McCarty Model, and planned a factory move for the end of the year. So 1995 saw just two new models: the 10th Anniversary, and the Santana.

The 10th Anniversary was the latest celebratory high-line guitar, a limited edition that listed for $6,600. "We had figured out that we could engrave the birds to put all the feathers in. It was new technology and it was

beautiful," remembers Smith. The problem, he says, is that the market gets bored easily, demanding ever-more-elaborate inlays.

The 10th Anniversary was obviously going to be a 22-fret guitar with McCarty electronics, top-notch timbers, and gold-plated locking tuners and Stop-Tail bridge. The engraved bird inlays, eagle headstock inlay and abalone-purfled ebony fingerboard gave the instrument a unique grace and beauty.

It was ironic that the PRS Santana guitar saw Smith returning to a design he'd hand-built 15 years before, with its old-style 24½" scale length and 11½" fingerboard radius, and yet was among the first to be crafted by the company's new CNC machinery.

"Carlos always liked his original [pre-factory] guitars," says Smith, "and he tried really hard to like the new, modern PRS design." PRS did make him some new guitars that he appreciated, but eventually said they'd make some like the old design, which pleased him more. Smith says

An attractive element of PRS's 1990s Santana model was the personalised backplate (seen in position, far right, and close-up in the inset picture here). When Carlos Santana's original pre-factory guitars were stolen, he had already ordered new replacements. Fortunately, his original guitars were returned to him after a nationwide search. Since 1998 the Santana model has been available from PRS only to special order. The most striking visual difference between the Santana and the "standard" PRS body is the markedly different outline, which goes back to the original design that Smith used before he put PRSs into production in 1985.

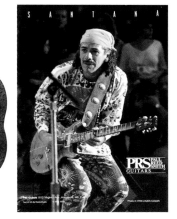

▼ 10TH ANNIVERSARY

PRODUCTION PERIOD: *1995*

THIS PROTOTYPE: *1994*

Back in the early days of PRS, few would have foreseen this model. It was issued in 1995 to celebrate the company's ten years of guitar-making since the first factory was set up in Virginia Avenue, Annapolis, back in the summer of 1985. Like all Artist guitars, it came with a certificate (pictured left) detailing precise specifications and construction. This 10th Anniversary featured a big-leaf quilted maple top, etched bird inlays and an ebony board. No-charge options included semi-hollow construction and the PRS Vibrato, while that quilted maple top added $200 to a $6,600 list price. Originally intended as a 100-piece limited edition, the run was increased to a proposed 200. This prototype is serial-numbered for 1994, but was completed during the first few days of 1995.

Since the late-1960s Carlos Santana (above) has developed an assured fusion of rock, blues and Afro-Cuban music, all tied together with Carlos's distinctively pure, sustained guitar style.

switches for pickup selection: both down for treble pickup; both up for bass pickup; top switch down and bottom one up for both pickups; reverse them and it mutes the guitar. Smith had originally used this dual-switch arrangement to enable him to get series linkage of two single-coil P-90s: not something you'd want with twin humbuckers, but Carlos liked the set-up so it stayed.

Inside the control cavity of the Santana is a small trim-pot that makes the treble pickup marginally darker, replicating a re-wound but broken pickup on Carlos's original. It's factory-set to recreate Santana's actual tone. Apart from the guitar, Smith says you also need a Mark I MESA/Boogie with an Altec 12" speaker. "He plays really loud with a lot of gain, the mid control on full, the treble at about two o'clock and the bass around ten o'clock."

In 1998 the Santana listed for $8,000, and became special-order only. At the same time a three-way toggle replaced the two mini-switches, and by the 1999 catalogue its name was changed to Santana II (see pages 90/91).

that people had been calling PRS for ten years asking for "the guitar Carlos plays"... which PRS didn't make. "So after we'd made some for Carlos we said we wanted to make it a production model and use his name. He was cool about it. We made a royalty deal, and he arranged for a large percentage of the money to go to charity."

Smith regards the Santana's sound as having more in the upper midrange than, for example, the McCarty. "The bridge pickup is really aggressive," he says, "and the neck pickup really warm and, as required, Minimoog-like. Carlos likes a powerful tone, though his amp is set quite dark." Unlike any other production PRS the Santana used a master volume and master tone but with two mini-

The 10th Anniversary model was the first instance where an eagle with "scrimshawed" engraving appeared on a PRS headstock (inset picture). The technique was

subsequently used on other high-line PRS guitars. The eagle on the 10th Anniversary also includes a suitable inscription below.

Long-serving PRS employee Marc Quigley (now Webmaster & Graphic Designer) wanted something different for his 1989 one-year employee guitar (back, left). He was inspired by Joe Knaggs's choice of having only a few fingerboard birds in atypical positions. "I realised you could use some together to look like a flock disappearing in the distance," says Quigley.

GUITARS OF THE MONTH AND EMPLOYEE GUITARS

PRS staff have the opportunity after one or two years and then again after seven years with the company to request an employee guitar, specially made for them and supplied more or less at cost. We show some examples of these often elaborate instruments over these pages.

While it's doubtful that Paul Reed Smith ever wanted to return to the penury of his early custom-building days, his need as a guitar-maker for artistic fulfilment was to some extent becoming buried under his newly-acquired skills in business and management. The various limited and artist instruments were certainly giving Smith and his team a chance to up the ante of modern guitar building. But it was the Guitars Of The Month series (GOTM) that kick-started an economically viable route to custom building.

The first prototype for the GOTM idea was Smith's amber Dragon (page 71). After two more prototypes, Joe Knaggs started making the 12 GOTM instruments, finalised between December 1994 and March 1996. The work by Knaggs on the design, prototyping and

development of key new models was about to have a major impact. The 12 GOTM instruments (plus three prototypes) gave PRS a means to experiment. They included some landmark instruments, some of which would eventually go into production or contribute features to production models. "My hope," said Smith, "is that these guitars will become the prototypes for the future of PRS."

Some GOTM instruments had special paint jobs, or fine inlay details – including the eagle headstock-inlay (Smith's "personal trademark") which would continue on the Private Stock guitars.

The GOTM guitars used timbers from Smith's Private Stash, a collection of highly-prized woods that Smith and Knaggs dip into for such special pieces. The GOTM designs included a scarlet 12-string prototype inspired by John Ingram, a baritone/tenor guitar, a re-designed EG, a left-handed McCarty, and the first PRS f-hole hollow-body guitar. Once the GOTM guitars had been evaluated, they were priced and sold.

▶ **MACHINEHEAD 10TH ANNIVERSARY**

PRODUCTION PERIOD: *1994*

THIS EXAMPLE: *1994*

PRS sometimes make special guitars for retailers. This is one of an edition of ten made for Machinehead's tenth birthday, in a unique deep purple hue. The UK dealer's name had come from a Deep Purple LP title.

◀ **EMPLOYEE GUITAR**

THIS EXAMPLE: *1996*

This employee guitar was made for Wes Bryant. The unique green translucent finish was custom-mixed to match the malachite birds inlaid on the guitar's ebony fingerboard. Also worth noting on this striking instrument is the unusual two-piece maple headstock, hand-signed in silver by Paul Reed Smith.

▲ **EMPLOYEE GUITAR**

THIS EXAMPLE: *1996*

Made for John Rausch, who was then Director of Sales at PRS, this is essentially a McCarty Model. It was the first PRS guitar coloured in what the company call tiger eye, after the semi-precious stone, and a finish now used only for PRS Private Stock and Archtop Artist models. The spectacular timbers, including a Brazilian rosewood fingerboard and a figured mahogany neck and back, were specially selected for a batch of three instruments. The other two guitars in the batch were made for action-movie star Steven Seagal and musician Robben Ford.

GUITARS OF THE MONTH

This was a sequence of 12 instruments that led directly to the current Private Stock scheme. It provided the opportunity to experiment with new ideas, and provided some features and models that went into production, including the McCarty Archtop. Here we show a selection of three Guitars Of The Month from PRS's picture archive. The complete run of 12 is detailed in the Model Key at the back of the book.

Two of the Guitars Of The Month (right), a red 12-string and a tortoiseshell Archtop. The "one of a kind 12-string prototype" was made in summer 1995, and features red coral and 14-carat gold inlay on a Brazilian rosewood fingerboard. Joe Knaggs went to Smith in spring 1995 with plans

to build this double-carved PRS hollow-body (far right), the first PRS with f-holes. Smith said: "The guitar will hopefully be the beginning of a line of very different guitars for us as a company." Prophetic words: it turned out to be the start of the McCarty Archtop and Hollowbody.

This Guitar Of The Month (right) was hand-painted by Enrica Ortega, whom Smith met on a fishing trip to Mexico. Smith and Dave Hazel designed the sterling silver fingerboard inlays "in the formations of the most prominent constellations in the sky".

PART THREE: STEVENSVILLE, 1995-

At the end of 1995 – their tenth anniversary year – PRS Guitars moved to their new factory on Kent Island, at Stevensville. This signalled a number of fundamental changes in the company which could simply be described as a more corporate attitude. Clearly, the transition from enthusiastic amateurs to the most respected new guitar brand in the industry amounted to a big success story.

"From a turnover of half a million dollars we've grown at 20 per cent per annum," Smith said in 1997, "and now we turn over $10 million gross." Smith confided that behind this tangible success were difficulties. "Both the company and me personally have our balls in the wringer all the time," he said in 1995. "It's tough doing something new. So often people walked past our NAMM trade-show booth and said, 'You still here? You haven't gone out of business?' They thought we'd be another minor company, here and then gone. But we're gonna make it."

Perhaps the biggest change was in Paul Reed Smith himself. For 20 years his vision, enthusiasm and ever-broadening skills had driven him from a student guitar-builder to the head of a highly successful manufacturing company – with all the responsibilities to his employees that went with such growth. Yet soon after the factory move, a different or at least changing man began to appear. The appointment of Doug Chandler as marketing director in 1997 was a case in point. "I gave Doug many of my responsibilities," said Smith in late 1997. "This monster is getting a little out of hand: I had to give up control of some things. I like people to have control of their jobs, to do what they think is right, obviously with some guidance and discussion. But I think there's a difference between being involved and being in the way. I'm working hard to understand that."

As PRS Guitars move through their second decade, the misguided impression that Paul Reed Smith himself still handcrafts all these guitars has faded. Even before the factory, Smith surrounded himself with assistants, advisors and mentors; these have ranged from Steve Hildebrand to Ted McCarty. The launch of the McCarty Archtop and the McCarty Hollowbody may have paid homage to the ex-Gibson president Ted McCarty, but Smith is nonetheless quick to praise Joe Knaggs – one of the factory's longest-serving employees – who conceived and developed those ground-breaking PRS models.

And if you're lucky enough ever to visit the PRS factory, you'll see for yourself that the strength of the company lies as much in the teamwork of the dedicated employees as in the vision of its founder.

▼ SWAMP ASH SPECIAL

PRODUCTION PERIOD: *1986-CURRENT*

THIS EXAMPLE: *1997*

Compare this Fender-flavoured guitar with the Custom 22 on page 37, for example, and you'll see a deeper, more comfortable chamfer inside the treble cutaway here. Early guitars had the deep chamfer, but as jigs were re-made it got smaller. When the programs were set for PRS's new CNC machines, the original "correct" chamfer was reinstated.

SWAMP ASH SPECIAL AND ROSEWOOD LTD MODELS

Paul Reed Smith had always believed that PRS guitars must appeal to both Fender and Gibson players. But as the 1990s had progressed it seemed that PRS were leaning much closer to the traditional flame of Gibson's heritage – exemplified by the McCarty Model, not to mention the overall look of the instruments.

The Classic Electric had, originally, hinted at a more Fender-oriented construction, using traditional Fender timbers such as alder for the body and maple for the bolt-on neck. But changes to pickups and, eventually, the body wood made the CE more like a cost-effective version of the Standard, and the CE Maple Top more a cut-price Custom.

As its name implies, the Swamp Ash Special restored some Fender flavour by using swamp ash, a lightweight timber favoured by Fender from the 1950s. The Swamp Ash's bolt-on curly-maple neck and fingerboard kept some of the luxuriant PRS vibe – as of course did the body outline, contouring and hardware. For the first time since

the Studio (and the optional Studio package and Ed King rig electronics) the arched-top Swamp Ash Special sported a middle pickup. It was a Seymour Duncan Vintage Rails single-coil-sized humbucker, squeezed in between two covered McCarty humbuckers. Smith felt at the time that the Vintage Rails was the best single-coil-sounding pickup on the market that didn't hum.

The guitar's unique switching allowed standard selection of the two humbuckers, but a pull-push switch on the tone control allowed introduction of the middle pickup and voicing of the slug coil of the neck humbucker, offering more single-coil-like permutations. Smith says the idea came from PRS salesman Ralph Perucci. "He wanted a swamp ash body and curly-maple neck, and asked us to put a pickup in the middle."

At its launch in 1996 the Swamp Ash Special listed for $1,980 (the same price as a CE Maple Top) but by August 1998 the price had increased to $2,400 (with the CE Maple Top lagging behind at $2,200). This was partly due

▶ **SWAMP ASH SPECIAL**

PRODUCTION PERIOD: *1996-CURRENT*

THIS PROTOTYPE: *1994*

This 1994 guitar became the prototype for the Swamp Ash Special model that was issued two years later. PRS sales representative Ralph Perucci requested what was then a PRS with strange specifications. The primary difference between this and the eventual production model is its set neck. Note also other non-Swamp Ash fittings like the Strat-style control knobs and five-way rotary pickup selector.

The Swamp Ash Special was intended by PRS to have a Fender-like tone, so naturally the production model features a bolt-on neck. But this early prototype has a set neck, as shown in the close-up picture (left) of the area around its neck-to-body joint.

▼ **ROSEWOOD LTD**

PRODUCTION PERIOD: *1996*

THIS PROTOTYPE: *1995*

This was certainly a spectacular-looking instrument, with its traditional tree-of-life inlay (close-

up, left). But the solid rosewood neck of the model makes what Smith and many others believe is an equally spectacular contribution to the sound of this PRS guitar. As a result, a rosewood-neck option was subsequently offered on the company's McCarty Model.

to the fact that finishing the ash body proved much more difficult and time-consuming than the factory had thought.

Along with the continuing Artist series in the form of the III and IV (see pages 92/93), the Rosewood Ltd fulfilled PRS's limited-edition high-line slot for 1996. Like the Dragon before it, the Rosewood brought a dual message. On one hand the tree-of-life inlay, based on a traditional theme, was a striking new design, never seen before on a PRS fretboard and headstock. This delicate inlay pattern further highlighted the work of Larry Sifel's Pearl Works team, and used a variety of materials including mammoth ivory, brown-lip mother of pearl, abalone, paua, mother of pearl, coral and gold, as well as fine etching techniques.

On the other hand, as the guitar's name implies, the Rosewood Ltd was the first PRS guitar made in any

quantity to use a rosewood neck. Smith's own amber-coloured Dragon guitar had been the first, and had convinced him of the timber's merit. (Rosewood had also been used for the neck of one of the 12 Guitars Of The Month, and according to Smith he'd made "a few rosewood-neck guitars for artists".)

Smith says that when PRS acquired a batch of Indian rosewood neck blanks it seemed like a once-in-a-lifetime chance, given his liking for his own rosewood-neck guitar. The initial plan was to offer two distinct models: one with rosewood neck, one with inlay. Bonni Lloyd suggested putting them together: the result was the Rosewood Ltd.

It used the East Indian rosewood neck blank with a rare Brazilian rosewood fingerboard. This was mated to a slightly thicker "McCarty-style" mahogany body back with an exceptional curly-maple top. The 22-fret design typically featured McCarty electronics – all gold-plated – along with anodised gold Stop-Tail and vintage tuners, or gold-plated vibrato and locking tuners.

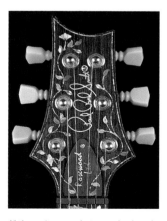

If the guitar market wasn't already convinced that Pearl Works were skilled in the art of inlay, then there could have been few disbelievers after the Rosewood Ltd, with its tree-of-life inlay continuing from the fingerboard on to the headstock (above).

▲ **PRIVATE STOCK #59**

COMPLETED: *NOVEMBER 11TH 1998*

This McCarty with camel inlays was built for Peter Wolf, now International Sales & Marketing Manager at PRS. Wolf, a key figure in the company, is "deeply involved in building our worldwide export business," compliments Paul Smith.

PRIVATE STOCK
ONE-OFF GUITARS

▲ **PRIVATE STOCK #86**

COMPLETED: *MARCH 10TH 1999*

PRS's special Private Stock guitars are all about ultimate-quality timbers. This Santana II has a "tiger-stripe" maple top as well as a tiger eye finish (see also its

exceptional back, below). The inlays are mammoth-ivory birds with 14-carat gold outlines. It was built for UK collector Garry Malone, designed and made by Joe Knaggs, Dave Hazel, Chris Bavaria and Paul Reed Smith, and assembled by Kevin Skaggs.

Mahogany is not a timber usually seen with any substantial figuring, so Private Stock #86 (back, right) is especially unusual. It uses figured South American mahogany: marbled for the neck, and curly for the back.

▲ PRIVATE STOCK #13

COMPLETED: *NOVEMBER 15TH 1996*

According to the letter that comes with each Private Stock guitar, this instrument is "the second of three Archtops hand-carved at PRS Guitars", and the owner is assured: "We love this guitar". It was hand-crafted by Joe Knaggs and assembled by John Ingram. The guitar features a curly-maple neck and black Brazilian rosewood fingerboard with gold-outlined onyx bird inlays. The top and back are "beautiful red maple" and, like the Santana II illustrated below, is in tiger eye finish.

▶ GOLDEN EAGLE

COMPLETED: *OCTOBER 23RD 1997*

Paul Reed Smith has a fascination with the work of his friend Floyd Scholz, an internationally renowned master-carver. Just ten Golden Eagles were planned, available with this golden eagle or an American bald eagle carved by Scholz into the basswood body. This one also came with curly-maple neck, engraved solid-gold bird inlays on the Brazilian rosewood board and, unusually, three McCarty humbuckers.

"Private Stock guitars are really like we've started the old workshop again with Joe Knaggs at the helm," says Smith. "Pretty much anything a customer wants, we'll make." Knaggs agrees, adding that Private Stock guitars are primarily customer-driven: PRS take orders directly from dealers and provide a quote. By way of example, Knaggs mentions a recent order for a McCarty Hollowbody II – but with a Roland GK-2a MIDI pickup and piezo electronics. "Another good example was a customer who had an old dog that died. He provided the artwork for some zany dog designs inlaid on the fingerboard, and we said yeah, why not?" While some guitars are based on existing production techniques, others need to be built fully or partially from the ground up.

Knaggs estimates the ratio of hand-work to machine-work on a Private Stock guitar is around 50/50 in the initial stages, but a double-neck, for example, would be all hand-made. The starting point for a Private Stock, he says, tends to be a McCarty with custom bird inlays, Brazilian rosewood fingerboard and double-stained "killer" top.

The first Private Stock guitar was completed on April 19th 1996. By the spring of 1999 over 85 pieces had been built, each carrying a sequential Private Stock number as well as a standard serial number. Around half have been up-scale McCartys, but there have been Archtops, double-necks, 12-strings and others. As with the Guitars Of The Month that prompted Private Stock, new ideas and designs can be prototypes for PRS production models. A Private Stock example of a McCarty Archtop was shown at the Winter NAMM show of 1997, and the positive reaction led it into production. "The mandolin is a weird one," says Knaggs. "Paul Schein at Washington Music Center asked for one, we had a few other requests, but a firm order got it rolling and we've built a few now."

Joe Knaggs at the racks of "Private Stash" timber (left), selecting some stunning figured maple headed for a Private Stock guitar. Knaggs has been with PRS since the first few months of production, and originally worked in the paint shop before he became production manager, and then what Smith describes as "my hands".

PRS promoted the high-quality neck inlay work on guitars at the top end of its line in this 1996 ad (left). The three fingerboards featured are from an Artist III (top), a Rosewood Ltd (centre) and an Artist IV (below).

ARTIST III AND ARTIST IV MODELS

The Artist III and Artist IV replaced the Artist II and Artist Limited, and completed the company's mid-1990s high-line production lines, harmonising with the similarly up-scale Rosewood Ltd and earlier 10th Anniversary models.

Both these new Artists were 22-fret guitars, with the Artist III closer to the design of the previous Artist guitars with its inlaid-signature headstock logo, open-coiled Artist pickups and five-way rotary switch. "The Artist III is full of rare paua, an iridescent shell that in the right light looks backlit," said Smith of the typically fine purfling around the fingerboard, rosewood-faced headstock and truss-rod cover. Timber specs were exceptional: mahogany necks and body backs with luxuriantly curly-maple tops, and rosewood fingerboards. "The woods remain our finest. I still play each and every Artist before it leaves our shop," commented Smith on the guitar's product flyer.

The Artist IV, however, seemed more in line with the 10th Anniversary and Rosewood Ltd models: it used gold-plated nickel-silver-covered McCarty pickups, as well as

electronics that, of course, included a three-way toggle pickup selector switch. Pearl Works excelled themselves when inlaying the IV's solid 14-karat gold fingerboard birds, headstock eagle and purfling.

"The engraving found on the solid-gold bird inlays of the Artist IV is extraordinary," said Smith. "The headstock bird alone contains over 3,900 lines." Pearl Works' Larry Sifel reckons that in fact the headstock bird contains nearer 5,000 engraved lines – and from his point of view the Artist IV was by no means plain sailing. "The first one had gold purfling, but that was a nightmare to do and it was switched to agoya, in laminate form. Without our Abalam laminate technique, agoya would have been too small a shell to use. But it's actually a fine pearl substitute."

Listing for $4,800, the Artist III came with gold-plated locking tuners and Stop-Tail bridge. The Artist IV, an altogether more up-scale piece, listed for $7,600. It too used the gold-plated Stop-Tail, but featured McCarty vintage-style non-locking tuners. Either could be ordered

▼ ARTIST III

PRODUCTION PERIOD: *1996-97*

THIS EXAMPLE: *1997*

This Artist III, number 312 of the run, was one of a select few made to commemorate the fifth anniversary of instrument retailer Garrett Park Guitars. Rick Hogue, the store's owner, added his ideas to the basic spec of the Artist III, resulting in an instrument with covered humbuckers, ebony tuner buttons, an exceptional quilted top (an option on the regular Artist III) and the rear electronics cover signed by Paul Reed Smith. The guitar naturally retains standard Artist III features such as the inlaid paua-shell headstock signature, and paua purfling.

▼ ARTIST IV

PRODUCTION PERIOD: *1996*

THIS PROTOTYPE: *1995*

Of the five Artist series guitars, the opulent Artist IV is in fact the rarest. "On the Artist I, II and III we ran under 500 of each," comments Larry Urie, Sales Manager at PRS Guitars. "The Artist Limited had a proposed run of 200, but only 165 were made. The Artist IV? We made under 70."

The engraved-gold 12th-fret bird inlay on the Artist IV (close-up, left). Smith described the work as "extraordinary", although the computer-assisted process is the same as that used for the 10th Anniversary model (see page 83).

with PRS vibrato or semi-hollow body at no extra charge; the extra for a quilted maple top was $240.

Both these Artist guitars illustrate how the "prototype" Guitars Of The Month influenced future models: the paua inlay of the Artist III was originally used on one of the three prototypes made for that programme. Smith says that the inlays on the second prototype guitar of the Guitars Of The Month series were made from New Zealand paua shell, "in my experience the most beautiful shell in the world". This was another inlay made possible by the Abalam laminate process developed by Pearl Works; previously, paua had been too small to use effectively. Larry Sifel from Pearl Works says they also use paua heart, from the area where the muscle attaches to the shell at the very centre, which can give an opal-like effect.

The solid-gold engraved birds and headstock eagle first surfaced on the second of the 12 Guitars Of The Month. "To my knowledge this has not been done before," said Smith of this inlay. Of course, Pearl Works had already supplied engraved pearl birds for the 10th Anniversary, and the Artist IV used the same computer-controlled engraving program.

The Artist III and IV were to be the last of the Artist Series, although the concept still lives on among the present PRS models with the top-of-the-line $10,000 McCarty Archtop Artist. Yet in the same way as the optional Studio Package was introduced after the Studio model itself was dropped, customers can order either a Custom 22 or 24 with an "Artist Package" (see page 38). This $1,200 option introduced on the August 1998 pricelist upgrades the instrument's specification with paua bird inlay, rosewood headstock facing, Artist-grade flame or quilt top, "translucent toned back" and leather case.

When Smith photocopied a T-shirt back in the pre-factory days to create his original eagle headstock motif, it's unlikely that he could have imagined that 20 years later it would be treated to this extravagantly engraved gold version (above) on the Artist IV.

▲ McCARTY STANDARD

PRODUCTION PERIOD: *1994-CURRENT*

THIS EXAMPLE: *1998*

Often overlooked and evidently under-promoted, the all-mahogany Standard models in the PRS line take us back to a time before Paul Reed Smith discovered the attractions of curly maple. It was the sound of early all-mahogany Juniors and Specials that had originally inspired him to make guitars. The McCarty Standard brings features introduced on the McCarty Model (see page 77) to an all-mahogany instrument.

McCARTY STANDARD AND McCARTY SOAPBAR MODELS

In the same way that the Custom is complemented by the non-maple-top Standard, so the McCarty Model has its own lower-priced all-mahogany McCarty Standard. Not that you'd know it. It's a guitar that has never received an ounce of advertising or promotion and doesn't even rate a photo in any PRS catalogue.

"We used to advertise the mahogany guitars, but we never got anywhere with them. We let it go," sighs Smith. "People buy them at their own rate. You can't force people not to buy curly maple when they really want it."

The McCarty Standard was actually first offered on the 1994 pricelist at $2,760, only then it had the same specification as the McCarty Model but with an opaque-finish maple top offered in the stock colours of just gold top or custom black. By the start of 1996 the McCarty Standard was offered in three more colours: vintage cherry, natural, and black. And, said PRS, "Vintage cherry and natural McCarty Standard models have solid mahogany bodies." Presumably to reflect this loss of the

maple top, the list price dropped to $2,480. By 1998 the guitar had stabilised at $2,300. The stock colours were now vintage cherry, natural, black sunburst and walnut, augmented by that year's list of custom opaque colours that included seven metallics, seafoam, black, antique white and ocean turquoise. By late 1998 more translucent colours were offered, although the only specification options remained as gold hardware or abalone bird inlays.

By the mid 1990s the guitar industry, like many other consumer businesses, was in the hold of a pronounced "retro" design craze. There had already been a certain return to classic guitar sounds, reflected in features like lower-output covered humbuckers emulating those classic Gibson PAFs of the 1950s. But other "old" pickups began popping up more frequently too: Danelectro-style lipstick-tube single-coils and, notably, the Gibson P-90 single-coil. The P-90 had been the forerunner of Gibson's humbucker and, of course, was one of Smith's favourite pickups in his pre-factory guitar-making days. So the announcement of

A McCarty Soapbar in turquoise from the 1998 catalogue (right) where PRS emphasise the retro vibe of this guitar, featuring a style of pickup first used by Gibson decades earlier.

The McCarty Soapbar

The old "Soapbar" single coil pickups had a clarity of tone—without sounds thin and weak—that had defined the sound of Rock and Roll and small combo jazz guitar playing in the 1940's and 1950's.

We wanted to try some on our McCarty Model, but the search for the "right" Soapbar proved difficult. It seems other guitar companies settled for second best. Our R & D Department worked with the experts at Seymour Duncan and designed a pickup with all the thick vintage punch of the original with a sparkling definition that's right up to the minute.

Andrew Fleming in the UK's *Guitarist* magazine says, "A fabulously retro take on PRS's established Strat meets Les Paul theme. An absolute cracker". Tom Wheeler says it "looks like an heirloom instrument and a '55 Chevy showcar at the same time".

Check out our Price List for more cool colors like the Ocean Turquoise shown opposite.

Our web site has our complete Accessory Shop online.

www.prsguitars.com

the McCarty Soapbar guitar in 1998, with its P-90-style soap-bar pickups, was no surprise. But according to Smith this was not a backward-looking instrument. "No, it wasn't really a return-to-roots guitar," he said, explaining that it was more to do with PRS men Doug Chandler and John Rausch urging for such an instrument. "I was saying: Please don't stick a stacked [humbucking] P90-style in there," recalls Smith. "Let's put a real P90-style single-coil in the guitar... but one that sounds good."

The P90-style single-coil with its soap-bar cover gives any guitar a distinctive look; the intended tone sits half way between the thinner and rawer Strat or Tele single-coil sound and the smoother, fuller-bodied Gibson humbucker. But the P-90 was notorious for picking up hum – which of course led to the invention of the humbucking pickup back in the 1950s. "Seymour Duncan worked with us on the pickups," says Smith of the non-hum-cancelling soap-bar pickup that graces the McCarty Soapbar. The immediate success of the McCarty Soapbar guitar prompted another model, the three-pickup Custom Soapbar (see page 38) launched in 1998.

The different single-coil pickups of the McCarty Soapbar mean that there's no need for the coil-split facility of the humbucker-equipped McCarty Model. Other than that, the two guitars are identically spec'd. Originally listing for $2,500 (with or without maple top, depending on colour), when the McCarty Soapbar appeared on PRS's late-1998 list the pricing confusion was cleared up by starting with the all-mahogany-body version at a base price of $2,300. Then, a maple top and opaque colour adds $200; maple top with translucent finish adds $400; and a 10-top option adds $500. Bird-inlays and the PRS vibrato and locking tuners were the only quoted options.

With the exception of its f-holes, the deep-body Archtop can look identical to a standard PRS, face-on. So this 1998 ad (right) highlighted the side of the body.

▲ McCARTY ARCHTOP (1st VERSION)

PRODUCTION PERIOD: *1998-CURRENT*

THIS PROTOTYPE: *1997*

The spruce-top/mahogany-back Archtop kicked off the line with a

list price of $3,200, which was $40 cheaper than a McCarty Model loaded with optional bird inlays and gold-plated hardware. This prototype has a single pickup, unlike the two-pickup layout that eventually went into production.

McCarty Archtop Models

Four years after the launch of the solidbody McCarty Model, PRS introduced probably their most innovative electric guitars to date: the hollow-body McCarty Archtop and McCarty Hollowbody.

The McCarty Model had been a reaffirmation of the constructional details that makes late-1950s Gibson Les Paul guitars so desirable. But the Archtop and Hollowbody used the company's mastery of their three-dimensional CAD software and CNC routing machinery to produce an instrument with a top and back carved inside and out, like a violin. It melded the modern PRS outline with the appearance of a traditionally hand-carved f-holed archtop guitar from a bygone age.

The first ever f-holed hollow-body PRS goes back to the Guitars Of The Month, and September's guitar, number nine of the 12. Subsequently, master luthier Joe Knaggs created two further prototypes. Private Stock number 13 (see page 91) and number 14, completed respectively on November 15th 1996 and January 15th 1997. "Those were

mostly hand-carved," explains Knaggs, "and not totally produced by the CNC machines like the eventual Archtop and Hollowbody models." Smith said the antique tiger eye-coloured number 13 was "an exceptionally fine instrument" and that "this will be a prototype for a future PRS model".

The idea of making a hollow-body PRS guitar came from Joe Knaggs, who describes himself today as a keen "ex-jazz guitarist". Knaggs relates: "What I hated about large-bodied L-5s and the like was that I never felt really comfortable. It was more like playing a big Martin. I didn't feel they allowed you to be versatile. To me the concept of a small-bodied archtop like, for example, an Ibanez George Benson was really cool – but that model really didn't sound as good as my L-5.

"I envisaged there being a compromise in the low-end response," Knaggs admits, pondering the physics of the small-bodied hollow design. "But I was surprised how much sound we pulled out of the Archtop." The Private

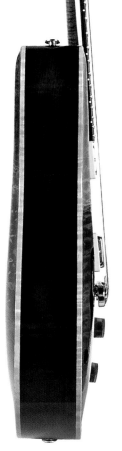

From the front, an Archtop can appear identical to a Hollowbody. It's only an inch in body depth that differentiates the two models. However, it has a profound effect on their feel and performance. Here we show an example of the Hollowbody (above left) and the deeper Archtop (above). Due to their unique construction, both guitars are remarkably resistant to unmusical feedback, a problem afflicting most hollow electrics.

McCarty Hollowbody Models

"I've asked Ted McCarty on a couple of occasions what his proudest achievement was during his time at Gibson," recounts PRS's Doug Chandler. "He's always said that it was the ES-335, because it was almost entirely his idea, and was an immediate success. Ted told me he thought that the solidbody guitars people were making back then sounded too sharp and, while he liked the idea of a larger hollow-body, he didn't like the feedback. Hence the 335.

"In the same way that the McCarty solidbody reflected the input Ted gave Paul on the things that made the original Les Paul so wonderful, we felt it only right to credit Ted on these hollow-body guitars. In many ways we were after a similar goal that he'd achieved with the 335."

Thus inspired by the ES-335, the Hollowbody essentially creates a link between the more traditional, deeper Archtop and PRS's solidbody designs. Paul calls it "a violin with a guitar attached". The only constructional difference between the Archtop and Hollowbody is one inch of body depth: the Hollowbody is 3" deep at the bridge and 1¾" at the side. But such an apparently small reduction creates a completely different guitar in feel, sound and performance.

While the Hollowbody may have been an afterthought and not part of the original Archtop concept, it has proved – at the time of writing, at least – to be the most successful of the two models. In terms of feel and "bulk", the Hollowbody is more familiar, but with the same compact shape of a solidbody PRS. Although semi-acoustic

The McCarty Hollowbody II

When we were developing the McCarty Hollowbody guitars we took a leaf out of Ted's own book and sent our prototypes out to key players to get feedback on improvements.
Problem is, nobody would give them back!
The beautiful solid curly maple top and back are carved inside and out, producing an acoustic tone and volume far in excess of the instrument's size. The specially wound McCarty Archtop pickups give the Hollowbody the ability to cover many musical bases, from traditional jazz/fusion to '90's rock. Dave Burrluck in the UK's Guitar Magazine puts it, "I haven't gone mad! This guitar is very versatile". He was equally impressed by the way we put them together, adding, "This is a guitar of stunning quality".

Our web site is constantly updated.

www.prsguitars.com

A spread from PRS's 1998 catalogue (left) dedicated to the Hollowbody II model hints at its major strength: versatility.

electric guitars enjoyed a highly visible resurgence, especially in the UK during the Oasis-led Britpop explosion that took place in the mid 1990s, generally it transpired that many PRS players were looking for a different feel and sound, and that their imagination was captured by the Hollowbody.

"I suspect we'll begin to see more and more hollow and semi-hollow electrics," Smith predicted, accurately, before the launch of the hollow PRSs. "I think there's a real move for cleaner and more acoustic-sounding guitars. Coming up with the Archtop and Hollowbody is a big deal." The

success of the hollow guitars is reflected by their impact on production. At the end of 1998, less than a year after their launch, PRS's raw-timber specialist Rob Martin told me that PRS production at that time was composed of around 40 to 50 per cent hollow-body guitars – and that a lot more of that part of the company's output were Hollowbody models than were Archtop models.

The hollow-body programme is in fact more significant than many realise. Like the solidbody McCarty Model, the guitars draw heavily from past techniques. But they simply would not have been possible without PRS's grasp of the CAD/CNC machinery that shapes them. Other hollow-body archtops and semi-acoustic guitars mostly use pressed-maple laminate tops and backs for production efficiency.

Conversely, archtop guitars whose tops and backs are literally hand-carved from solid wood command a very high price and are impossible to produce in any significant numbers. PRS realised that by using solid wood and shaping it on the CNC machines they could produce a

▼ **McCARTY HOLLOWBODY**

PRODUCTION PERIOD: *1998-CURRENT*

THIS PROTOTYPE: *1998*

Although the regular Hollowbody, which lists at $3,000, features a spruce top with mahogany back and sides (like this example), a figured maple top is optional, as well as a high-grade 10-top in flame or quilt figure. Whatever the top, the regular Hollowbody always features a mahogany back, unlike the Hollowbody II which has a maple top and back as standard.

Paul Reed Smith (left) with Ted McCarty at the 1998 NAMM trade show, where McCarty was on hand to help launch the PRS Archtop and Hollowbody models that bear his name. "He handed the baton on to us," said Smith.

superior tone – but with the production and cost-efficiency of laminated hollow or semi-hollow instruments. "It's extremely simple inside the hollow-body guitars," says Joe Knaggs of the Archtops and Hollowbodys. "But getting it to that point... that was *not* simple. There was an awful lot of R&D and computer programming."

Time aside, Knaggs's original design seems to have been accurately replicated from prototype stage into production. "There wasn't a lot of experimenting," he remembers. "Obviously, using the CNC you have the ability to really fine-tune everything. But I said to Paul that I really don't know how the spruce-and-mahogany guitar, for example, could sound any better. Everyone who's played them so far agrees. Most who've tried them want to buy one."

Importantly, both the Hollowbody and Archtop fit perfectly into the direction that Smith sees for the future of PRS. The doubts that he had about the sound of his guitars in the early 1990s seem to have receded. "I think the [solidbody] McCartys are going very well because they

hang really well with Boogie and Marshall amps and with Fender, Riviera, Bogner... all of them," he said toward the end of 1997. The McCarty line is indeed expanding the sonic breadth of the PRS line. Eight out of 21 models listed in the 1999 catalogue are McCartys.

Maybe PRS are somehow tapping into an historic legacy that they never had. After all, Smith wasn't even born when classic electrics were rolling off production lines in the early 1950s. Or it could be that Ted McCarty really is passing on the baton, linking the past with the future.

Long-time PRS user David Grissom was on hand at the launch of the company's piezo bridge system at the winter NAMM trade show of 1999, emotively demonstrating the potential of the new acoustic-sounding hollowbody guitars. He is in no doubt whatsoever about the quality of the late-1990s PRS guitars. "Playing them is kind of like using an open canvas. There's no pre-conception about the way they're supposed to sound. The new guitars coming out of the factory are definitely the best that Paul's ever made."

▲ **McCARTY HOLLOWBODY II**

PRODUCTION PERIOD: *1998-CURRENT*

THIS EXAMPLE: *1998*

The Hollowbody II first listed at $3,600 with its Custom-grade maple back and front. Unlike the Archtops, both Hollowbody models come as standard with the non-adjustable Stop-Tail bridge (the adjustable is an option) and both are available with a number of upgrades. This example has an "Artist Package" which adds paua bird inlay, rosewood headstock facing, Artist grade flame or quilt top, "translucent toned back" and leather case.

▼ **PRIVATE STOCK #218**

COMPLETED: *FEBRUARY 20TH 2001*

Should your taste go beyond the sheer playability of the Singlecut, there is always the Private Stock scheme, PRS's custom shop that is able to come up with stunnning examples of guitar craft such as

that pictured below. The spectacular wood is a "curly" East Coast maple made all the more attractive by a finish that is matched to the turquoise inlays with 14-karat gold outlines. Also placing it beyond the regular Singlecut is the Brazilian rosewood fingerboard and headstock veneer.

The PRS Singlecut

SINGLECUT AND TREMONTI MODELS

All the production-line guitars made by PRS – aside from bolt-on-neck electric basses and the Santana models – had been based on just one classic body outline. It's certainly unconventional for a guitar maker to be so single-minded, but this unusual working method did eventually change – at the start of the new millennium as the wraps were finally taken off the long-awaited PRS single-cutaway guitar, the Singlecut model. Priced at $3,000 at its Winter 2000 NAMM launch, the Singlecut became the most expensive standard solidbody in the line (apart from the special-order Santana II).

The Singlecut had been prototyped the previous year in the company's exclusive Private Stock line, and the new model enjoyed a successful if contentious launch. Since the introduction of its first model, the Custom, PRS had always claimed that its instruments combined the two

great icons of the modern electric guitar world: Gibson's Les Paul and Fender's Stratocaster. Some people now felt that the Singlecut – a guitar clearly more inspired by the Les Paul than any previous PRS – was too radical a departure from the company's existing double-cutaway designs. Yet Smith's justification for the new instrument seems typically honest. "We've always wanted to do a single-cutaway guitar, but we never came up with a design I liked," he says. "I've tried to draw one for the past 20 years – I still have hundreds of drawings of my attempts. I've always thought the Telecaster and the Les Paul were really well done, and now I think we finally have a good single-cutaway shape."

The first advertising for the Singlecut (see above) showed Ted McCarty in the foreground with an out-of-focus Singlecut behind him. The copy read: "Ted McCarty introduced the single cutaway, carved top solid-body to the world in 1952. We learned a lot from Ted while we were working on ours." Not surprisingly, the Gibson company

▲ SINGLECUT

PRODUCTION PERIOD: *2000-CURRENT*

THIS EXAMPLE: *2001*

The new single-cutaway model finally went into production during 2000, and a comparison between this and the prototype (right) reveals the design changes that PRS made, subtly modifying the overall shape of the body, as well as radically altering the layout of the instrument's controls.

The particular design of the relatively new Singlecut model has resulted in a heel (seen on the prototype, right) that is different to a regular 22-fret double-cutaway PRS. Here, the shoulder on the non-cutaway side provides the required stiffness – a job performed on the double-cut guitars by an extended heel.

over in Nashville had a problem with this, and the ad was dropped. However, the Singlecut is a very different animal to the Les Paul. "There are about 30 differences between a PRS Singlecut and a Les Paul," suggests Smith. "There are more differences than similarities. There's the front of the headstock colour, headstock shape, headstock thickness, our double-action truss rod, and the scale length.

"There's no binding on the neck or the body on the Singlecut," he continues, "and there's no pickguard on the body. There's a different bridge set-up, the knob positions are different, the knob wiring is different, the jack-plate is a different material, and the guitar bodies are a different thickness. The heel carve is completely curved, the body outline is different in six places by at least a quarter of an inch [6mm], and there's a PRS scoop in the lower horn. There's a lot when you start looking! The pickups are different, and there are bird inlays. It's one of our guitars."

While the outline shape of the Singlecut arguably lacks the elegant simplicity of the Les Paul, it is indeed a highly

intelligent and thorough re-appraisal of this 50-year-old classic solidbody. Typically, it echoes all the benchmark construction methods that were pioneered by Gibson but adds the tone-based design flourishes that are hallmarks of PRS's instruments.

"The Singlecut is all about the neck joint," says Smith. "The way we did ours is completely different to the way that Gibson did theirs. Gibson's Les Paul has a narrow tongue-and-groove joint; ours is a dovetail. You couldn't even think about swapping the necks on these guitars. I was trying to get a PRS neck joint underneath the fingerboard. The Singlecut's joint is more like a single-cutaway Les Paul Junior."

The PRS 7 pickups of the Singlecut were another new design. Smith says they were developed by the in-house team, and then the bridge pickup was modified following a suggestion by Jeff Lanahan, the company's artist-liaison man, regarding the kind of magnet and the number of coil turns. "It's worked perfectly," Smith says. "They're made

▲ PRIVATE STOCK #78

COMPLETED: *MARCH 30TH 1999*

This was the first prototype (smaller guitar, above) of what at the time was the new, unseen PRS single-cutaway guitar, designed and hand-made by Joe Knaggs, Dave Hazel, Chris Bavaria, John Ingram and Paul Reed Smith. It featured a Brazilian rosewood fingerboard and East Coast curly-maple top with South American mahogany neck and back, and was subtly hollowed to reduce weight and add resonance. While this guitar is a prototype, it fell within the Private Stock scheme.

very differently from the pickups we normally produce." Smith is unwilling to give too much away, but it's claimed that a unique process gives the 7s a vintage performance combined with the ability to function at today's high levels of gain and volume. He says that compared to the McCarty Model – the most Les Paul-sounding PRS up to this point – the Singlecut has a cleaner bass pickup and a rather more powerful treble pickup.

The layout of the Singlecut's four controls is also different to the layout that has always been used on a Les Paul. For the PRS Singlecut model, the set of two volume and two tone controls is flipped compared to a Les Paul's. The knob closest to the bridge on a Singlecut governs bridge pickup volume.

Directly below that knob is the Singlecut's neck pickup volume, while the two controls furthest away from the guitar's bridge are for bridge-pickup tone (top) and neck-pickup tone (below). Smith says the company interviewed players and discovered that the bridge-position treble

pickup's volume knob is the most used Les Paul control. That's why it was positioned closest to the bridge on the Singlecut. But surely these important differences in the layout will just confuse Les Paul players? "I hope so," laughs Smith. "Seriously, I don't see it as a problem, because I know that some of those players wished their Les Paul was wired the way we've done it. I can't look into the future. But we did it like that because we thought it was a better way to play this type of guitar."

Wood choice is identical to PRS's Custom but, as ever, creating the "right" weight is of paramount importance. Smith says that the Singlecut's maple top and mahogany back are both different thicknesses than a Les Paul. "A Les Paul is thicker," he says. "It can be too heavy. Our back is thinner. The mahogany backs we buy are fairly light, and the mahogany necks are as strong and heavy as we can get them."

A year after the launch of the Singlecut, PRS launched at Winter NAMM 2001 the Mark Tremonti Model. Bearing

▼ TREMONTI MODEL

PRODUCTION PERIOD: *2001-CURRENT*

THIS EXAMPLE: *2001*

Creed guitarist Mark Tremonti is only the second ever artist to be blessed with a PRS signature model – and Carlos Santana is a tough act to follow. Never mind – Creed has proved to be one of the

most successful new American acts of recent years. The band's guitarist (seen in action in PRS's promotional ad, near left) chose a personally appointed version of the company's Singlecut model (an ad for the regular edition of which is pictured, far left). The Tremonti Model came in two special finishes: black, like the one pictured here, or platinum.

► SINGLECUT BRAZILIAN ROSEWOOD

PRODUCTION PERIOD: *2001*

THIS EXAMPLE: *2001*

An especially attractive version of the Singlecut was this limited-run edition that came with a solid Brazilian rosewood neck and fingerboard. Supplies of this hallowed guitar-making wood have been severely curtailed since trade in Brazilian rosewood was embargoed some years ago. PRS now use it for some Private Stock instruments, as well as for this special run of 250 Singlecuts.

in mind that Carlos Santana is the only other PRS signature artist, this was an important accolade for the Creed guitarist. As one of the biggest rock acts in the US in recent years, with over 12 million records sold and seven number-one singles, Creed and Tremonti have been instrumental in proving that the Singlecut is a viable alternative to a Les Paul.

The Tremonti Model, which originally appeared on PRS's pricelist for $3,400, is in fact identical to the company's regular Singlecut model, except that it comes with a special 12th-fret signature inlay, as well as a customised truss-rod cover, and a choice of either a black or platinum finish. And, emphasises Smith, the pickups are different. "Mark wanted a very powerful treble pickup. He was insistent that it be his exact sound. It's a ceramic-loaded high-output pickup at the bridge, while the neck unit is a version of our 7 bass pickup."

Later in 2001, a 250-only limited edition Singlecut appeared with a Brazilian rosewood neck, brushed nickel

pickup covers, and a satin gold-anodised Stop-Tail bridge. This is close in specification to the guitar that Smith himself plays (though he still favours a double-cutaway outline). "The two that I bought for myself, Carlos Santana took from me," he laughs. "They sounded ridiculous! I lent them to Carlos to record the follow-up to *Supernatural*, and he said, 'Can I have them? Please?' They were pretty special to him."

Smith says that the satin gold-anodised bridge and the brushed nickel pickup covers started the company's system of providing "half and half" hardware. "We'll be doing more of that as time goes on.

"I like the half-and-half look way better than all-gold hardware," Smith continues. "We're breaking new ground with this concept, and I don't know of any other maker right now who's using an aluminium bridge – you can only anodise aluminium. Most other manufacturers are using zinc or brass. So, yes, in a way you could say that it's me bringing my guitar to the industry."

Artist liaison man Jeff Lanahan has done much to increase PRS's popularity with high-profile new bands, which by 2000 had reached near endemic proportions and prompted a slew of ads such as this for the Electric Bass (right).

▲ **PRIVATE STOCK #199**

COMPLETED: *FEBRUARY 28TH 2001*

By mid 2001 the new Electric Bass and fancier Electric Bass Maple Top models were being fitted with a new internal pre-amp to provide an active boost that gives the instrument's tone a

helpfully improved bottom-end. This early Private Stock example (main guitar) incorporates the new unit, which is brought into circuit by that extra mini-toggle switch positioned near the bridge. This particular Electric Bass has a beautiful curly maple top enhanced by its satin finish, and features a Brazililan rosewood fingerboard.

ELECTRIC BASS AND ELECTRIC BASS MAPLE TOP

Nearly ten years after the first-series PRS basses were discontinued, a new electric bass design appeared in the company's catalogue in the form of the bolt-on-neck Electric Bass and Electric Bass Maple Top models. Launched at the Winter NAMM 2000 trade show, the Electric Bass Maple Top listed for $2,600, while the plainer Electric Bass at $1,980 was the lowest-priced US-made PRS instrument.

The new bolt-on PRS Electric Bass bears little resemblance to the first-series basses, many of which are now collectors' items. The project was kick-started in 1997 when Paul Reed Smith suggested to Joe Knaggs that he should make a five-string bass for the 1998 Winter NAMM show, coinciding with an increasing number of requests from customers for a bass model.

"We all felt it was a good idea to be a broader-based musical instrument maker," says Knaggs, who headed up the new bass project, "and that part of that should be a line of basses. The bass has been more of a team design

than, for example, the hollowbody guitars. I had a lot to do with the bass, but Paul Reed Smith and I worked on it together. There was a lot of teamwork involved."

The bolt-on-neck design, with its flat-fronted-body, takes in some obvious influences. "I always describe it as a combination of a Fender Jazz, a Music Man, and a PRS bass," says Knaggs. "It's like a melding of those three." The new basses saw a return to the PRS lines of alder, a wood the company hadn't used since 1995 when the CE body changed from alder to mahogany. "Now that we're using computer-assisted (CNC) routing machines we have the ability to make a more consistent part," says Knaggs.

When PRS made alder bodies before, they used the old dupli-carver, the original routing machine that carved the arched tops of the company's guitars and original basses. "With that it was harder to control the end product. Also, we now have a very reliable source of alder, and we're getting a better grade of wood." Swamp ash was initially offered as an optional body wood for the Electric Bass,

▲ **ELECTRIC BASS MAPLE TOP**

PRODUCTION PERIOD: *2000-CURRENT*

THIS EXAMPLE: *2000*

Here's one of the earlier passive-only versions of the Electric Bass, without the pre-amp and associated mini-switch of the later

incarnation (see main guitar). This is the more expensive Maple Top variation, and shows a typically impressive piece of PRS construction. The maple top is in fact set into the instrument's alder back, and thus leaves an attractive outline of alder around the figured slab of maple.

while the Maple Top version – available only with an alder body – uses a figured maple slab that's inset into the top, leaving an alder edge.

The new basses were originally offered with an optional piezo pickup system closely related to the one offered on the Hollowbody and Archtop guitars. The bass version was designed in conjunction with LR Baggs who helped develop the circuit. Baggs built the system for PRS, and it was their piezo element in the saddles. This piezo option for the new basses featured a three-band EQ, a volume control, and a three-way "mode" switch. It was designed to augment the passive magnetic bass tone rather than provide a separate "acoustic" sound as well as the standard magnetic tones. "We didn't think players would want the bass to be both an 'acoustic' (piezo) and 'electric' (magnetic) instrument," says PRS's Winn Krozack.

However, at the time the bass was launched PRS's regular guitars were on a year's back-order, and significant orders were building up for the new Singlecut model. So

production of the bass faltered. "One of the problems was that we stopped bass production and spent time developing a pre-amp for it," explains Smith. Knaggs adds: "We decided to give people the option of going passive or going active, and then gave it a really powerful bottom-end punch with the new pre-amp. We discontinued the piezo [officially from January 1st 2002] because it was not really selling. But it is a wonderful system, and we will probably use it on the exotic basses that we make within the Private Stock programme."

Larry Urie, PRS's National Sales Manager, reckons that PRS made about 72 basses in 2000. "Thirteen of those were for the NAMM show, and there were some artist models made, but I remember shipping only about 40 or so – maybe 50 – to dealers. The new basses, now with the 'high-end audio' pre-amps, started shipping in late May and early June of 2001."

Although bass production is just a small part of PRS's output, on the eve of the Winter NAMM 2002 show Smith spoke passionately about the new non-piezo basses with pre-amps. "We're fired back up! See, the bass market is busted up: there's no one king, but a thousand contenders. I really like the way the new basses sound and the way they play. We decided from day one it was going to be a slow growth. But, for example, the new Creed record was recorded on a PRS bass. We're just going to take our time ... and it's getting better every day."

▲ SANTANA III

PRODUCTION PERIOD: *2001-CURRENT*

THIS EXAMPLE: *2001*

The latest model to adopt the early-style Santana double-cutaway body shape is the Santana III, which on launch in 2001 was

offered at around half the list price of the continuing Santana II. Paul Reed Smith is pleased with the III's unique style. "It's definitely a PRS, but it's got a different feel," he says. "It's a bit like saying, 'Do you want corned beef, or roast beef?' It's really still beef ... but they taste completely different."

SANTANA III AND SANTANA SE (FIRST VERSION)

As we've discovered, Carlos Santana has played a crucial part in PRS's history and is a wonderful ambassador for the quality and tone of the company's guitars. Nonetheless, his favoured pre-factory-era guitars with their different body outline weren't offered as production models until 1995. The original Santana (which became the Santana II, see p82-83) was an expensive special-order instrument.

In the mid 1990s, Carlos Santana was a fading light commercially. His classic albums were way behind him. But the release of *Supernatural* in 1999 marked a clever collaboration with contemporary artists and turned his career around spectacularly. In February 2000 he won eight Grammys for the album, equalling Michael Jackson's previous record for *Thriller* in 1993. Santana was seen and heard everywhere – playing his signature PRS guitars.

But PRS was slow to capitalise on this success. It wasn't until the Winter NAMM trade show of 2001 that the company launched an "affordable" Santana model. In fact there were two new models. The Santana III was – at last –

a version of the guitar that Carlos played at a production-model price. With a US list of $3,700 the simplified model was under half the price of a Santana II.

The III was the affordable version of Carlos's guitar, the fourth flavour of the PRS solidbody recipe behind the Custom, the McCarty, and the Singlecut. Not only does the Santana body outline have its own effect on the strapped-on feel of the guitar, but the shorter 24 ½-inch (622mm) scale-length and flatter 11 ½-inch(292mm) fingerboard radius contribute to a subtly different playing feel. The neck's fuller and rounder shape compared to the wide-fat neck is noticeably different too.

"It's thicker front-to-back," says Smith, "the thickest neck we make. The Santana III's shape is a little more 'pregnant', and it's a little slinkier sounding because the scale length is shorter – like tuning down to E-flat. Carlos calls it 'handsome' and says it's a big, thick, 'male' guitar."

Yet the 2001 launch of the Santana III was totally overshadowed by a very different guitar, the Santana SE.

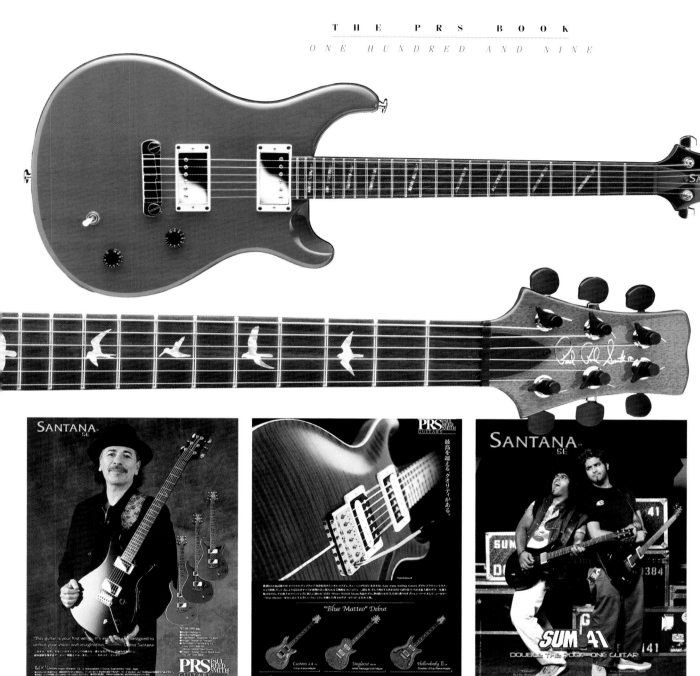

Although the first version of the Santana SE only lasted a year, it was a well received instrument. At the Frankfurt Musikmesse 2002 it won the show's International Press Award for best electric guitar. Deemed the Grammys of the musical instrument and pro audio industries, the awards were voted for by 51 international gear-related magazines. Paul Reed Smith was on hand to accept the award. "This is our first real approach with quality into a commodity market," he said of the first-version SE. A new SE appeared during 2002.

Carlos poses with a first-version Santana SE (far left), while a 2002 ad (centre) features the continuing Santana II model in that year's featured "blue matteo" finish. A further example of PRS's growing acceptance among newer bands has Sum 41 with Santana SEs.

This was the first PRS guitar to be made overseas, in Korea. While the cheapest US-made guitar, the CE Maple Top, listed for $2,300, the Santana SE ("Student Edition") had a list-price of just $738. This would have been impossible to achieve in the US factory, and provided a guitar clearly aimed at a younger market. There was concern that the SE would cheapen the brand. "It was a very understandable reaction from very proud US craftsmen," explains Doug Chandler, at the time Marketing Manager at PRS and the prime instigator of the SE project. "But to the company's credit, they reviewed all the facts and figures, and the commercial sense was inescapable."

Nonetheless, no PRS logo appeared on this first version of the Santana SE. Instead, the back of the headstock read: "Made by World Musical Inst. Co. Ltd under exclusive license from PRS Guitars." Carlos Santana's success gave PRS the name they needed. "Carlos wanted a guitar a student could buy," says Smith. "He gets lots of letters from players who want to play a guitar like his but can't

afford his signature model. We said we could pull it off. I think he's proud of it."

Rather than being a copy of the Custom, the simple, all-mahogany flat-top design of the SE harked back to the second-series EG models. Yet it had a glued-in neck that closely replicated the company's wide-fat neck profile. The guitar came with Korean-made PRS hardware (with vibrato and Stop-Tail bridge options), twin covered humbuckers made in China and designed by EMG's Rob Turner to PRS's approval, plus a simple three-way toggle pickup selector switch and volume and tone controls.

PRS then appointed a project manager, Doug Shive, who now divides his time between the US and Korea overseeing the model. The company also employs a full-time Korean factory inspector on-site to maintain quality at source. (As we'll see, the SE was later modified for a second version.) The SE was a brave move, and a guitar that allowed PRS to compete at a lower price – something the various CE and EG models had failed to do.

▼ PRIVATE STOCK

COMPLETED: 2001

Some especially pretty quilted maple was used for the top of this superb McCarty Model. Notable too are the snakewood inlays with 14-karat gold outlines, while a more expected touch on a Private Stock guitar is this instrument's Brazilian rosewood fingerboard and headstock veneer. The purfling on the headstock too is very fine, and snakewood has been used again for the tuner buttons. The overall result is a beautiful example of Private Stock art.

THE GROWTH OF PRIVATE STOCK

The Private Stock programme began back in 1996 (see p90/91) and by the spring of 1999 over 85 instruments had been completed. By the start of 2002, the total had risen dramatically to just under 400. The Private Stock team – primarily Joe Knaggs, Dave Hazel, Chris Bavaria and Kurt Tilling – now build an average of 140 instruments per year. To celebrate the craft, PRS produced a Private Stock calendar for 2002 that featured 12 of the guitars that emerged from what is in effect PRS's custom shop.

Like any manufacturer, PRS can offer only a certain number of options for its regular production instruments. If you want something a little different – and are prepared to wait between six to nine months – then you enter the Private Stock programme. But it's not simply about a slightly different specification. From the ground up, Private Stock instruments use the best quality woods, not to mention some of the most beautiful inlays you'll see on a musical instrument. Joe Knaggs says that the base list-price for a Private Stock guitar in early 2002 was around

$11,000. "That would be something like a McCarty Model with tiger-eye finish, a 'killer' figured top, and a beautiful mahogany back. It would have a curly maple neck stained in tiger-eye, a Brazilian rosewood fingerboard inlaid with abalone birds that have 14 karat gold outlines, plus a Brazilian rosewood headstock veneer and an abalone eagle inlay, again with a 14 karat gold outline. The guitar would be signed by Paul Reed Smith and it would come with a certificate describing the guitar's special points." Compare that with the specifications of a standard McCarty, which lists for $3,000, and you begin to see why such personalised one-off Private Stock guitars command such value.

Bearing in mind the number of high-profile artists currently using PRS, you might expect that they would be clamouring to place Private Stock orders. In fact, Knaggs reckons that around 95 per cent of orders are taken from

▲ PRIVATE STOCK #107

COMPLETED: *OCTOBER 26TH 2000*

The number seven features prominently in this Private Stock creation, the first all-original seven-string PRS guitar. Note the custom "7" inlays on the fingerboard – and even the Private Stock edition number is 107. You will be relieved to hear that there are only two 7s in the guitar's serial number.

▼ PRIVATE STOCK #235

COMPLETED: *APRIL 2ND 2001*

This has become a well known McCarty Model in charcoal finish – if, that is, you've seen a particular

PRS ad (see following page) or have their excellent 2002 Private Stock calendar. For it is this guitar that features in both the ad, and on the cover as well as inside the calendar. Just as well, then, that it wasn't completed a day earlier.

private buyers, including music stores, but in fact only a minuscule half of one per cent are ordered by artists. And although numerous recent models, notably the Singlecut, were fully prototyped in the Private Stock line, such R&D projects only occupy about three per cent of the instruments that PRS produces.

In early 2002 Knaggs admitted that he wasn't working on any particular prototypes within the Private Stock programme that were planned to become production models later. "But we are working on some large hollowbody models," he said, "some exotic basses, and some Archtop 12-strings." Dave Hazel from the Private Stock team says that of the two Archtop 12-strings in production in early 2002, one has a Brazilian rosewood neck, the other a mahogany neck. "They're actually

Archtop Artist models for Excel – the company that manufactures PRS's bridges and hardware – in exchange for making prototype parts, including a new 12-string bridge. They're essentially Private Stock items, although they are numbered as Archtop Artists."

Hazel says PRS also have a 28-inch-scale baritone Hollowbody in production as a Private Stock guitar. "That's a new one. We've made a couple of baritones in the past but this is the first Hollowbody version. We've also just completed some Singlecuts with a 25½-inch scale length instead of our usual 25-inch scale.

"While the outer body dimension is the same as our regular Singlecut they have a thinner, McCarty-thickness body, three Lindy Fralin single-coils, an LR Baggs X-bridge piezo-loaded vibrato, and a five-way lever pickup selector switch. At least two had swamp ash backs; the others had mahogany backs. They've certainly attracted some attention, but as to whether they'll lead to a production instrument … who knows?" Although PRS recently

A rare ad (right) for the Private Stock programme – which is usually oversubscribed anyway.

declined a request from an unnamed artist to build a guitar shaped like a unicorn, Knaggs pauses only briefly to consider the oddest commission recently taken on. "The guitar in the 2002 Private Stock calendar with the waterfall on the fingerboard has been the most unusual over the last year, I guess," he says. The "waterfall" guitar, pictured on the following pages, brightened up the month of January in that Private Stock calendar. A slate blue Custom 24 with "killer top", the guitar had a distinctive waterfall fingerboard inlay that featured mother of pearl, paua, paua heart, orange-red spiney and malachite.

As we've seen, the Pearl Works operation usually handles the inlay work on PRS guitars, but this particular fingerboard inlay, depicting a Norwegian waterfall scene, was carried out by Joe Knaggs and Danny Dedo. "Larry Sifel at Pearl Works likes to do inlays when a run is ordered, which makes it worth their while setting up all their programming," explains Hazel. "The waterfall was designed by Joe Knaggs and Danny Dedo. Danny, one of

▲ **PRIVATE STOCK #207**

COMPLETED: *APRIL 6th 2001*

Custom built for Bobby Bonilla, this McCarty Model has a strong baseball theme for the special inlays designed by Joe Knaggs, and unusually includes a motif on the body as well as the fingerboard. It's rare too for a Private Stock guitar to have a signature on the headstock as well as the regular eagle logo of the programme.

▶ **PRIVATE STOCK #314**

COMPLETED: *DECEMBER 15th 2001*

One of three guitars made especially for exhibition at the NAMM instruments trade show of January 2002, this superb custom 12-string has a striking copperhead finish and snakewood fingerboard, headstock veneer and inlays, all topped with gold-plated hardware. The other two – a Singlecut and a Hollowbody I – were similarly appointed.

our CNC operators in R&D, did the programming for the various inlay parts. Some parts were scribed into the maple fingerboard, then painted by Joe. So there was plenty of inlay – but painted parts too."

Paul Reed Smith estimates that the Private Stock instruments amount to about one-twentieth of PRS's revenue. Knaggs says that among these notable guitars, the most expensive item was an instrument produced in April 1995 for the Guitar Of The Month programme, the precursor to the Private Stock scheme. "It was purchased by Jim Jannard from Oakley Sunglasses," says Smith, recalling that the McCarty-spec guitar required a replica of the Dragon I fingerboard inlay … in solid gold.

"I remember doing two solid-gold Dragons," says Larry Sifel at Pearl Works. "One was in a plaque for Paul Reed Smith that was presented to him for his 40th birthday, but the other was for the guitar we're talking about. We ran all the same individual parts of the Dragon I inlay but in gold instead of shell and stone. Theoretically we could have

done it out of one piece and then engraved it – but we didn't," he smiles.

Yet for all their fabulous decoration, Private Stock guitars aim to capture spectacular tone. As any PRS fans will know, that starts with the wood. Not surprisingly, the Private Stock wood is of the highest quality. "It's a guess, but I'd say we have 200 highly figured maple tops stashed away," says Hazel about PRS's private wood stock.

"When we get a load of wood, Mike Reid, PRS's main wood supplier, and the guys in rough-cut go through it and separate out stuff that might be of Private Stock level. Say we get in 200 tops – there might be three that are classified in this manner. But of course we don't make a final call until the wood has been dried and acclimatised. Even then we don't decide until we start milling, and sometimes something that looked like it might be Private Stock quality might only make an Artist level or a 10-top.

"As for mahogany," continues Hazel, "we're looking for quarter-sawn wood that's highly figured. A lot of it is

▲ **PRIVATE STOCK #184**

COMPLETED: AUGUST 17th 2001

Nominated by Joe Knaggs as the most unusual and striking commission so far undertaken by PRS's Private Stock programme, this Custom 24 has a remarkable inlay on the fingerboard depicting

nothing less than a Norwegian waterfall. Aside from the Dragon instruments it represents the peak of the company's inlay work. The waterfall was designed by Knaggs and Danny Dedo, and Dedo also programmed the inlay parts. Ole Akre's other special requirements included custom horn carving and ebony headstock veneer.

'ribbon stripe' figure, which means it has shiny stripes, which is not the same as flame. But we do get a lot of flame and quilt as well. When I see people cutting up boards in the factory, if it looks spectacular I try and snitch it for Private Stock. There's also the weight to consider. A lot of people are particular about that and with mahogany it varies more than maple. Weight is as important for some people as the figure. We have certain weight criteria for specific models, and we even use internal hollow chambers sometimes to reduce weight. Our thickest solidbody guitar is the Singlecut, so we try to keep its weight down."

Although Private Stock guitars rarely use unusual or "exotic" timbers like some makers, Hazel says the main PRS wood that comes into this category at the time of writing is Brazilian rosewood. "A large percentage – more than half – of our Private Stock orders request a Brazilian rosewood neck. We also do curly maple and blistered maple necks. 'Blistered' means very figured but not in a

consistent way – more of a combination of quilt and curl, a little like a burl."

And what is Paul Reed Smith's involvement in the Private Stock guitars? "His main contribution is not so much getting his hands dirty," laughs Hazel, "because this whole show has gotten so big he can't do everything. But we'll take something to him and get approval or opinion. He definitely gets his hands on every Private Stock guitar before it leaves the building. He plays every one, and sometimes suggests different pickups, hardware, set-up or whatever. He's even more involved with artist guitars, for example the guitars for Carlos Santana.

"We ran a few guitars personally for Paul last year, almost Private Stock – though they didn't have numbers – and with those he would come back into the shop every day to see how it was going. He wanted to try some new ideas. He'd be tapping the necks – Paul is very much about sound, tapping the wood and listening to its resonance." Clearly, old habits die hard.

◀ **PRIVATE STOCK #255**

COMPLETED: *MAY 31st 2001*

There aren't too many left-handers among Private Stock output, but this is still a perfect example of the kind of upscale McCarty Model that the programme can offer.

▼ **PRIVATE STOCK #116**

COMPLETED: *FEBRUARY 29th 2000*

More unusual among the McCarty Models and Singlecuts that make up a good deal of the work of the Private Stock team is something

like this, a McCarty Soapbar. This particular example has its "perfectly quartersawn" African mahogany body enhanced by a custom vintage natural sunburst finish, while the virgin Brazilian rosewood fingerboard is, unusually, unsullied by inlays.

PRS's 2002 Private Stock calendar included the company's 50,000th set-neck guitar, and featured 12 spectacular pieces from the custom shop, captured by Jim Noble Photography and shown here in order from January (top left) to December (bottom right). Top row, left to right: #184, Custom 24, the renowned "waterfall guitar" (see also main guitar here); #255, McCarty Model left-hander ; #274, custom 12-string; #201, Singlecut with quilted top. Middle row, left to right: #125, custom 12-string with beautiful inlay; #218, Singlecut with quilted top; #107, custom seven-string with "7" inlays; #200, Santana II with quilted top, and PRS's 50,000th set-neck guitar. Bottom row, left to right: #271, Singlecut with etched birds; #199, Electric Bass Maple Top; #75 & 64, a couple of custom Electric Mandolins; and #235, McCarty Model in charcoal.

▼ SINGLECUT TREM

PRODUCTION PERIOD: *2003-CURRENT*

THIS EXAMPLE: *2003*

A lot more than just a Singlecut with vibrato, the Singlecut Trem came too late to prevent the forthcoming PRS/Gibson lawsuit (see page 122). Thinner-bodied *than the Singlecut, and with the usual two-control layout, it was much more PRS-like than the original Singlecut design. Relatively few were made before the 2004-injunction but since its return in late 2005 the SCT has found its voice as the PRS player's Singlecut.*

THE RETURN OF THE DRAGON AND THE SINGLECUT TREM

The news about PRS models was unexciting at the start of 2002. There was a simplified McCarty Archtop. There was the loss of the Custom 22 Soapbar. And there was an upgraded Santana SE. But then along came the fifth Dragon guitar.

The Dragon 2002 was made in a run of only 100, and had an equivalent-to-list price of $30,000. It was the first Singlecut Dragon, and the inlay and artwork was the most dramatic to date. Using over 300 pieces of shell and stone, the dragon was designed by Jeff Easley – who had already created the Dragon III and the Dragon 2000 – and the inlay was devised by Paul Reed Smith, Joe Knaggs and Larry Sifel. It was assembled in two dimensions and then "bent" over the face of the Singlecut and glued to the body in a vacuum bag. Once Pearl Works had inlaid the design, the guitar was sunbursted, airbrushed, and even engraved to create the fine details. Otherwise, specs on the Dragon 2002 were virtually identical to the 2001 PRS Singlecut Brazilian Rosewood Limited Edition model.

"When I saw an original rough sketch from Jeff Easley to get some ideas, all I could see in my mind was that scene in Jurassic Park where the monster looks in the window of the car," remembers Paul Reed Smith. "I called up Jeff and gave him the idea. We tried to lay his newly drawn design over our double-cut body but realised it would look better over the Singlecut. Joe Knaggs and I were working on it for a long time. We asked people for their opinions, and I hung it up in my bedroom to get a feel for it, but the whole thing smelt good from the beginning. This is a combination of guitars, guitar art, inlay art, three-dimensional inlay art, drawings of dragons, painting, air-brushing, sunbursting, and even scratched lines. There's a lot to it."

The Dragon 2002 again illustrated the significant market for such "collectors' guitars" when orders for all 100 instruments were taken by the end of the first day of the Winter NAMM 2002 trade show where it was officially announced.

2003 was similarly light on new core models – the

◄ DRAGON 2002

PRODUCTION PERIOD: *2002*

THIS EXAMPLE: *2002*

This latest Dragon has 312 inlaid parts, with 12 different kinds of shell, five types of reconstituted stone, and mastodon ivory for the teeth. "It's the largest area we've ever covered on any guitar," says Pearl Works' Larry Sifel. The Dragon 2002 includes PRS's new locking tuners (right), which says Paul Reed Smith, are the same design concept as those on Carlos Santana's pre-factory guitars. Compared to the previous types, the new ones have a smoother feel, and are more straightforward in use. "Don't clamp them too tight," advises PRS's John Ingram. "A quarter to half a turn on the locking bolt is all you need to hold the string firmly in place."

▲ McCARTY ARCHTOP (2ND VERSION)

PRODUCTION PERIOD: *2002-2004*

THESE EXAMPLES: *2002*

This revised version of the 1998

original is the last surviving deep-bodied Archtop model in the line. It has PRS's Baggs-developed piezo system in addition to the two regular magnetic humbuckers. This new set-up is now governed by

three control knobs, for humbucker volume and tone plus piezo blend/volume. There's also a three-way toggle magnetic pickup selector, and a mini-toggle to choose magnetic, piezo, or both.

exception was the long-awaited Singlecut Trem. If the Singlecut itself may have been too un-PRS-like for many with its thick body, four controls and Stop-Tail-only bridge option, the Singlecut Trem could have been called the Singlecut Custom. "That's *exactly* what it is, that's a great name," says Smith. "Maybe we should have called it that." Spec'd with a 2.098-inch (53.3mm) thick body as opposed to the Singlecut's 2.29-inch (58.2 mm)*, the Singlecut Trem featured two zebra-coil 6 humbuckers with standard volume and tone controls (with push/pull coil-split switch) and only a PRS vibrato (to give the misnamed "tremolo" its correct term).

"I think some players look to us for a graceful middle of the road," says Smith referring to the tonal duality of PRS guitars such as the Custom: "a balance between single-coil and humbucking sounds. The Singlecut may have been too much on the humbucker side. But having said that, the Singlecut is doing very well. Something like 60 per cent of the bands on VH-1 are playing our guitars – 40 per cent of

them are playing Singlecuts. But the Singlecut Trem is offering something we don't offer, and there are guys out there that grew up on single-cutaways but always wanted one with a vibrato."

At $2,680 it was purposely priced lower than the Singlecut ($3,200), only $80 more than the non-maple topped Standard and bolt-on Swamp Ash Special and only $180 more than the CE Maple Top. Smith maintained, "We made the Singlecut Trem more simply. It initially came with a gigbag, not a case, though now it does come with a case. There were no covers on the pickups and limited colours. We made it come in at a price."

It's doubtful that the differences on the Singlecut Trem would account for the price difference. In reality it seems it was aggressively priced to gain market acceptance (by 2006 it was priced identically to the Singlecut at $3,100); as Smith says the Singlecut was popular with artists, less so with die-hard PRS players at which the Singlecut Trem was undoubtedly aimed.

Mike Einziger of Incubus with his McCarty Archtop Spruce typifies the move by several key new players to PRS. "In the past few years the bands using our stuff are younger, and they look to different idols," says PRS's Jeff Lanahan.

*NB: These thicknesses were provided by PRS in 2006 and refer to the specification before sanding and finishing.

This moody shot of Paul Reed
Smith playing a 513 Rosewood was
taken by PRS's art director Marc
Quigley and was used for the
company's Christmas card.

THE 513 & MODERN EAGLE

Behind the scenes PRS had become involved in legal wranglings with Gibson over the "legality" of the Singlecut. While this would become very public later in the year, January's Winter NAMM 2004 introduced two brand-new PRS double-cutaway guitars, the 513 and the Modern Eagle.

"What do guitar players want?" muses Paul Reed Smith of the origins of the 513. "Do they want our guitars to play better? Not really. Do they want them to look better? Not really. They don't even want them to sound much better… but they do want a lot more sounds." To achieve this goal the 513 amounts to a virtually complete redesign of the PRS guitar.

Fundamental changes included the scale length, increased from 25-inch (635mm) to 25¼-inch (641mm), and the neck-to-body joint. "It's a stronger neck joint," says Smith. "It (the body) holds onto the neck further out under the heel. We were trying to get more of the core sound of the Singlecut neck joint but on a double-cutaway

guitar." Along with newly designed bird inlays (created by Joe Knaggs) there was a slightly different fretwire – slightly taller and slightly flatter on top as opposed to the domed profile on the Brazilian rosewood fretboard and neck.

A new, model-specific neck profile was created "very close to that of the wide fat profile, but the nut width is in between our wide fat and regular at about 1 43/64-inch" (42.5mm), says PRS. The top nut, white instead of black friction-reducing plastic, for the first time in PRS's history was called "truly compensated". "I've always use a compensated nut (moved slightly forward to improve low fret intonation) but this one's got more compensation," says Smith. It's not just moved slightly forward, it's angled – slightly closer to the first fret on the bass-side than the treble.

It is the 513's pickup and switching system, however, that provided the secret to the sounds of the 513. Utilising five single-coil pickups, the outer four grouped in

► MODERN EAGLE

PRODUCTION PERIOD: *2004-CURRENT*

THIS EXAMPLE: *2004*

The Modern lies at the pinnacle of PRS production – above the Artist Package and below Private Stock. It's the guitar Paul Reed Smith chooses to play. "The first 22-fret Dragon I, you know, you've heard me play that guitar for years. I didn't want to take it to China. I didn't want to risk it. The guys

said, well we've got a Modern Eagle in final assembly that's a second because it's got these two pieces of (maple) heartwood on it. A lot of people think it looks really beautiful and from the first moment it was done it sounded great. I've been playing it for a couple of years now," said Smith in 2006, "and haven't plugged it into any amp and have it not do what I need it to do. It sounds gorgeous – it's got a really balanced sound spread out across all the frequencies."

◄ 513 ROSEWOOD

PRODUCTION PERIOD: *2004-07*

THIS EXAMPLE: *2004*

Not quite 20 years into PRS's history, the 513 amounts to a complete redesign of the original Custom centred around a new neck-joint, five pickups and 13 sounds – achieved with both

five-way and three-way lever switches. The patent-pending pickup design, along with the Brazilian rosewood neck and fingerboard, added greatly to the cost. It wouldn't be until 2007 that a more standard mahogany-necked version, simply called the 513, would replace this original model and introduce the versatile guitar to a wider audience.

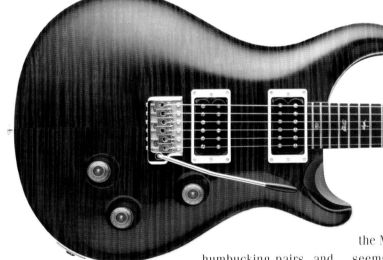

▲ CUSTOM 24 BRAZILIAN

PRODUCTION PERIOD: *2003*

THIS EXAMPLE: *2003*

Announced in the summer of 2003, the Brazilian series compromised a Custom 22 and 24 and a McCarty – 500 of each listing at $4,150. The base specification included flamed maple 10-top (West Coast) with a $200 up-charge for quilt. Brazilian rosewood fingerboard, pink abalone heart bird inlays, Brazilian rosewood headstock overlay with inlaid pink abalone heart signature and the word "Brazilian" inlaid in green abalone ripple. Like the Dragon 2002 and 2001 PRS Singlecut Brazilian Rosewood Limited Edition model, the guitars featured nickel/gold-plated combination hardware. Standard neck and bridge options applied to the appropriate models and aside from a $600 up-charge for an East Indian rosewood neck option on the McCarty, no other options were available. Each guitar has a signed and numbered backplate.

humbucking pairs, and two lever-style pickup selector switches, the system is unlike any other PRS.

According to Paul Reed Smith, each coil "is basically a mini version of our bass pickup. When you put a whole bunch of turns on a humbucker, it gets too dark but you need a whole bunch of turns on a single-coil otherwise it sounds too thin. So Winn Krozak came up with a way of winding right onto the metal (pole-piece). He did an extraordinary job: there are circuit boards on the bottom of the pickups otherwise they'd be so hard to wire". One five-way lever switch selects the pickups in the usual Strat-like selections (Treble, Treble and Middle, Middle, Middle and Bass, Bass); the other, a three-way lever, selects the "mode": "heavy humbucking" (both coils), "clear humbucking" (both coils, tapped output) and single-coil.

If the technology to create the 513 seems complicated,

the Modern Eagle, a production Private Stock-style guitar seems like a distillation of everything PRS has learnt about the electric guitar. "I'd agree but it's also a very simple guitar built to do its job," says Smith. "It's like a runner – he gets in his box and wins the race, it's as simple as that. We're in a competition with other guitar manufactures for the artists. Many of these artists have enough money to buy the nicest vintage pieces made in the 1950s by Fender or by Gibson in whatever year – whatever they want. We're in competition with those 'days of grace'. We're held to a standard: 50 years of history, 20 factories and hundreds of thousands of people – these people made their living and put their children through school with those days of grace. We're in competition with all that. That's what I've come to realise a Modern Eagle needs to be. You pull it out and it's competitive with everything that's ever been made – not so easy to do. Some of our guitars are like museum pieces, but the Modern Eagle is also a players' guitar."

▲ SE SOAPBAR II

PRODUCTION PERIOD: *2004-06*

THIS EXAMPLE: *2004*

With the suspension of the original single-cutaway SE Soapbar, this double-cut version was intended as a stop gap. In fact, not least with its Les Paul Special vibe, it proved a runaway success, edged out of the line by the later maple veneer-faced version.

▲ SE EG

PRODUCTION PERIOD: *2004-05*

THIS EXAMPLE: *2004*

Recalling the original EG 3, the SE EG is the only other PRS production guitar to feature the Fender Strat-like three single-coils. The SE EG, however, like all SE's to-date, is a set-neck guitar and, although the SE EG wasn't critically acclaimed, it sold more than PRS anticipated.

SE EXPANSION

In 2002 the second version of the original Santana SE appeared priced at $738. Although PRS had shipped some 10,000 of the original 2001-specification SE, the new version was "redesigned, modified, updated and enhanced". Among the primarily cosmetic changes were an added forearm contour, a bound neck and headstock, a pickguard, expanded colour options, and different colour fingerboard inlays. A block-style PRS logo also appeared on the truss-rod cover – the first model to feature this logo since the original late-1980s Classic Electric. The 2002 version also featured a pair of new PRS-designed and Korean-made uncovered humbucking pickups.

"It's the same money, but we're trying to give people more," explains Smith. "I come from a world where a great guitar is a great guitar, even if it's a little plain looking. But this is the video age and people want it to be spruced up somewhat, so that's what we did."

2003 saw the Tremonti SE based on the USA model but with thinner all-mahogany body and contoured rather than carved top. The following year saw the second Singlecut design, the SE Soapbar, like the Tremonti but without the bound fingerboard or body and utilising a pair of Korean-made soapbar single-coils. The 2004 EG SE revisited the previous low-end EG in name but, like all SEs to date, was a set-neck guitar, not a bolt-on, and used the same outline as the Santana SE. The Strat-alike pickguard and three-single-coil configuration drew criticisms from some quarters as being overly derivative.

"I think there's a bit of a misconception with the three single-coil version, that it wasn't successful," says Doug Shive, the SE's Project manager. "But in the year we introduced it we sold more of that model than any other SE. I think it was a pretty big success actually although internally it was felt it didn't hit the mark."

In December 2004, PRS announced its third SE signature model, the Billy Martin, although, uniquely, unlike Santana and Tremonti, he didn't have a USA signature. "Billy is a local guy and his band Good Charlotte

▲ SE BILLY MARTIN MODEL

PRODUCTION PERIOD *2004-5*

THIS EXAMPLE: *2004*

Originating from Waldorf, Maryland in the mid-1990s, Good Charlotte, with their modern punk rock-inspired sound, achieved three times platinum-selling mainstream success with their 2002 release The Young and the Hopeless. Original band member Billy Martin has been a long-time PRS user and his distinct SE signature model was designed as a 'thank-you' to a local band by PRS. Despite its Day-Glo inlays it went on to surprise PRS by selling in large numbers.

▼ TREMONTI SE

PRODUCTION PERIOD: *2003-CURRENT*

THIS EXAMPLE: *2003*

Mark Tremonti's high-profile with mega-selling Creed and, later, Alter Bridge has made him a true PRS ambassador. He was also fundamental in the design of the USA Singlecut model. His SE signature was the first single-cutaway design to grace the Korean-made range and aside from its suspension during the Singlecut court case has remained in production from 2003 to the present day. Although officially offered in just two colours – black and platinum metallic – the Tremonti SE has been offered in, for example, white in the UK.

Unlike the later SE Singlecut, or indeed Tremonti's USA signature, the Tremonti SE features an all-mahogany body.

▼ SANTANA SE (2ND VERSION)

PRODUCTION PERIOD: *2002-06*

THESE EXAMPLES: *2002*

The latest version of PRS's Korean-made sub-$750 guitar has mainly visual changes over the original SE. These two (with and without the optional PRS vibrato) show that the new SE has a pickguard, a contour on the front of the body for player comfort, and binding to the neck and headstock. "We had to get our Korean factory to agree to do it the way it works for us," says Smith. "It was guitar makers talking to guitar makers."

is from Annapolis so we thought it would be nice to say thanks for helping us out by playing PRS guitars." explains Shive. "Originally we were just going to do a 500-piece run worldwide but we ended up doing several thousand! But there is, of course, a limited audience for a guitar with Day-Glo green dots and a funny looking bat at the 12th fret! It ran its course then we phased it out."

Dan Spitz, aside from being a long-time member of thrash metal merchants Anthrax, is also a watchmaker and in his decade-long hiatus from the band opened a watch repair shop. In 2005 he reunited with the band and this led to this highly customised PRS with the first six-in-a-line "Spitz" headstock, closely based on the PRS 12-string head shape.

END OF THE SINGLECUT?

When PRS introduced the Singlecut in 2000 it was instantly controversial. Some PRS fans felt it was simply too un-PRS-like with its four controls and shoulder placed toggle pickup selector switch. Others felt it was just too close to Gibson's iconic Les Paul. Smith maintained that he'd "always wanted to make a single-cutaway guitar because of the neck joint", but Gibson didn't agree. On March 27th 2000 Gibson sent a letter demanding that PRS cease and desist from producing and selling the Singlecut. In November, Gibson sued PRS for among other things trademark infringement. PRS counterclaimed and a lengthy legal battle ensued.

It wasn't until January 2004 that it was ruled that the Singlecut had "imitated" the Les Paul and that the two parties had 90 days to sort out damages. The future of the Singlecut looked bleak and, while the legal wrangling continued, another court action was taken to prevent PRS, as of July 2nd 2004, from "manufacturing, selling, or distributing... the PRS Singlecut". There was little that

PRS could do but comply and all Singlecuts – including the SE models – were suspended from production. Any existing work-in-progress bodies and necks were stored and a limited run of the Tremonti Tribal was stopped halfway through. Images of the Singlecuts couldn't be used in catalogues or PRS marketing.

The musical instrument industry was stunned. Who next would be prevented from making a single-cutaway electric guitar? There were even concerns from acoustic guitar makers. After all, wasn't the Les Paul outline conceived from an acoustic guitar with an added cutaway? PRS launched an appeal that would be heard later in the year. Paul Reed Smith certainly wasn't happy with the events thus far. "There's no actual evidence of confusion between the Singlecut and the Les Paul but there's confusion in my mind between trade dress, trademarks and design patents," he said in the fall of 2004.

▼ **CUSTOM 22/12**

PRODUCTION PERIOD: *2004-CURRENT*

THIS EXAMPLE: *2004*

Officially launched in January 2004 (though it took a long time to ship) the Custom 22/12 was the first production PRS 12-string – some 27 years after Paul Reed Smith made his first, "a Flying V 12-string for Peter Johnson. The second one was for Al DiMeola", then with Return To Forever.

Heart's Nancy Wilson bought a 12-string while both Neil Schon and Carlos Santana purchased 6/12 double-necks in the pre-factory days. The first PRS 12-string, however, goes back to 1995's Guitars of the Month programme and Private Stock has produced a small number of one-off 12-strings. Although it appears to just be a 12-string Custom, the 22/12 features a raft of new features that inevitably delayed production. There's the elongated headstock

(around 40mm longer than the six-string) necessary to hold the additional six locking tuners, a new nut moulding that had to be designed and produced, a new neck carve, new 12-string pickups (based on those designed in West St by John Ingram and Paul Smith), and probably most complex: a 12-string version of PRS's adjustable Stop-Tail wrap-over bridge.

PUDDLE OF MUDD   NICKELBACK

▲ **TREMONTI TRIBAL**

PRODUCTION PERIOD: *2004-06*

THIS EXAMPLE: *2004*

Had PRS not won its legal wrangle with Gibson, this Limited Edition model would have been

prematurely curtailed. Just over half of the 100-only run was built prior to the injunction in 2004, the remainder finished in 2005 and into 2006 – probably the longest production span in PRS's history for such a small limited run.

To some insiders this whole legal situation surrounding the Singlecut was ironic because, although the guitar had proved highly popular with artists, it hadn't been a strong-selling PRS guitar. The UK's PRS distributor, Gavin Mortimer of Headline Music, for example, had mused that the instrument might well fall from the line in favour of the Singlecut Tremolo – a more PRS-like single-cutaway instrument.

Did Smith think PRS would have avoided legal problems if the Singlecut Trem had preceded the Singlecut? "No. This is about the trademark of the outline shape, a two-dimensional trademark on the outside shape not anything inside the guitar," he commented in the midst of the proceedings. "The case has nothing to do with trade dress anymore. There is a theory of initial interest confusion for concert-goers sitting at the back of the arena... that's what the (court) documents say. I don't believe we've done anything wrong in terms of anything that the documents say. I've had a lot of time to soul search this whole thing

and... I don't see what we've done wrong. Are we too good a competitor? I've been to NAMM – there are single-cutaway guitars in hundreds of booths, it's almost uncountable. So how come I'm not 'let in' when everyone else is?"

"We intended to confuse nobody," he continued. "There's not any shred of evidence in this case that anyone bought a PRS thinking they were buying someone else's guitar. In fact we put as many identifying features on this thing as we possibly could. And when you put a PRS Custom and Singlecut next to a Les Paul, it's clear that the Singlecut was spawned from the Custom, not the Les Paul. I mean you can just see it! That's my belief, that's just me. I regret that the industry has had to be dragged through this but I think it has been coming for a long time. I'm surprised that I'm in the middle of it but I am."

Eventually the appeal was heard on December 10th 2004 but, as the company moved into its 20th Anniversary year, the Singlecut remained out of the line and it wouldn't be until nearly a year later that sense prevailed.

(TOP) PUDDLE OF MUDD/NICKELBACK
Nickelback are typical of the post-grunge rock wave that hit big in the late 1990s/early 2000s. The track "How You Remind Me" from the band's third album Silver Side Up was massively successful and, despite critical disinterest, Nickelback also had the biggest-selling rock album Stateside in 2006 with All The Right Reasons. Puddle of Mudd's major-label debut Come Clean, released in 2001, went on to sell five times platinum. Phillips left the band after disappointing sales of the second album and "musical differences" but not before his PRS's had been seen by millions.

PART FOUR: 20 YEARS OF PRS

Undoubtedly assisted by the attention that was drawn to the brand by the Singlecut/Les Paul tousle, PRS's 20th Anniversary brought a massive amount of media exposure.

"In 1986," says PRS President Jack Higginbotham, "we had a party because we'd made the 1,000th guitar. I remember thinking that was unbelievable – who would believe there are a thousand people out there that want these things? What are we gonna do next? It can't last. I'm amazed at the success and the longevity of this company."

How did Paul Reed Smith feel of this landmark? "I'll tell you how I feel. I feel older because I haven't exercised enough. My hair is grey, I hate that. But I don't feel like I've lost my youthful vitality at all, I don't feel like an old man. I don't feel out of touch musically with what's going on in the world. I don't feel out of touch with what's going on technically."

It was a time to reflect on successes such as the PRS Custom, the original PRS and still the best-selling guitar in the line. "I'm always surprised when I plug in a Custom 24," says Smith. "It always sounds good, it's just a good guitar." But aside from the guitars themselves, PRS's contribution to the industry as a whole has been dramatic. Few would argue that over two decades the company has raised the bar in terms of production quality.

"When we came to market there were file marks on Fender's frets," says Smith. "Gibson's necks were 'S'-d. There was no curly maple. Finishes had become 'interesting': the polyester on maple fretboards was almost ⅟₁₆th of an inch thick – there was almost no fretwire left. Three-bolt necks and bullet truss-rods had become a thing, some rods didn't work at all. I mean, how many of those U-shaped truss-rods go into overseas guitars – they just don't work. As a repairman that's scary. I think we said; hey, let's remember our art here: neck shape, set-up, fret jobs, glue the frets in, get it to play in tune, get the tuner pegs not to slip. Let's put vibratos on guitars that don't normally get them, let's get the taper of the pots right, let's make the pickups sound acceptable.

"Some people hadn't forgotten, some people had. Jol Dantzig (Hamer) hadn't forgotten, nor had Tom Anderson. Fender Custom Shop necks are good these days; Tom is making good guitars, as are Collings. You can buy a good Martin, a good Taylor guitar. Now, there are a lot of people busting their butts to make good guitars."

Jack Higginbotham understands the company better than most. "Why is PRS PRS? There's always going to be debates about what makes a good guitar and what makes a good guitar sound. But the goal of creating an instrument with great tone and great playability is just saturated inside of PRS. That's not to say we all agree on what that is but we all have the same intention. That, I believe, is paramount. We couldn't be PRS unless that was the case."

▲ **20TH ANNIVERSARY CUSTOM 24**

PRODUCTION PERIOD *2005-07*

THIS EXAMPLE: *2005*

Unlike some celebratory PRS instruments, the 20th Anniversary guitars were understated. Note the subtle redesign of the bird inlays – exclusive to these models – and the "20th" truss-rod cover that featured on all USA-made PRS guitars during 2005. The pictured Custom features PRS's five-way rotary pickup switch and the "lampshade" knobs originally conceived for the 513 Rosewood.

PRS's 20TH ANNIVERSARY

It was no surprise that PRS would centre on its original guitars – the Custom and the Standard – to lead its 20th Anniversary celebrations. The 20th Anniversary Custom was unveiled in both 24- and 22-fret formats, the Standard as just a 24-fret model. All three guitars featured new green ripple abalone 20th Anniversary bird inlays with brown lip mother-of-pearl wisps, once again designed by Marc Quigley and Joe Knaggs. "It's like a pattern of birds flying on the board with wisps that kind of represent flow. The green ripple abalone is what we use on the Santana inlays," Joe Knaggs explained. The three guitars also featured a black anodized truss-rod cover – engraved with "20th" – that were features on all PRS's USA-made production models during 2005.

While both the Customs were listed at $3,370, slightly higher than the regular models, and both were offered with Artist Package upgrades, the 20th Anniversary Standard came in at the same price, $2,730, as the regular model as it was only offered in a new satin nitro-cellulose finish

with four colour options: vintage cherry, mahogany, orange and charcoal.

"We thought it would be a nice thank-you to everyone who has supported us in the last 20 years if, rather than having a limited number of guitars for our anniversary, we had 20th Anniversary 'packages' so a lot of people would be able to buy such a guitar," explained Peter Wolf at the launch. "We don't want to do something that only a few rich people can afford – our guitars are expensive enough already."

Orders were taken on the new guitars after they were announced in late December 2004 through to around the end of July/August 2005. "The idea is we want to make these guitars in 2005 and we're trying to keep it as close to the original price as possible," said Joe Knaggs.

Twenty years on the appeal of the Custom remains undimmed. "I think people gravitate to the Custom because it's the original, like original Levi's or Coca-Cola. Yeah, Paul came up with a really nice guitar and it caught

▲ 20TH ANNIVERSARY STANDARD 24

PRODUCTION PERIOD: *2005-06*

THIS EXAMPLE: *2005*

This 20th Anniversary Standard, the most affordable of all the 20th Anniversary guitars, marked the introduction of a new satin nitro-cellulose finishing process that would lead, in 2006, to the Satin finish guitars. The all-mahogany Standard 24 was available in just four colours: vintage cherry, mahogany, orange (pictured), and charcoal.

20TH ANNIVERSARY DRAGON 2005

PRODUCTION PERIOD: *2005-06*

THIS EXAMPLE: *2005*

"The concept and rough layout of the two dragons fighting was developed by me and the product development team," says PRS's Private Stock maestro Joe Knaggs. "The drawing was done by Jeff Easley [the famous Dungeons and Dragons artist who'd designed the inlays for Dragon four and five]. I fine-tuned the drawing to make it inlay-able, and designated the shells and other inlay materials." The 863 parts include "red orange spiny, green heart abalone, paua, pink heart abalone, snakewood, gold mother of pearl, mother-of-pearl, black lip mother-of-pearl, brown lip mother-of-pearl, silver, gold, ebony, korean awabi, green ripple abalone, red coral, sucalite and abalone sparkle". Like the previous Dragons, the inlay work was executed by Larry Sifel and his team at Pearl Works "with a lot of help from the Private Stock team", adds Joe.

on... and now it's kinda normal," reflected Joe Knaggs in 2005.

Washington Music's Paul Schein has been selling PRS guitars for 20 years and vividly remembers the initial appeal. "In 1984 the vintage thing hadn't come around," he reflects. "But the PRS guitar with its beauty, quality and innovation came at a time when guitars were really just crap wrapped around a Floyd Rose. I mean look at Kramers of that era. We sold 'em, God bless 'em, but they were really just a vibrato with something to support it. The PRS was like an Aston Martin in a sea of Austin Marinas. It was obvious how much better Paul's guitars were than anything else that was around at that point."

More quietly the PRS Bass, for the second time, was removed from the line. PRS's bass-playing Larry Urie

mused, "I believe they weren't what people expected of us. When they're thinking PRS they're thinking wildly flamed maple tops and really an esoteric kinda bass. Which it wasn't. It was a really good bass, I like them a lot but the more affordable end was too plain Jane for people. They weren't gonna pay that kinda money for a painted bass. You can buy a Jazz bass for $600 that pretty much gets the job done. I think that was the main reason for the demise. We went to great lengths with the maple-top basses – we actually inset the maple into the top but, at the end of the day, people didn't believe it, it looked like veneer. However, I think we got a lot closer to a real player's bass this time. The Private Stock Gary Grainger bass (see page 140), I think that's more of what people would expect from us – a high dollar fancy-looking piece."

▼ **CE MAHOGANY 24**

PRODUCTION PERIOD: *2005-CURRENT*

THIS EXAMPLE: *2005*

▼ **CE MAHOGANY 22**

PRODUCTION PERIOD: *2005-CURRENT*

THIS EXAMPLE: *2005*

Aside from the ill-fated EG models, the bolt-on CE (originally known as the Classic Electric) has always been the entry point to the USA range.

The mahogany-bodied version dropped out of the line in 2000 in favour of the CE Maple Top but returned in 2005 dressed in smart new colours such as blazing copper pictured here on the CE 22. Both pictured guitars would also have featured "20th" embossed truss-rod covers.

THE CE MAHOGANY, CARS & ROCK STARS

Outside of the 20th Anniversary brouhaha, PRS introduced the CE Mahogany creating the most cost-effective entry into the USA-line. With a list price of $2,400 it undercut the existing maple-topped CE by $250. Available in both 22- and 24-fret formats (with corresponding wide-fat and wide-thin neck profiles), though only with the PRS vibrato. The only options listed were gold hardware and either the five-way rotary selector or pull/push tone control with three-way toggle pickup selector switch.

Originally just called the CE, the CE Mahogany is technically a reissue of the mahogany-bodied CE, which had replaced the alder body CE around 1995. Aside from the Singlecut's forced exit from the PRS line, previous models had all been axed for the simple reason of dwindling sales. The previous mahogany-bodied CE was no exception. "Although I really liked the instrument, we weren't selling very many – they weren't selling through at

the stores at a rate that was comfortable for everyone," was Smith's explanation. Its return was equally honest: "because there seems to be a demand again".

The CE's return brought new finishing technology in the form of "Hot Hues" colours – cappuccino, blazing copper, indigo and purple (offered alongside 12 more standard opaques and 'bursts) – developed by DuPont for the hot-rod racing market. "It is actually a complete finish system, but we are just using the colour, not the clear," relates PRS President Jack Higginbotham. "It is more user-friendly than any other metallic colours we have ever sprayed. We were so impressed by the colours that we brought back the mahogany CE guitar offered, primarily, in the Hot Hues colours."

The tie-up with DuPont had been created by Jack Higginbotham who was keen to broaden PRS's image outside of the music industry – the automotive industry seemed an obvious target. A partnership with GM Motors seemed equally logical and, in the same year, two Corvette

▲ **CORVETTE STANDARD 22**

PRODUCTION PERIOD: *2005-06*

THIS EXAMPLE: *2005*

Part of PRS's expanding brand expansion, this tie-up with GM Motors exposed the company to new market areas with some success. Two versions were available with different fingerboard inlays: a 427 logo or the pictured Z06. These colourful guitars, in Corvette-accurate colours, are bound to feature in guitar collections of the future.

▼ **DAVE NAVARRO SIGNATURE MODEL**

PRODUCTION PERIOD: *2005-CURRENT*

THIS EXAMPLE: *2005*

Dave Navarro is another long-time PRS user who eventually got his own signature model in 2005. Best known for stints in Jane's Addiction and the Red Hot Chili Peppers he formed The Panic Channel in 2004. Compared to his tattoos his signature is extremely plain: an all white Custom 24.

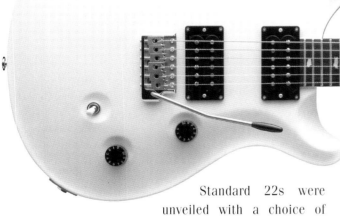

Standard 22s were unveiled with a choice of Corvette colours, and PRS logo's adorned the new Corvette C6-R race car during 2005. The guitar referenced Corvette's Z06 model – optional fingerboard inlays offered were "Z06" or the "427" logo (after the 427 cubic inch engine of the Z06). At a much higher price, the Private Stock Z06 with highly figured maple top was also offered.

Fast cars, what next? Oh, yes, rock stars. Dave Navarro, the high-profile Jane's Addiction and Red Hot Chili Peppers guitarist had been a PRS user for some years and joined the PRS ranks as only the third artist, after Carlos Santana and Mark Tremonti, to garner a USA signature model. His signature is a vibrato-equipped jet white Custom 24 with wide-thin neck, mother-of-pearl bird inlays, "Dave Navarro" logo'd truss-rod cover and no options.

The final 2005 introduction was the PRS 20th Anniversary Dragon 2005 – the first 6/12 double-neck Dragon, (see page 127), conceived by Larry Urie, Joe Knaggs and the Private Stock team. Supremely over-the-top, the inlay work was the most complex ever undertaken on an electric guitar. It was to be the last Dragon worked on by Larry Sifel, the founder of Pearl Works, who passed away in 2006.

20TH ANNIVERSARY SINGLECUT TREM

PRODUCTION PERIOD: LATE 2005-7

THIS EXAMPLE: 2005

The court case between PRS and Gibson was only resolved late in PRS's 20th Anniversary year allowing versions of the Singlecut and Singlecut Trem to receive the Anniversary treatment. This spectacular example features the Artist Package upgrade including Artist grade quilted maple top, Brazilian rosewood fingerboard and headstock facing and gold hardware.

THE RETURN OF THE SINGLECUT

As 2005 progressed, the absence of news in regard to the Singlecut's appeal made many wonder if the guitar would ever be seen again. Enterprising individuals were already forcing up the second-hand price of existing "pre-injunction" Singlecuts sensing a negative outcome. On September 12th, however, an announcement was made.

"In a long-pending trademark dispute between PRS Guitars and Gibson Guitars Corp, the United States Court of Appeals for the Sixth Circuit today reversed a lower court decision and ordered the dismissal of Gibson's suit against PRS. The decision also immediately vacates the injunction prohibiting the sale and production of PRS's award-winning Singlecut Guitar. Paul Reed Smith Guitars announced today that it will immediately resume production of its Singlecut guitars," said a PRS press release. It continued...

"In the litigation, Gibson alleged that concert-goers in a smoky concert hall might not be able to differentiate a PRS Singlecut from a Gibson Les Paul. The appellate court rejected that trademark theory out-of-hand, emphasizing Gibson's concession in court arguments that 'only an idiot' would confuse the two products at the point of sale."

"I feel relieved," said Paul Reed Smith in December 2005. "I agree with the [appeal] court documents: there was so much wrong with this case we're not even gonna talk about most of it. That's what it said. There was so much wrong [with the original court hearing] it didn't feel right. Now it feels right again. So, I feel like it's time to get back to business: normal has returned. People that play Singlecuts think that they're their own animal. I feel relieved, feel good about it and that the judges finally heard what was going on."

While PRS celebrated, Gibson then requested that all 12 judges from the Sixth Circuit rehear the case. This was rejected leaving one last hope for Gibson that the United

The Pre-injunction Singlecuts

Examining PRS's USA production records reveals some interesting statistics on the Singlecut family – just 5,090 were made in total prior to the July 2004 injunction that stopped the model. Of that total, 1,911 standard Singlecuts were shipped, another 371 with Artist Packages and a further 1,657 with 10-tops. Of the 250 Singlecut Brazilian Rosewoods shipped, 219 were 10-tops. Of the 1,035 Singlecut Trems made before the injunction 526 were standard models, 139 had Artist Packages, and 370 had 10-tops. The Tremonti model notched up 635 and, of a limited run of 100 Tremonti Tribals, roughly half shipped before the injunction. In other words, it was quite a lot of fuss about relatively few guitars.

Reflecting the importance of the outcome of the Gibson versus PRS court battle, the UK's Guitarist magazine went to town with their front cover feature. Conceived by the magazine's art team Phil Millard and Matt Ward, it was shot by Future Publishing's in-house photography studio. It all helped to make the Singlecut the most notorius electric guitar of the early 21st century.

States Supreme Court would decide to review the case.

On June 5th 2006, PRS issued the following release. "Paul Reed Smith Guitars is very pleased to announce that the United States Supreme Court today denied Gibson Guitar's final appeal of a Court of Appeals decision upholding PRS's right to make a single cutaway-style guitar... The Supreme Court's decision today leaves the Sixth Circuit opinion in place and ends Gibson's multi-year effort to thwart legitimate competition under the guise of intellectual property law."

"I am delighted for our employees, our distributors, our dealers, our customers and the industry," said Smith. "Everyone was extremely supportive of our cause and our company over the last six years, fully embracing our decision to fight back against Gibson's charges. My thanks especially go to those in the industry who helped educate the court: the media, our industry peers, guitar craftsmen and industry scholars. Their help was invaluable."

It was that September 2005 date that signalled the return of the Singlecut though "we didn't instantly start production back up", explained Larry Urie at the time. "We did have the unfinished Tremonti Tribals in work-in-progress. We began taking new orders that same day but we were about eight months back-ordered. To start Singlecuts back up right away we would have had to bump someone's existing order. We have had to squeeze in the Singlecuts for the Winter NAMM 2006 show as well as some for review but, by and large, Singlecuts ordered from Sept 2005 onwards should start shipping around March or April 2006."

That said, PRS still managed to create 20th Anniversary versions of the Singlecut and Singlecut Trem just at the tail end of 2005. Meanwhile, in early 2006, numerous magazines featured the Singlecut on their covers. This "difficult" guitar that might well have been dropped in favour of the vibrato version was back – much more famous than when it had left.

▲ **SE SINGLECUT**

PRODUCTION PERIOD: *2006-CURRENT*

THIS EXAMPLE: *2006*

Although the Singlecut name is borrowed from the USA line, this SE version takers the standard two control layout of the Singlecut Trem and its thinner body depth. Conversely, for what appears to be

an SE "Singlecut Trem", it was only offered with a Stop-Tail bridge. It was yet another example of how the SE line was evolving not into "copies" of the USA-made guitars but a range filled with unique designs. And, finally, PRS had a proper maple-topped guitar that would compete with instruments like Epiphone's Les Paul Standard in the lower-priced market.

MAPLE MOVES TO SE

The injunction on the Singlecut had also affected the SE line – the SE Soapbar and Tremonti SE were not offered during this period. To compensate, the double-cutaway Soapbar II was announced in December 2004 and quickly became popular. "Before the injunction the Tremonti and the Soapbar were the two best-selling SEs by far," says SE project manager Doug Shive. "We couldn't do anything about the Tremonti – it is was it is: a single-cutaway guitar. But the Soapbar was very easy to change. It was intended as a stop-gap but has proved to be very successful on its own."

At the end of 2004 a satin camouflage-finished SE, simply referred to as the "Camo", also surfaced with a Standard designation on the truss-rod cover. "We took orders at Winter NAMM 2005 but we didn't actually have a

guitar as our supplier had flipped the decal so the black was white. Peter Wolf had the idea. He thought there was a market for that primarily in Europe. The camouflage decal is pretty expensive actually so you have to do enough to make it worthwhile. I combined that idea with the idea, why don't we just offer a satin finish guitar? As we couldn't make Singlecuts, and the planned maple-top SE guitars were a little way off, it gave us something to freshen up the line temporarily. As the interest died on the Camo, within about six months I guess, we'd by then figured out what we wanted to do: the satin finish Standard."

"We formally announced the SE Standard – the same as the Camo but in opaque flat black, translucent cherry and mahogany – at Summer NAMM 2005. It started to ship to dealers at the end of 2005 although its big launch was at the Winter NAMM 2006 as a lot more people attend that show, by which time the Camo was phased out."

Other changes for 2005 included the SE EG that was now

▲ SE CUSTOM

PRODUCTION PERIOD: *2005-CURRENT*

THIS EXAMPLE: *2005*

The first SE to feature a solid maple front under a figured maple veneer, the SE Custom has a flat front instead of the graceful carve of PRS's flagship model. Nonetheless it's proved, as anticipated, a big-selling SE model. Like all SEs to this point, it's a 22-fret guitar – a 24-fret SE "Custom" wouldn't appear until 2007 in the guise of the Paul Allender model.

▼ SE SOAPBAR II MAPLE

PRODUCTION PERIOD: *2005-CURRENT*

THIS EXAMPLE: *2006*

A cosmetic upgrade of the Soapbar II, this version adds just a figured maple veneer facing to the mahogany body. The lightweight mahogany guitar, however, has proved well-liked by numerous players – young and old – including many existing PRS owners.

▲ SE CAMO

PRODUCTION PERIOD: *2005*

THIS EXAMPLE: *2005*

Despite its headstock logo, the "Camo" officially predated the launch of the SE Standard. But, like the Billy Martin, it helped expand PRS's appeal to a younger audience and proved the SE Standard – now a cornerstone of the SE line – was a viable proposition.

▲ SE EG

PRODUCTION PERIOD 2005-CURRENT

THIS EXAMPLE: *2005*

Originally the SE EG appeared with three single-coils, this version with a bridge humbucker was added later. Both version's are exclusive to the PRS range – no USA-made guitars, at the time, featured either pickup configuration.

offered with a bridge humbucker and two single-coils. "Both the guitars are routed the same way," says Shive. "It's actually a hum/single/hum route under the pickguard – we did that by design from the start: all we had to do was change the pickguard and pickups and essentially you had a new model."

In late 2005 PRS announced the first maple-topped SE models: the SE Custom and SE Soapbar II Maple followed swiftly by the SE Singlecut brought into the line, along with the reinstated Tremonti SE, after the injunction was lifted. The Custom uses a thin and flat solid maple top with a figured maple veneer facing and natural edge. The Soapbar II Maple simply adds a maple veneer body facing to the Soapbar II. The SE Singlecut's top is contoured maple, again with a natural edge and a figured maple veneer facing.

"It was pretty hard selling Paul on using maple tops," explains Shive. Smith had originally been concerned that using maple on the SEs, such a hallmark of the USA line, could confuse the market and dilute sales. "I presented it in a way that it wouldn't confuse the market," he says. "The SE Custom is a flat-top guitar so there'd be absolutely no confusion with the carved-top USA-made Custom. You see them side-by-side and you know exactly which one is which. Likewise the Soapbar II Maple – it's not just unique to the SE line but to the whole PRS range." The same is true of the SE Singlecut – another model unique to the SE line "We did the electronics like the USA Singlecut Trem, we made the body thinner – all these different things to distinguish the SE version from the USA model. We don't want to trade sales – we want them to be very different things."

▲ **SINGLECUT STANDARD SOAPBAR SATIN**

PRODUCTION PERIOD: *2006-CURRENT*

THIS EXAMPLE: *2006*

▼ **SINGLECUT STANDARD SATIN**

PRODUCTION PERIOD: *2006-CURRENT*

THIS EXAMPLE: *2006*

This all-mahogany, twin humbucking guitar and its soapbar- equipped stablemate are both available with either PRS Vibrato or Stop-Tail. Unlike the original Singlecut they both feature the standard PRS dual-control configuration and the thinner body depth of the Singlecut Trem. The Singlecut Standard Satin is pictured in vintage cherry and the Singlecut Standard Soapbar Satin in vintage orange.

SATIN EXPANSION

Moving into its third decade, PRS started 2006 with some vigour. Aside from the return of the Singlecut, Singlecut Trem and Mark Tremonti signature, PRS's 2006 price list split the range into two: the High-Gloss Finish models and the virtually all-new Satin Finish models.

The Satin range featured four all-mahogany models inspired by the successful 20th Anniversary Standard of 2005 that had also featured a satin nitro-cellulose finish. Along with the non-Anniversary, all-mahogany, Standard 22 & 24, for the first time two all-mahogany Singlecuts were introduced – the Singlecut Standard Satin and the Singlecut Standard Soapbar Satin. All four guitars listed at $2,730.

"The success of the 20th Anniversary Standard made me think that, because we already know the process, it would be really nice to come out with a series of satin guitars for 2006," reflected Peter Wolf. "It's not only to help our customers to save money but to allow less involved production. But most importantly I also felt the

20th Anniversary Standard was one of our best sounding guitars. I really like the way they sound and feel. And if you can offer a guitar a couple of hundred dollars cheaper that's a good thing."

To create these cost-savings the guitars not only featured a quicker finish but limited options too. On the Standard 22 and 24 it was just a choice of Stop-Tail or vibrato (22 only, the 24 is only offered with vibrato), gold hardware, four colours, neck profile and electronics package. The two all-mahogany Singlecuts had even fewer choices, just gold hardware and the same four-colours. All featured bird inlays as standard. PRS has always charged, on standard models, an upgrade for this hallmark feature so this inclusion added more to the apparent value of these models.

The all-mahogany Singlecuts were the really new guitars – the only previous all-mahogany single-cutaway had been the original SE Soapbar. Both new models used the thinner Singlecut Trem body depth and likewise the same

▲ **(TOP) STANDARD 22 SATIN**

PRODUCTION PERIOD: *2006-CURRENT*

THIS EXAMPLE: *2006*

▲ **(ABOVE) STANDARD 24 SATIN**

PRODUCTION PERIOD: *2006-CURRENT*

THIS EXAMPLE: *2006*

It was the 2005 20th Anniversary Standard that inspired the Satin Finish models of 2006 and here are the Standard 22 Satin (pictured in vintage mahogany)

and the Standard 24 Satin with vibrato in vintage cherry. Less fancy than the 20th Anniversary models they are the same specification but with standard bird inlays and blank black plastic truss-rod covers. The 22 is offered with both Stop-Tail or vibrato, the 24 is vibrato-only; both are pictured with 'McCarty electronics' although the five-way rotary switch, along with gold hardware, is an option. Hopefully, these satin Standards will be gigged hard not coveted in collections.

◀ **SINGLECUT SATIN**

PRODUCTION PERIOD: *2006-07*

THIS EXAMPLE: *2006*

This short-lived Singlecut Satin was launched in 2006 and discontinued a year latter, along with the Singlecut itself, when PRS introduced the SC 250 and SC 245. Due to PRS's production backlog the Singlecut Satin was still being made and shipped in early 2007 and remains effectively a limited edition in all but name and could well become a collectible.

two knob/three-way pickup selector switch control layout.

According to PRS's Richard Ames, the satin finish is "relatively simple, but it's got to be right because there's no top-coat later on. Although the process is simpler – it cuts out the whole of the finish hall – the satin process has to be done more carefully". At the time, Ames was the only employee who did this and, in 2005, he stained all the 20th Anniversary Satin Standards, "yeah, 10-20 a day – it was all I did".

The coloured stains are applied onto the bare wood that, like any other PRS, has been perfectly sanded. The vintage orange gets two coats of orange stain applied by hand with a rag. The charcoal uses two coats of gray black stain, "the same as we use for the Gray Black High-Gloss finish", says Ames. Vintage cherry has a brown basecoat then a red oil-stain topcoat; vintage mahogany also gets a brown base then "about three coats" of red/orange.

Next, a very thin coat of "isolator" is applied to protect the stain from the grain filler. The grain filler is applied

next – it's literally wiped on then wiped off by hand and left over night to dry. The following day a vinyl sealer is applied that helps the nitro cellulose coats adhere. After that, two coats of nitro-cellulose are sprayed then scuffed up, another coat is sprayed and scuffed before the final, fourth, nitro coat. There's no labour intensive hand sanding between coats and no final buffing. "Sanding is the most labour-intensive area of our production," says Joe Knaggs. "People are sanding away every day and they can easily make or break the instrument, ruin the shape. With our quality standards you can have someone ruin a guitar in a couple of seconds. And it happens. Then there's the finishing – which involves a lot more sanding between coats – that's why we're working here to save the customers some money."

With the introduction of these mahogany Satins the under-marketed all-mahogany McCarty Standard and McCarty Soapbar Standard (see pages 94-95) were dropped from the line.

As with the original double-cut Modern Eagle, the Singlecut Trem Modern Eagle represents the top-dollar PRS guitar before Private Stock. Essentially the specs and options are the same as the previous Modern Eagle but, oddly, these top-of-the-line guitars are classed with the most affordable PRS instruments, such as the Singlecut Standard Satin, under the general "Satin Finish" range umbrella. They are certainly very different guitars. The SCT Modern Eagle features a Brazilian rosewood neck and fingerboard, above-Artist grade woods and a smoother, more complex – and more time consuming – satin nitro-cellulose finish.

MAPLE SATINS, MODERN EAGLES AND MR JOHNNY HILAND

2006's all-mahogany Satins were augmented by two $3,000 maple-topped Singlecuts – the Singlecut Satin (see page 135) and Singlecut Trem Satin. Listing at $100 less than the High-Gloss equivalent models, like the all-mahogany Satins both came with limited options: gold hardware, 10-top, Artist Package (flame only, not quilt) and just eight colours as opposed to the 27 colour options of the High-Gloss Singlecut pair.

An all-new Singlecut Trem Modern Eagle was also added into this Satin Finish range but, like the existing double-cut Modern Eagle, listed for $8,400 – the most expensive PRS guitars before the five-figure Private Stock one-offs.

While both Modern Eagles technically have a satin finish it's a smoother more labour-intensive finish that shouldn't be confused with the finishing process of the lower-cost Satin models – a simplified extension of the satin nitro finish used on the Modern Eagle guitars.

Back in 2004 Paul Reed Smith remarked that "there's a tremendous amount of time in the finishing of our guitars", referring to the then standard, now called High-Gloss, polyester basecoat/acrylic topcoat finish. "I wanted the guitars to ring really well and so I said can we finish them with nitro and just, you know, sand them down and steel wool them, wax them and kiss 'em off? They looked pretty good and it takes around two days to do, not like a week."

In reality the Modern Eagle's finish proved far from simple on the production line but it reflected a growing

▼ **SINGLECUT TREM SATIN**

PRODUCTION PERIOD: *2006-CURRENT*

THIS EXAMPLE: *2006*

Although the Satins were launched at the start of 2006, the combination of a substantial back order, and

the fact that spraying nitro-cellulose and polyester/urethane finishes alongside each other caused PRS some problems. Satin Finish maple-tops were slow to ship especially to export markets such as the UK where only a handful had arrived by the end of the year.

JOHNNY HILAND SIGNATURE MODEL

PRODUCTION PERIOD: *2006-CURRENT*

THIS EXAMPLE: *2006*

Hiland's signature guitar, based on a CE 24 Maple Top, is the most distinctive artist guitar in the line. Aside from a special neck carve, there are the over-sized dot markers, a recessed truss-rod cover to allow precise behind-the-nut bends. JH pickups (the bridge unit is based on a pickup Paul Reed Smith has been working on with David Grissom), and unique wiring – it's also the only PRS to use a three-way lever switch for pickup selection.

desire for lower-gloss, thinner finishing. "Certainly, in the industry, more people are going back to a thin finish because they feel it will sound better," offered Joe Knaggs in 2005. "For so long it was that it had to be dipped in glass. So, many makers just piled on the finish so they could flat it out. To keep a really thin finish with such a high gloss is a very difficult thing to do. I'm glad that people are becoming more receptive to the grain showing through because it allows you to keep the finish thin."

PRS guitars, though used by a stylistically wide community of musicians, are not the default choice of the archetypal country gunslinger. Johnny Hiland – "legally blind and illegally talented", as he was referred to by *The Tennessean* newspaper back in 2001 – could well change that perception via his PRS signature guitar which was officially launched at Winter NAMM 2006. Its 24-fret bolt-on maple neck suggests a hot-rod Swamp Ash Special, probably PRS's twangiest guitar to date, but the Hiland signature draws on broader influences, like his playing.

The body is the typical maple-topped mahogany blend, with custom-shaped neck, dual custom-wound covered JH humbuckers, vibrato and three-way lever pickup selector. The tone control has a push/pull switch that splits just the JH Bass pickup, not both, as is usual. The enlarged black dot inlays aid Hiland's restricted vision but, hearing him play, you wonder if he actually needs them.

"I think Johnny Hiland is the most versatile guitar player I've ever heard," said Ricky Skaggs. "From Bill Monroe to Eddie Van Halen, he can play it all." Hiland, meanwhile, has become an ambassador for PRS at numerous concerts and clinics and with his Musician's Hotline column where he states: "My PRS JH signature model is 'untouchable'. I love my guitar! It looks great, feels great, has the best craftsmanship in the world, and sounds unbelievable. I can play any show (from rock, to country and swing, jazz, to blues) anywhere at anytime. You have to be as excited about your guitar as I am about mine."

▼ **PRIVATE STOCK 10TH**
ANNIVERSARY SINGLECUT #1229

COMPLETED: *13TH JAN 2006*

The 10th Anniversary of PRS's Private Stock programme was celebrated with two celebratory models: a double-cut Custom 24 and a single-cutaway (pictured) based on the Singlecut Trem.

Clearly intended as collectors pieces they epitomise the craft of the Private Stock luthiers, from the outrageously quilted maple top seen here, the engraved pickup covers, ornately inlaid Brazilian rosewood fingerboard, not to mention the inlaid body and bound fingerboard and body edge.

PRIVATE STOCK CELEBRATES 10TH ANNIVERSARY

Emerging from the Guitars of the Month project back in 1995, Private Stock one-offs began in 1996 and, not surprisingly, 2006 saw a 10th Anniversary model. By mid 2006 a total of 1,400 Private Stock guitars had been made and currently the small team of elite guitar makers build around 200 a year. The Private Stock team "now includes myself, my assistant Tina Benson, David Hazel, Paul Miles, Dana Seidmen, Michael Byle, Rich Hubbard, Scott Bloomfield – who's really running the repair department but he's a part of it – Danny Dido and Brian Lutz", explains Joe Knaggs, head of both Private Stock and, since 2000, PRS's Research and Development.

Despite Knaggs's dual role, Private Stock and R&D are fairly separate entities at PRS. "This team makes pretty much all Private Stock. The only way that it relates to R&D is that we build prototypes of what may become new models. So we handle Private Stock, artist guitars where a special order is required, prototypes and any other thing that's out of the ordinary. We prototyped the Satin guitars,

for example, and at the other end it might be a guitar for someone like Derek Trucks."

"For the prototype Satin guitars we mixed that with production-made parts, but we would handle running them through. For example, if we're doing a Singlecut Trem thickness guitar but with a Stop-Tail, not a vibrato on it, we'd have to reset the necks and hand-carve the heel ready for the NAMM show launch. When we get back we write all the programs for the CNC to get that guitar into production."

"In R&D, I have Bill Oertel working with me; he's managing the engineers. There are probably 50 to 60 projects going on at the moment. Right now we're working on the new factory layout to writing the program for new-design divets where the controls go, to finding a jig to round the fingerboards over... it's not just the instruments that come through us."

In mid 2006 PRS's production guitars were back-ordered nearly a year and Private Stock had a two-year

PRS's Private Stock team hard at work. Brian Lutz (above) finish sands a Singlecut; long-time PRS employee Dave Hazel (above right) works on a fingerboard; Joe Knaggs hand-carves the maple top of a Gary Grainger bass in his England football t-shirt. A keen football fan Knaggs hoped it would help England at the 2006 World Cup finals. It didn't.

back-order. "We could be making more," says Knaggs, "but we don't want to pump them out and devalue the project. But we get 10-25 orders or people asking for quotes every day."

PRS's new factory, which will be up and running in 2007, will provide a lot more space and resources for, amongst other things, Private Stock. "There are other areas we could go into," suggests Knaggs. "For example, the large hollow-body SCJ. I could be making probably 25 a month. We haven't put them out because we don't have the time but I firmly believe we could make a number of those in Private Stock every month and they'd all sell. It won't detract from the normal Private Stock instruments because it's a completely different guitar."

Few would disagree that PRS's Private Stock instruments are among the most luxuriant guitars money can buy. If you can only dream of affording one, the annual Private Stock calendar, with sumptuous photographs by Jim Noble, gives you a taste of what you're missing.

The 2006 calendar features (below left, top row, left-to-right) #784, a ruby red Hollowbody II; #615, an aquamarine Singlecut jumbo; and #627, a black burst Singlecut Hollowbody II. Below those, (from l-to-r), are a pair of Hollowbodies – #727, with an outrageously quilted

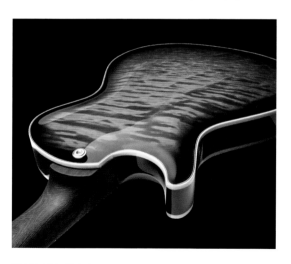

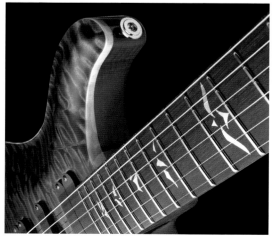

PRIVATE STOCK GARY GRAINGER BASS

PRODUCTION PERIOD: *2006-CURRENT*

THIS EXAMPLE: *2006*

Experienced bassist Grainger, who's played with a host of musicians including John Scofield, regularly plays with Paul Reed Smith at performances and clinics. His Signature is now the only bass offered by PRS but it's exclusive to Private Stock.

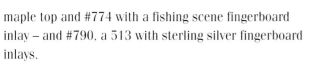

Gary Grainger (left) with PRS's Peter Wolf at Winter NAMM 2007.

maple top and #774 with a fishing scene fingerboard inlay – and #790, a 513 with sterling silver fingerboard inlays.

Below (top row, l-to-r) is #841, a McCarty with gold outlined snakewood inlays; #849, another McCarty with another fabulous quilted maple top; and #886, a 513 with finely striped curly maple top. Underneath those (from l-to-r) is #889, a Custom 24 with Brazilian rosewood top; #895, a 20th Anniversary white wash McCarty; and #900, a McCarty with custom phoenix fingerboard inlay.

▶ PRIVATE STOCK AMPLIFIER

PRODUCTION PERIOD: *2007-CURRENT*

THIS EXAMPLE: *PROTOTYPE, 2006*

One of PRS's new projects is this 'boutique' amp. Substantial orders were taken, at it's behind-the-scenes launch at NAMM 2007, for this high-dollar product which will begin shipping in 2007.

▼ MARK TREMONTI MODEL

PRODUCTION PERIOD: *2007-CURRENT*

THIS EXAMPLE: *2007*

With the original Tremonti Model becoming the basis for the new SC

250, Mark's new-for-2007 signature reflects his current playing needs. It's still a deep-bodied, four control Singlecut but adds an up-routed vibrato. It's also unchambered – Tremonti likes his Singlecuts "the heavier the better."

▼ 513 MAHOGANY

PRODUCTION PERIOD: *2007-CURRENT*

THIS EXAMPLE: *2007*

Replacing the original Brazilian rosewood-necked 513 Rosewood, the 513 Mahogany uses PRS's standard mahogany neck. It means the new 513 is considerably more affordable and is hoped that the innovative guitar, a substantial redesign of the original PRS Custom, will reach more players.

THE EVOLUTION OF THE SINGLECUT

Just a year after the Singlecut returned to the PRS line it was discontinued. In fact, for 2007, it became two guitars: the SC 250 and the SC 245. The former retained the same 25-inch scale, though now Phase II locking tuners and an adjustable Stop-Tail were standard along with new 250 Treble and Bass uncovered pickups based on the Tremonti designs. In reality, the SC 250 is the modern player's Singlecut: "it's a Tremonti without the Tremonti name on it," says Paul Reed Smith.

The SC 245, on the other hand, moves closer to vintage single-cutaway territory with a shorter 24½-inch scale (as used on the Santana, slightly shorter than Gibson's current

24⅝-inch scale). This one uses a non-adjustable Stop-Tail and again new PAF-style 245 pickups with scuffed covers. "We made a few Singlecuts with the Santana scale and they were lovely," says Smith. "We're using these wonderful alnico-loaded 'ancient' pickups. It sounds gorgeous. It's an old-style guitar."

Aside from the 10-top (flame and quilt), bird inlays and gold hardware options on both models, the 245 was offered with a gold anodized Stop-Tail (only available with gold hardware). Both models bear the new names on the truss-rod cover and both use slightly chambered bodies to enhance resonance and reduce weight.

Two more signature Singlecuts joined the line too: a modified Tremonti replaces the previous model but comes with up-routed vibrato – the first time a PRS has featured this since the 1987 Special. Unlike the Singlecut Trem it featured four controls and the full-depth Singlecut thickness mahogany back. The Chris Henderson (3 Doors

▲ **SC 250**

PRODUCTION PERIOD: *2007-CURRENT*

THIS EXAMPLE: *2007*

Announced at the January 2007 NAMM show, the original Singlecut split into two new guitars: the SC 250 and the SC 245. The SC 250 retains the original PRS scale length of 25-inches but is essentially a non-signature Tremonti and is aimed at the modern rock player. It features new 250 humbuckers and also uses the adjustable Stop-Tail so players can intonate heavier gauge strings, often down-tuned.

▲ **SC 245**

PRODUCTION PERIOD: *2007-CURRENT*

THIS EXAMPLE: *2007*

This Singlecut moves to the shorter 24½-inch scale previously used on the PRS Santana guitars. It's designed to capture a more vintage single-cut tone reflected in its lower-powered PAF-style pickups. Both this and the SC 250 have sound chambers to reduce weight and increase resonance.

▼ **CHRIS HENDERSON MODEL**

PRODUCTION PERIOD: *2007-CURRENT*

THIS EXAMPLE: *2007*

Joining PRS's elite signature artists, 3 Doors Down guitarist Chris Henderson has created the first production three-pickup Singlecut. Like Mark Tremonti, Henderson has been a big advocate of the Singlecut, originally using the Tremonti model both live and in the studio. "These guitars will shoot out against any (Gibson) Les Paul you put in a room with them and they will kill them. They'll crush them."

Down) signature is the first three-pickup production Singlecut. This uses a 250 Treble with 7 Middle and Bass; it has the same four control layout as the other Singlecuts but a push/pull on the tone control of the bass pickup control introduces the middle pickup. Both of these Singlecuts use the standard 25-inch PRS scale length.

A late addition was the 513, with standard mahogany neck and rosewood fingerboard that replaced the previous Brazilian neck/fingerboard 513 Rosewood. Not only is this a more affordable 513 but indication that the increasingly hard-to-find and highly expensive Brazilian rosewood is in short supply.

◄ **SE CUSTOM SEMI-HOLLOW**

PRODUCTION PERIOD: *2007-CURRENT*

THIS EXAMPLE: *2007*

Unique to the PRS line, this new SE takes the SE Custom and adds a semi-hollow construction with Rickenbacker-inspired 'slash' soundhole.

▼ **SE ONE**

PRODUCTION PERIOD: *2007-CURRENT*

THIS EXAMPLE: *2007*

Thirty two years after Paul Reed Smith made his first guitar, based on the Gibson Les Paul Junior (see page 9), PRS introduced its first single-pickup guitar that could easily have been called a SE Singlecut Junior.

Paul Reed Smith, flanked by a number of PRS artists introduces the SE One at winter NAMM 2007. SE project manger Doug Shive (below) with his latest creation: the SE Custom Semi-Hollow.

MORE SE'S, A 'REISSUE' AND A NEW FACTORY

In the 2007 SE line, the SE One – a single-pickup, single-cutaway – was added, all mahogany with single bridge soapbar and pickguard – along with the double-cut SE Custom Semi Hollow, with slash-style single soundhole, and the fourth SE signature: the maple-topped SE Paul Allender (Cradle of Filth) model. This latter guitar is the first SE to feature a 24-fret neck and wide-thin type neck carve on a glued-in maple neck.

To make way for all the new 2007 models the original SE, the Santana, was dropped along with, in the USA line, the Santana III, the Singlecut, the Corvette Standard, the Hollowbody II's Artist Package and the Singlecut Satin that was replaced with the new SC 250 Satin.

For some time PRS has been working with David Grissom on a new guitar but it still hadn't surfaced at the January 2007 NAMM show. According to Paul Reed Smith, "The DGT – the David Grissom Trem – based on Grissom's own PRS McCarty will be released later in 2007. You'll have to wait and see."

▲ **SE PAUL ALLENDER MODEL**

PRODUCTION PERIOD: *2007-CURRENT*

THIS EXAMPLE: *2007*

All previous SEs have been 22-fret guitars. The Paul Allender Model is the first 24-fret SE and the first to use new SE pickups modelled on the popular USA HFS/Vintage Bass combo.

▲ **1980 WEST ST. LTD.**

PRODUCTION PERIOD: *2007*

THIS EXAMPLE: *PROTOYPE, LATE 2006*

The 1980 West St. Ltd. was unveiled at the start of 2007, virtually a reissue of a pre-factory Paul Reed Smith guitar. The name refers to West Street, Annapolis, the site of Paul's attic workshop, and 1980 is the approximate date that Paul would have made a guitar like this. "It's not exactly a reissue," says Smith, because it has a sapele top" – a beautifully figured African mahogany. "And it's really like a new model as so few people have seen, or played, the guitars we made before 1985." The all-mahogany guitar uses what we now call the Santana shape, headstock and scale length with a small dragon inlaid on the top.

PRS'S NEW FACTORY

During 2006 work got underway on a new factory to expand PRS's USA manufacturing base. Adjacent to the current facility that's been home to PRS for the past decade, the new building – around five times larger than the existing factory – is hoped to come on line in 2007.

"We built our first factory in 1985. We moved to Kent Island in 1996. We seem to be expanding in ten-year cycles. I never imagined we would need to drastically increase the size of our facility so soon," said Jack Higginbotham at a celebration to launch the project in October 2006. Aris Melissaratos, Secretary, Maryland Department of Business & Economic Development, said, "PRS Guitars represents America's manufacturing future – a blend of advanced technology and superb, proprietary craftsmanship."

"If all we were going to do was to make more of what we already do that would be the worst mistake we could make and we'd go out of business almost immediately. What we can do is other things – that's the key. Those projects are in planning. But I believe we can do more of what we do now and I believe that will create more demand too. We also don't put 100 per cent marketing potential behind certain products because we know we have limitations in terms of supplying that product. For example, what would happen if we put a blitz on the piezo Hollowbody? We haven't done anything marketing wise with that. That's typical of the opportunities we have for growth," said Higginbotham.

PRS also stated that, "the additional square footage will provide room for an expansive PRS museum that highlights the history, innovations and progress of the PRS guitar line. New zones of creativity are also planned that include more room for the research and development team to design, create and perfect new guitar models, a sound-recording studio and additional photography/art studio space for the in-house creative team".

PART FIVE: THE MODEL KEY

Over the following pages we've assembled a comprehensive guide to the models that PRS Guitars has produced since the company's formation back in 1985. The Model Key should serve to give an overall picture of the development of PRS's individual models, as well as the general changes made from time to time to features, construction and so on.

Used in conjunction with the wealth of information contained in the rest of the book, the Model Key provides a crucial addition to the growing database of information about the past and present of PRS instruments.

We have not sought to identify the pre-factory guitars that Paul Reed Smith and his collaborators made in Annapolis before the establishment of PRS in 1985. As custom-made instruments, these rarely fall precisely into strict model specifications – after all, that is what a custom-built guitar is all about. If you are lucky enough to come upon one of these guitars today, then what you see is what you've got. The Model Key deals solely with the PRS instruments made from 1985, which for the most part divide into specific, identifiable models.

Within the Model Key you'll find several different sections. There is an extensive, major listing of all the PRS production models made from 1985 to 2007, organised in a simple-to-use A-to-Z format that includes dates of production and detailed specifications for each model. In combination with the unmatched collection of high-quality photographs displayed in *The PRS Guitar Book*, this should assist in the identification of any regular PRS instrument you may come across.

In addition to the primary alphabetical model inventory, the Model Key also charts PRS's special one-off models, including the shortlived Guitars Of The Month series and the Private Stock scheme. Unique access to the company's records for these guitars enables us to bring you these important details for the first time in any book.

As well as analysing PRS's regular production models, including the Korean-made SE range, and one-off items such as Private Stock instruments, the Model Key also presents information on all the various types of pickups used by the company during the 22-year period that we are investigating.

We have also detailed a number of other significant changes in the use of hardware and, significantly, have provided simple and straightforward translations of the serial-numbering systems used by PRS that will enable readers easily to allocate reasonably accurate dates of production to particular instruments.

THE PRS MODEL KEY

The Model Key is designed as a one-stop reference section for PRS guitars. The main sections include an A-to-Z of all the production models from 1985 to 2007 (page 148-157) as well as listings of the Guitars Of The Month series (page 158) and the Private Stock instruments (page 158-165). Finally, a comprehensive round-up of information useful to date PRS guitars is presented (page 166-169), including notes on hardware changes and a series of serial-number charts.

PRODUCTION MODELS A-to-Z

HOW TO READ THE ENTRIES

This reference listing uses a simple, condensed format to convey a large amount of information about every PRS production model made between the start of the first PRS factory in summer 1985 and spring 2007.

Each model is listed by the alphabetical order of its model name. At the head of each entry is the model name in bold type. Some models that have been known by different names through the years have "aka" (also known as) in brackets with the previous names – which are also cross-referenced in the A-to-Z listing.

The model name or names is followed by a date or range of dates showing the production period of the instrument. These dates are necessarily approximate, primarily because catalogues, pricelists and other evidence does not always relate to actual production periods. However, our extensive research has resulted in the most accurate dates possible.

SPECIFICATION POINTS

Most main guitar entries provide a list of bulleted points. These are a summary of the model's main specifications, separated into groups. In the order presented, the points refer to: neck, fingerboard, headstock; body, finish; pickups; controls; pickguard; bridge/tailpiece. Of course, not every model will need all the points.

COMMON FEATURES

All PRS guitars have a 25" (635mm) scale unless stated otherwise. All instruments have truss-rod adjustment on the headstock, behind the nut. Unless stated, all rosewood fingerboards are East Indian. All humbuckers are uncovered unless stated otherwise.

PRS have offered a number of feature "Packages" at various times:

Artist Package (1997-current): paua bird inlays; rosewood headstock veneer; Artist-grade flame or quilted top; translucent toned back; gold hardware; leather case.

Special Package (1991-93): wide-thin neck; vibrato up-routing; tone control replaces sweet switch.

Studio Package (1991-96): one Hot Vintage humbucker and two PRS single-coils.

All USA-made PRS guitars constructed during 2005 featured black anodized "20th" truss-rod covers to celebrate PRS's 20th Anniversary.

All this information is designed to tell you more about your PRS instrument. By using the general information and illustrations earlier in the book combined with the knowledge obtained from *The PRS Guitar Book's* unique Model Key, you should be able to build up a very full picture of your instrument and its pedigree.

ACOUSTIC GUITAR

Eleven prototypes were made of the PRS acoustic flat-top guitar, in the early 1990s. The models were never put into production.

AMPLIFIERS

Made 1988 to late 1989. HG-70 Top. 412 Cabinet and HG-212 Combo. Amplifier section features: 70 watts RMS; two separate pre-amps (for "Vintage American" and "Vintage English" sounds); backlit front panel; built-in reverb; effects loop; high-gain noise gate; footswitchable channels and reverb; 16/8/4-ohm speaker impedance switching; equalised direct XLR out; auxiliary amp out; luminescent rear panel. Controls: Channel switch; Rhythm channel: Reverb; Master; Bright; Bass; Mid; Treble; Gain; Solo Channel: Master; Pres; Bass; Mid; Treble; Gate; Gain.

ARTIST I 1991-94

● One-piece mahogany wide-fat set-neck, Brazilian rosewood fingerboard, abalone bird inlays, 24 frets, inlaid signature on headstock, chrome-plated locking tuners.
● Solid mahogany PRS-shape body with 10-plus maple top, special "thin" finish. Colours: amber; dark cherry sunburst; indigo; teal black.
● Two humbuckers (Artist Treble and Artist Bass).
● Three controls (five-way rotary pickup selector, tone, volume).
● Nickel-plated PRS vibrato.
Limited Edition of "under 500".
Options included semi-hollow body; gold hardware; PRS Stop-Tail bridge; quilted maple top; Studio Package; humbucker/single-coil/humbucker.

ARTIST II 1993-95

● One-piece mahogany wide-fat set-neck, maple purfling on Brazilian rosewood fingerboard, abalone bird inlays, 22 frets, inlaid signature on headstock; maple purfling on headstock and truss-rod cover; gold-plated locking tuners.
● Solid mahogany PRS-shape body with 10-plus maple top, special "thin" finish. Colours: amber; dark cherry sunburst; indigo; teal black.
● Two humbuckers (Artist Treble and Artist Bass).
● Three controls (five-way rotary pickup selector, tone, volume).
● Gold-plated PRS Stop-Tail.
Limited Edition of "under 500".
Some examples with: semi-hollow body; PRS vibrato; quilted maple top; Studio Package; humbucker/single-coil/humbucker.
Some PRS literature lists this as the "Artist 22" model.

ARTIST III 1996-97

● One-piece mahogany wide-thin or wide-fat set-neck, paua purfling on Brazilian rosewood fingerboard, paua bird inlays, 22 frets, paua purfling on headstock and truss-rod cover, inlaid paua-shell signature on headstock, gold-plated locking tuners.
● Solid mahogany PRS-shape body with Artist-grade maple top, special "thin" finish. Colours: amber; dark cherry sunburst; indigo; teal black.
● Two humbuckers (Artist Treble and Artist Bass).

ACOUSTIC GUITAR

● Three controls (five-way rotary pickup selector, tone, volume).
● Gold-plated PRS Stop-Tail.
Limited Edition of "under 500", issued with certificate of authenticity.
Some examples with: semi-hollow body; gold-plated PRS vibrato; quilted maple top.

ARTIST IV 1996

● One-piece mahogany wide-thin or wide-fat set-neck, agoya (early examples gold) purfling on rosewood fingerboard, engraved 14-carat gold bird inlays, 22 frets, engraved 14-carat gold eagle on headstock; agoya (early examples gold) purfling on headstock and truss-rod cover; gold-plated locking tuners.
● Solid mahogany PRS-shape body with Artist-grade maple top. Colours included amber; dark cherry sunburst; indigo; teal black.
● Two humbuckers (McCarty Treble and McCarty Bass) with gold-plated covers.
● Two controls (tone, volume), three-way toggle pickup selector; pull-push on tone control operates coil-tap.
● Gold-plated PRS Stop-Tail.
Limited Edition of "under 70", issued with certificate of authenticity.

ARTIST LIMITED 1994-95

● One-piece mahogany wide-fat set-neck, abalone purfling on Brazilian rosewood fingerboard, 14-carat gold bird inlays, 22 frets, abalone purfling and "Artist Ltd" inlaid in abalone on truss-rod cover, inlaid mother-of-pearl and abalone eagle on headstock, abalone purfling on headstock; gold-plated locking tuners.
● Solid mahogany PRS-shape body with 10-plus maple top; sunbursts or colours.
● Two humbuckers (Artist Treble and Artist Bass).
● Three controls (five-way rotary pickup selector, tone, volume).
● Gold-plated PRS Stop-Tail.
Limited Edition planned at 200, only 165 made, issued with certificate of authenticity.

BASS-4 / BASS-5 1986-92

● One-piece maple set-neck, Brazilian rosewood fingerboard (fretted or fretless – fretless soon changed to ebony 'board), moon inlays, 22 frets (or fretless), 34" (864mm) scale, signature logo on headstock; chrome-plated tuners; four-string (Bass-4) or five-string (Bass-5).
● Solid mahogany PRS-bass-shape body; sunbursts or colours.
● Three PRS single-coil pickups, plus hum-cancelling coil in rear of body.
● Four controls (volume, five-way pickup selector, plus "deep" and "clear" EQ) and active circuit bypass switch;.
● Nickel-plated PRS bass bridge/tailpiece.
Options included bird inlays; gold hardware; figured maple top (but soon became Curly Bass model – see separate entry).

CE see CE 24 entry

CE MAPLE TOP see CE 22 MAPLE TOP and CE 24 MAPLE TOP entries

CE 22 1994-2000

● One-piece maple wide-fat bolt-on neck, rosewood fingerboard, abalone dot inlays,

22 frets, signature logo on black-faced headstock; chrome-plated locking tuners.
● Solid mahogany PRS-shape body; colours.
● Two humbuckers (Dragon Treble and Dragon Bass until 1998; Dragon II Treble and Dragon II Bass from 1998) with nickel-plated covers.
● Three controls (five-way rotary pickup selector, tone, volume).
● Nickel-plated PRS Stop-Tail.
Options included PRS vibrato; gold-plated hardware; McCarty Electronics (two controls [volume, tone] plus three-way toggle pickup selector); wide-thin neck.

CE 22 MAHOGANY 2005-current
● One-piece maple wide-fat bolt-on neck, rosewood fingerboard, abalone dot inlays, 22 frets, signature logo on headstock, black anodized "20th" truss-rod cover, chrome-plated locking tuners.
● Solid mahogany PRS-shape body; sunbursts or colours.
● Two humbuckers (Dragon II Treble and Bass) with nickel-plated covers.
● Three controls (five-way rotary pickup selector, volume, tone).
● Nickel-plated PRS Vibrato.
Options include McCarty electronics (two controls [volume, tone] plus three-way toggle pickup selector); gold-plated hardware. Models made after 2005 revert to standard truss-rod cover.

CE 22 MAPLE TOP (aka CE MAPLE TOP) 1994-current
● One-piece maple wide-fat bolt-on neck, rosewood fingerboard, abalone dot inlays, 22 frets, signature logo on black-faced headstock; chrome-plated locking tuners.
● Solid mahogany PRS-shape body with figured maple top; sunbursts or colours.
● Two humbuckers (Dragon Treble and Dragon Bass until 1998; Dragon II Treble and Dragon II Bass from 1998) with nickel-plated covers.
● Three controls (five-way rotary pickup selector, tone, volume).
● Nickel-plated PRS Stop-Tail.
Options include PRS vibrato; gold-plated hardware; McCarty Electronics (two controls [volume, tone] plus three-way toggle pickup selector); wide-thin neck.

CE 24 (aka CLASSIC ELECTRIC, CE) 1988-2000
● One-piece maple regular bolt-on neck, rosewood fingerboard (maple until 1989), abalone dot inlays, 24 frets, signature logo on black-faced headstock; chrome-plated locking tuners.
● Two-piece alder PRS-shape body (solid mahogany from 1995); colours.
● Two humbuckers (early examples Vintage Treble and Vintage Bass; replaced by 1991 with HFS Treble and Vintage Bass).
● Three controls (five-way rotary pickup selector, tone, volume). (Early examples with two controls [volume, tone] plus three-way toggle pickup selector.)
● Nickel-plated PRS vibrato.
*Options included PRS Stop-Tail (from 1995); gold-plated hardware; McCarty Electronics (two controls [volume, tone] plus three-way toggle pickup selector); wide-thin neck.
Known as Classic Electric 1988-89; CE 1989-98; CE 24 1998-current .*

Early examples with "PRS Electric" logo on un-faced maple headstock.
*Some PRS literature lists this as the "CE Bolt-On" model.
Also 22-fret version from 1994, see CE22.*

CE 24 MAHOGANY 2005-current
● One-piece maple wide-thin bolt-on neck, rosewood fingerboard, abalone dot inlays, 24 frets, signature logo on headstock, black anodized "20th" truss-rod cover, chrome-plated locking tuners.
● Solid mahogany PRS-shape body; sunbursts or colours.
● Two humbuckers (HFS Treble and Vintage Bass) with nickel-plated covers.
● Three controls (five-way rotary pickup selector, volume, tone).
● Nickel-plated PRS Vibrato.
Options include McCarty electronics (two controls [volume, tone] plus three-way toggle pickup selector); gold-plated hardware. Models made after 2005 revert to standard truss-rod cover.

CE 24 MAPLE TOP (aka CE MAPLE TOP) 1989-current
● One-piece maple regular bolt-on neck, rosewood fingerboard (early examples maple), abalone dot inlays, 24 frets, signature logo on black-faced headstock; chrome-plated locking tuners.
● Two-piece alder (solid mahogany from 1995) PRS-shape body with figured maple top; sunbursts or colours.
● Two humbuckers (early examples Vintage Treble and Vintage Bass; replaced by 1991 with HFS Treble and Vintage Bass).
● Three controls (five-way rotary pickup selector, tone, volume).
● Nickel-plated PRS vibrato.
*Options include PRS Stop-Tail (from 1995); gold-plated hardware; McCarty Electronics (two controls [volume, tone] plus three-way toggle pickup selector); wide-thin neck.
Known as CE Maple Top 1989-98; CE 24 Maple Top 1998-current.
Early examples with "PRS Electric" logo on un-faced maple headstock.
Some PRS literature lists this as the "CE Bolt-On Maple Top" model.
Also 22-fret version from 1994, see CE22 Maple Top.*

CE BASS-4 / CE BASS-5 1990-91
● One-piece maple bolt-on neck, rosewood (or maple) fingerboard, dot inlays, 22 frets, 34" (864mm) scale, signature logo on headstock; chrome-plated tuners; four-string (CE Bass-4) or five-string (CE Bass-5).
● Solid alder PRS-bass-shape body; sunbursts or colours.
● Three PRS single-coil pickups, plus hum-cancelling coil in rear of body.
● Four controls (volume, five-way pickup selector, plus "deep" and "clear" EQ) and active circuit bypass switch.
● Nickel-plated PRS bass bridge/tailpiece.
Options included bird inlays.

CE BASS-4 MAPLE TOP / CE BASS-5 MAPLE TOP 1990-91
● One-piece maple bolt-on neck, rosewood fingerboard, dot inlays, 22 frets, 34" (864mm) scale, signature logo on headstock; chrome-plated tuners; four-string (CE Bass-4) or five-string (CE Bass-5).

● Solid alder PRS-bass-shape body with figured maple top; sunbursts or colours.
● Three PRS single-coil pickups, plus hum-cancelling coil in rear of body.
● Four controls (volume, five-way pickup selector, plus "deep" and "clear" EQ) and active circuit bypass switch;.
● Nickel-plated PRS bass bridge/tailpiece.
Options included bird inlays.

CE BOLT-ON see CE 24 entry

CHRIS HENDERSON SIGNATURE MODEL 2007-current
● One-piece mahogany wide-fat set-neck, rosewood fingerboard, mother-of-pearl bird inlays, 22 frets, signature logo on headstock, "Chris Henderson" on truss-rod cover, chrome-plated locking tuners.
● Solid mahogany single-cutaway PRS-shape body with figured maple top; sunbursts or colours.
● Three humbuckers (250 Treble and 7 Middle and Bass).
● Four controls (volume and tone for treble and bass pickups), plus three-way toggle pickup selector; pull-push bass pickup tone control activates middle pickup.
● Nickel-plated PRS Adjustable Stop-Tail.
Options include 10-top maple top (flame or quilt); gold hardware.

CLASSIC ELECTRIC see CE 24 entry

CORVETTE STANDARD 22 2005-06
● One-piece mahogany wide-fat set-neck, rosewood fingerboard, "Z06" or "427" inlays, 22 frets, signature logo on headstock, chrome-plated locking tuners.
● Solid mahogany PRS-shape body with "crossed flag" inlay; Corvette colours.
● Two humbuckers (Dragon II Treble and Bass) with nickel-plated covers.
● Three controls (five-way rotary pickup selector, volume, tone).
● Nickel-plated PRS Stop-Tail.
Options included PRS vibrato; fingerboard inlay.

CURLY BASS-4 / CURLY BASS-5 1986-92
● One-piece maple set-neck, Brazilian rosewood fingerboard (fretted or fretless – fretless soon changed to ebony), moon inlays, 22 frets (or fretless), 34" (864mm) scale, signature logo on headstock; chrome-plated tuners; four-string (Curly Bass-4) or five-string (Curly Bass-5).
● Solid mahogany PRS-bass-shape body figured maple top; sunbursts or colours.
● Three PRS single-coil pickups, plus hum-cancelling coil in rear of body.
● Four controls (volume, five-way pickup selector, plus "deep" and "clear" EQ) and active circuit bypass switch;.
● Nickel-plated PRS bass bridge/tailpiece.
*Options included bird inlays; 10-top or quilted maple top; gold hardware.
For non-maple-top version, see Bass-4 / Bass-5.*

CUSTOM see Custom 24 entry

CUSTOM 22 1993-current
● One-piece mahogany wide-fat set-neck, rosewood fingerboard, moon inlays, 22 frets, signature logo on headstock; chrome-plated locking tuners.

THE PRS MODEL KEY

- Solid mahogany PRS-shape body with figured maple top; sunbursts or colours.
- Two humbuckers (Dragon Treble and Dragon Bass until 1998; Dragon II Treble and Dragon II Bass from 1998) with nickel-plated covers.
- Three controls (five-way rotary pickup selector, tone, volume).
- Nickel-plated PRS Stop-Tail.
Options include 10-top or quilted maple top; PRS vibrato; McCarty Electronics (two controls [volume, tone] plus three-way toggle pickup selector); gold hardware; Artist Package; semi-hollow body (1988-98: right-hand only 2000-current); left-handed version (1999); bird inlays; wide-thin neck.

CUSTOM 22 BRAZILIAN 2003
- One-piece mahogany wide-fat set-neck, Brazilian rosewood fingerboard, pink abalone heart bird inlays, 22 frets, Brazilian rosewood headstock overlay with inlaid pink abalone heart signature logo and Brazilian inlaid in green abalone ripple, chrome/gold-plated locking tuners.
- Solid mahogany PRS-shape body with 10-top West Coast maple top; sunbursts or colours.
- Two humbuckers (Dragon II Treble and Bass) with nickel-plated covers and gold-plated polepiece screws.
- Three controls (five-way rotary pickup selector, volume, tone).
- Gold-anodised PRS Stop-Tail.
Options included quilt maple top; PRS vibrato; McCarty electronics (two controls [volume, tone] plus three-way toggle pickup selector); wide-thin neck.
Limited Edition of 500 each with signed and numbered backplate.

CUSTOM 22 SOAPBAR 1998-2002
- One-piece maple regular-D set-neck, maple fingerboard, moon inlays, 22 frets, signature logo on headstock; chrome-plated locking tuners.
- Solid mahogany PRS-shape body with figured maple top; sunbursts or colours.
- Three Seymour Duncan soapbar single-coil pickups.
- Two controls (volume, tone) plus five-way lever-switch pickup selector.
- Nickel-plated PRS vibrato.
Options included 10-top or quilted maple top; gold hardware; bird inlays.

CUSTOM 22/12 2004-current
- One-piece mahogany special 12-string carve set-neck, rosewood fingerboard, moon inlays, 22 frets, signature logo on elongated headstock, chrome-plated locking tuners.
- Solid mahogany PRS-shape body with figured maple top; sunbursts or colours.
- Three pickups (12-string Treble and Bass) with nickel-plated covers and one Lindy Fralin single-coil.
- Two controls (volume, tone) plus three-way toggle pickup selector; pull-push tone control operates coil-split (Treble pickup only) and activates centre single-coil.
- Nickel-plated PRS 12-string adjustable Stop-Tail.
Options include quilt maple top; 10-top (flame and quilt), gold-plated hardware, bird inlays.

CUSTOM 24 (aka PRS CUSTOM GUITAR, CUSTOM) 1985-current
- One-piece mahogany regular set-neck, rosewood fingerboard (Brazilian until 1991), moon inlays, 24 frets, signature logo on headstock; chrome-plated locking tuners.
- Solid mahogany PRS-shape body with figured maple top; sunbursts or colours.
- Two humbuckers (Standard Bass and Standard Treble until 1991; HFS Treble and Vintage Bass from 1991) with nickel-plated covers.
- Two controls (five-way pickup selector, volume) and two-way "sweet switch" tone filter until 1991; three controls (five-way rotary pickup selector, tone, volume) from 1991.
- Nickel-plated PRS vibrato.
Options include tune-o-matic-style bridge and stud tailpiece; 10-top or quilted maple top; McCarty Electronics (two controls [volume, tone] plus three-way toggle pickup selector); PRS Stop-Tail; gold hardware; Artist Package; bird inlays; semi-hollow body; wide-thin neck (from 1987). Known as PRS Custom Guitar (earliest examples). Custom 1985-98; Custom 24 1998-current. New 22-fret version added 1993; see Custom 22.

CUSTOM 24 BRAZILIAN 2003
- One-piece mahogany regular set-neck, Brazilian rosewood fingerboard, pink abalone heart bird inlays, 24 frets, Brazilian rosewood headstock overlay with inlaid pink abalone heart signature logo and "Brazilian" inlaid in green abalone ripple, chrome/gold-plated locking tuners
- Solid mahogany PRS-shape body with 10-top West Coast maple top; sunbursts or colours.
- Two humbuckers (HFS Treble and Vintage Bass) with nickel-plated covers and gold-plated polepiece screws.
- Three controls (five-way rotary pickup selector, volume, tone).
- Nickel/gold-plated PRS vibrato.
Options included quilt maple top; McCarty electronics (two controls [volume, tone] plus three-way toggle pickup selector); wide-thin neck.
Limited Edition of 500 each with signed and numbered backplate.

DAVE NAVARRO SIGNATURE MODEL 2005-current
- One-piece mahogany wide-thin set-neck, rosewood fingerboard, mother-of-pearl bird inlays, 24 frets, signature logo on headstock, custom "Dave Navarro" truss-rod cover, gold-plated locking tuners.
- Solid mahogany PRS-shape body with maple top; jet white (without natural maple edge).
- Two humbuckers (HFS Treble and Vintage Bass).
- Two controls (volume, tone) plus three-way toggle pickup selector; pull-push tone control operates coil-split.
- Gold-plated PRS vibrato.
No options.

DRAGON I 1992
- One-piece mahogany wide-fat set-neck, Brazilian rosewood fingerboard with first-style Dragon inlay, 22 frets, abalone inlaid signature on headstock; gold-plated locking tuners.

- Solid mahogany PRS-shape body with figured maple top. Colours: amber; dark cherry sunburst; indigo; or teal black.
- Two humbuckers (Dragon Treble and Dragon Bass).
- Three controls (five-way rotary pickup selector, tone, volume).
- Gold-plated PRS Stop-Tail.
Limited Edition of 50.
Options included wide-thin neck; semi-hollow body; PRS vibrato; quilt maple top.

DRAGON II 1993
- One-piece mahogany wide-fat set-neck, Brazilian rosewood fingerboard with second-style Dragon inlay, 22 frets, gold inlaid signature on headstock; gold-plated locking tuners.
- Solid mahogany PRS-shape body with figured maple top. Colours: amber; dark cherry sunburst; indigo; or teal black.
- Two humbuckers (Dragon Treble / Bass).
- Three controls (five-way rotary pickup selector, tone, volume).
- Gold-plated PRS Stop-Tail.
Limited Edition of 100.
Options included wide-thin neck; semi-hollow body; PRS vibrato; quilt maple top; Studio package; multi-tap pickup system; humbucker/single-coil/humbucker.

DRAGON III 1994
- One-piece mahogany wide-fat set-neck, rosewood fingerboard with third-style Dragon inlay, 22 frets, "Dragon III" on truss-rod cover; gold inlaid signature on headstock; gold-plated locking tuners.
- Solid mahogany PRS-shape body with figured maple top. Colours: amber; dark cherry sunburst; indigo; or teal black.
- Two humbuckers (Dragon Treble and Dragon Bass).
- Three controls (five-way rotary pickup selector, tone, volume).
- Gold-plated PRS Stop-Tail.
Limited Edition of 100.
Options included wide-thin neck; semi-hollow body; PRS vibrato; quilt maple top.

DRAGON 2000 1999
- One-piece Brazilian rosewood wide-fat set-neck, Brazilian rosewood fingerboard with no inlay, 22 frets, truss-rod adjuster at headstock; signature logo on headstock; gold-plated locking tuners.
- Solid mahogany PRS-shape body with figured maple top and 3-D dragon inlay; sunbursts or colours.
- Two "PRS Model" humbuckers with gold-plated covers.
- Two controls (volume, tone) plus three-way toggle pickup selector.
- Gold-plated PRS Stop-Tail.
Limited Edition of 50.

DRAGON 2002 2002
- One-piece Brazilian mahogany wide-fat set-neck, Brazilian rosewood fingerboard, 22 frets, signature logo on headstock, gold-plated new locking tuners.
- Solid mahogany single-cutaway PRS-shape body with figured maple top and 3-D "dragon's head" inlay; whale blue, black cherry and grey black only.
- Two humbuckers (7s) with brushed nickel-plated covers.
- Four controls (volume and tone for treble

and bass pickups) plus three-way toggle pickup selector.
● Gold-anodised PRS Stop-Tail.
Limited Edition of 100.

EG 3 1990-91
● One-piece maple wide-thin bolt-on neck, rosewood fingerboard, dot inlays, 22 frets, signature logo on black-faced headstock; chrome-plated tuners.
● Solid alder first-EG-shape body; sunbursts or colours.
● Three Seymour Duncan single-coil pickups.
● Three controls (volume, two tones) plus five-way pickup selector lever-switch.
● Plastic pickguard.
● Nickel-plated PRS vibrato.

EG 4 1990-91.
● One-piece maple wide-thin bolt-on neck, rosewood fingerboard, dot inlays, 22 frets, signature logo on black-faced headstock; chrome-plated tuners.
● Solid alder first-EG-shape body; sunbursts or colours.
● Two Seymour Duncan single-coil pickups, one HFS humbucker (early examples with HFS II coverless humbucker pickup).
● Three controls (volume, two tones) plus five-way pickup selector lever-switch.
● Plastic pickguard.
● Nickel-plated PRS vibrato.

EG II 1991-95
● One-piece maple EG-wide-thin bolt-on neck, rosewood fingerboard, dot inlays, 22 frets, signature logo on black-faced headstock; chrome-plated locking tuners.
● Solid alder second-EG-shape body; sunbursts or colours.
● Three optional pickup layouts: (i) three Fralin Zero Noise "domino" hum-cancelling single-coil pickups; (ii) one HFS humbucker pickup plus two Fralin Zero Noise "domino" hum-cancelling single-coil pickups; (iii) two HFS humbuckers plus one Fralin "regular" single-coil pickup.
● Two controls (volume, tone) plus five-way pickup selector lever switch; pull-push tone control operates coil-tap or dual-tone system.
● Plastic pickguard.
● Nickel-plated PRS vibrato.

EG II MAPLE TOP 1991-95
● One-piece maple EG-wide-thin bolt-on neck, rosewood fingerboard, dot inlays, 22 frets, signature logo on black-faced headstock; chrome-plated locking tuners.
● Solid alder second-EG-shape body with three-piece figured maple top; sunbursts or colours.
● Three optional pickup layouts: (i) three Fralin Zero Noise "domino" hum-cancelling single-coil pickups; (ii) one HFS humbucker pickup plus two Fralin Zero Noise "domino" hum-cancelling single-coil pickups; (iii) two HFS humbuckers plus one Fralin "regular" single-coil pickup.
● Two controls (volume, tone) plus five-way pickup selector lever switch; pull-push tone control operates coil-tap or dual-tone system.
● Plastic pickguard.
● Nickel-plated PRS vibrato.
Options included three-piece maple 10-top.

ELECTRIC BASS 2000-05
● One-piece maple bolt-on neck, rosewood fingerboard, abalone dot inlays, 21 frets, 34" (864mm) scale, signature logo on headstock, chrome plated tuners.
● Solid alder new-PRS-bass-shape body; inset figured maple top; sunbursts or colours.
● Two PRS high inductance passive pickups.
● Three controls (master tone and volume for each pickup); passive electronics (active "high end audio pre-amp" with mini toggle switch by 2001).
● Nickel-plated PRS machined brass bridge.
Options included maple fingerboard; figured maple neck with either rosewood or figured maple fingerboard; abalone bird inlays; swamp ash body; gold-plated hardware; piezo bridge with three-band EQ (discontinued by 2002).

ELECTRIC BASS MAPLE TOP 2000-05
● One-piece maple bolt-on neck, rosewood fingerboard, abalone dot inlays, 21 frets, 34" (864mm) scale, signature logo on headstock, chrome plated tuners.
● Solid alder new-PRS-bass-shape body; sunbursts or colours.
● Two PRS high inductance passive pickups
● Three controls (master tone and volume for each pickup), passive electronics (active "high end audio pre-amp" with mini toggle switch by 2001).
● Nickel-plated PRS machined brass bridge.
Options included maple fingerboard; figured maple neck with either rosewood or figured maple fingerboard; 10-top maple top; abalone bird inlays; swamp ash body; gold-plated hardware; piezo bridge with three-band EQ (discontinued by 2002).

513 2007-current
● One-piece mahogany 513 set-neck, rosewood fingerboard, mother-of-pearl 513 bird inlays, 22 frets (513 fretwire), 25.25" (641mm) scale, signature logo on headstock, "513" inlaid on truss-rod cover, chrome-plated locking tuners.
● Solid mahogany PRS-shape body with figured maple top; sunbursts or colours.
● Five single-coil pickups (513).
● Two controls (volume, tone) plus five-way blade pickup selector switch and three-way blade tone selector switch.
●Nickel-plated PRS vibrato.
Options include 10-top maple top (flame), gold-hardware.

513 ROSEWOOD 2004-07
● One-piece Brazilian rosewood 513 set-neck, Brazilian rosewood fingerboard, gold mother-of-pearl 513 bird inlays, 22 frets (513 fretwire), 25.25" (641mm) scale, inlaid gold mother-of-pearl signature logo on headstock, "513" inlaid on truss-rod cover, chrome-plated locking grommet tuners.
● Solid mahogany PRS-shape body with 10-top maple top; sunbursts or colours.
● Five single-coil pickups (513).
● Two controls (volume, tone) plus five-way blade pickup selector switch and three-way blade tone selector switch.
●Nickel-plated PRS vibrato.
Options included gold-hardware.

GOLDEN EAGLE 1997-98
● One-piece maple set-neck, Brazilian

rosewood fingerboard, engraved 14-carat gold bird inlays, 22 frets, inlaid engraved 14-carat gold eagle on headstock; gold-plated locking tuners.
● Basswood PRS-shape body (some semi-hollow) with hand-carved golden eagle (one made with American bald eagle design) by Floyd Scholz; suede brown finish.
● Two (or three) McCarty humbuckers.
● Two controls (volume, tone) plus three-way toggle pickup selector.
● Gold-plated Stop-Tail.
Options included PRS vibrato.
Limited Edition planned at ten; possibly only seven made.

JOHNNY HILAND SIGNATURE MODEL 2006-current
● One-piece maple JH bolt-on neck, maple fingerboard, black large dot inlays with 513 bird at 12th fret, 24 frets, signature logo on headstock, custom "Johnny Hiland" truss-rod cover, chrome-plated locking tuners.
● Solid mahogany PRS-shape body with figured maple top; sunbursts or colours.
● Two humbuckers (JH Treble and Bass).
● Two controls (volume, tone) plus three-way blade pickup selector; pull-push tone control operates coil-split (bass pickup only).
● Nickel-plated PRS vibrato.
Options include 10-top maple top (flame only).

LIMITED EDITION 1989-91
● One-piece mahogany regular or wide-thin set-neck, Brazilian rosewood fingerboard, abalone bird inlays, 24 frets, handsigned signature on headstock; gold-plated locking tuners.
● Semi-hollow mahogany PRS-shape body with figured cedar top; sunbursts or colours.
● Two humbuckers (Vintage Treble and Vintage Bass).
● Three controls (five-way rotary pickup selector, tone, volume).
● Gold-plated tune-o-matic-style bridge and stud tailpiece.
Limited Edition of 300.
Options included chrome/nickel hardware; multi-tap pickup system.

McCARTY ARCHTOP first version 1998-2000
● One-piece mahogany wide-fat set-neck, rosewood fingerboard, moon inlays, 22 frets, "McCarty" on truss-rod cover, signature logo on headstock; chrome-plated tuners, ebony tuner buttons.
● Hollow mahogany PRS-shape deep body (2.75"/70mm at rim), spruce top with two f-holes; vintage natural finish (originally satin, changed to gloss in 1999).
● Two humbuckers (McCarty Archtop) with nickel-plated covers.
● Two controls (volume, tone) plus three-way toggle pickup selector.
● Nickel-plated PRS Adjustable Stop-Tail.
Replaced by McCarty Archtop Spruce.
Options included abalone bird inlays; piezo bridge system; gold-plated hardware.

McCARTY ARCHTOP second version 2002-04
● One-piece mahogany wide-fat set-neck, Brazilian rosewood fingerboard, Brazilian rosewood headstock facing with paua signature logo, "McCarty" on truss-rod

THE PRS MODEL KEY

cover, paua bird inlays, 22 frets, gold-plated tuners, ebony tuner buttons.
● Hollow mahogany PRS-shape medium-deep body (2.75"/70mm at rim), spruce top with two f-holes. Artist grade figured maple back; vintage natural finish, colours and sunbursts.
● Two humbuckers (McCarty Archtop) with nickel-plated covers, piezo system.
● Three controls (magnetic volume and tone, piezo blend/volume) plus three-way toggle magnetic pickup selector, mini-toggle for magnetic/piezo/both; dual output jacks.
● Gold-plated PRS Adjustable (piezo) Stop-Tail.

McCARTY ARCHTOP I 2000-01
● One-piece mahogany wide-fat set-neck, rosewood fingerboard, moon inlays, 22 frets, "McCarty" on truss-rod cover, signature logo on headstock, chrome-plated tuners, ebony tuner buttons.
● Hollow mahogany PRS-shape deep body (2.75"/70mm at rim), figured maple top with two f-holes; vintage natural finish and colours.
● Two humbuckers (McCarty Archtop) with nickel-plated covers.
● Two controls (volume and tone) plus three-way toggle pickup selector.
● Nickel-plated PRS Stop-Tail.
Options included quilted maple top; 10-top (flame and quilt); abalone bird inlays; Adjustable Stop-Tail; gold-plated hardware, piezo bridge system.

McCARTY ARCHTOP II 1998-2001
● One-piece mahogany wide-fat set-neck, rosewood fingerboard, moon inlays, 22 frets, "McCarty" on truss-rod cover, abalone inlaid signature on rosewood-faced headstock; chrome-plated tuners, ebony tuner buttons.
● Hollow mahogany PRS-shape deep body (2.75"/70mm at rim), figured maple top with two f-holes and figured maple back; sunbursts or colours.
● Two humbuckers (McCarty Archtop) with nickel-plated covers.
● Two controls (volume, tone) plus three-way toggle pickup selector.
● Nickel-plated PRS Adjustable Stop-Tail.
Options included abalone bird inlays; piezo pickups/electronics; gold-plated hardware; double-10-top in flame or quilted maple.

McCARTY ARCHTOP ARTIST 1998-2002
● One-piece mahogany wide-fat set-neck, Brazilian rosewood fingerboard, abalone bird inlays with 14-carat gold outlines, 22 frets, abalone inlaid signature on rosewood-faced headstock; gold-plated tuners, ebony tuner buttons.
● Hollow mahogany PRS-shape deep body (2.75"/70mm at rim), Artist-grade maple top with two f-holes and Artist-grade figured maple back; sunbursts or colours including double-stain types.
● Two humbuckers (McCarty Archtop) with gold-plated covers.
● Two controls (volume, tone) plus three-way toggle pickup selector.
● Gold-plated PRS Adjustable Stop-Tail.
Special order only.
Options included piezo bridge system.

McCARTY ARCHTOP SPRUCE 2000-2001
● One-piece mahogany wide-fat set-neck,

rosewood fingerboard, moon inlays, 22 frets, "McCarty" on truss-rod cover, signature logo on headstock, chrome-plated tuners, ebony tuner buttons.
● Hollow mahogany PRS-shape deep body (2.75"/70mm at rim), spruce top with two f-holes; vintage natural finish and colours.
● Two humbuckers (McCarty Archtop) with nickel-plated covers.
● Two controls (volume and tone) plus three-way toggle pickup selector.
● Nickel-plated PRS Stop-Tail.
Replaced earlier McCarty Archtop.
Options included abalone bird inlays; Adjustable PRS Stop-Tail; gold-plated hardware, piezo bridge system.

McCARTY BRAZILIAN 2003
● One-piece mahogany wide-fat set-neck, Brazilian rosewood fingerboard, pink abalone heart bird inlays, 22 frets, Brazilian rosewood headstock overlay with inlaid pink abalone heart signature logo and "Brazilian" inlaid in green abalone ripple, gold-plated "vintage" tuners.
● Solid mahogany PRS-shape body with 10-top West Coast maple top; sunbursts or colours.
● Two humbuckers (McCarty Treble and Bass) with nickel-plated covers and gold-plated polepiece screws.
● Two controls (volume, tone) plus three-way toggle pickup selector; pull-push tone control operates coil-split.
● Gold-anodised PRS Stop-Tail.
Options included quilt maple top; East Indian rosewood neck.
Limited Edition of 500 each with signed and numbered backplate.

McCARTY HOLLOWBODY 1998-2000
● One-piece mahogany wide-fat set-neck, rosewood fingerboard, moon inlays, 22 frets, "McCarty" on truss-rod cover, signature logo on headstock; chrome-plated tuners, ebony tuner buttons.
● Hollow mahogany PRS-shape medium-deep body (1.75"/44mm at rim), spruce top with two f-holes; vintage natural finish (originally satin, changed to gloss in 1999).
● Two humbuckers (McCarty Archtop) with nickel-plated covers.
● Two controls (volume, tone) plus three-way toggle pickup selector.
● Nickel-plated PRS Stop-Tail.
Replaced by McCarty Hollowbody Spruce. Options included abalone bird inlays; flame, quilted or 10-top maple top (sunbursts or colours), replaced by McCarty Hollowbody I model (2000); piezo bridge system; gold-plated hardware; Adjustable PRS Stop-Tail.

McCARTY HOLLOWBODY I 2000-current
● One-piece mahogany wide-fat set-neck, rosewood fingerboard, moon inlays, 22 frets, "McCarty" on truss-rod cover, signature logo on headstock, chrome-plated tuners, ebony tuner buttons.
● Hollow mahogany PRS-shape medium-deep body (1.75"/44mm at rim), figured maple top with two f-holes; sunbursts and colours.
● Two humbuckers (McCarty Archtop) with nickel-plated covers.
● Two controls (volume and tone) plus three-way toggle pickup selector.
● Nickel-plated PRS Stop-Tail.

Replaced earlier McCarty Hollowbody with figured-maple-top option.
Options include quilted maple top; 10-top (flame and quilt); abalone bird inlays; Adjustable PRS Stop-Tail; gold-plated hardware, piezo bridge system.

McCARTY HOLLOWBODY II 1998-current
● One-piece mahogany wide-fat set-neck, rosewood fingerboard, moon inlays, 22 frets, "McCarty" on truss-rod cover, signature logo on headstock; chrome-plated tuners, ebony tuner buttons.
● Hollow mahogany PRS-shape medium-deep body (1.75"/44mm at rim), figured maple top with two f-holes and figured maple back; sunbursts or colours.
● Two humbuckers (McCarty Archtop) with nickel-plated covers.
● Two controls (volume, tone) plus three-way toggle pickup selector.
● Nickel-plated PRS Stop-Tail.
Options include abalone bird inlays; flame, quilted or 10-top maple top; piezo bridge system; gold-plated hardware; Adjustable PRS Stop-Tail; Artist Package (discontinued 2007).

McCARTY HOLLOWBODY SPRUCE 2000-current
● One-piece mahogany wide-fat set-neck, rosewood fingerboard, moon inlays, 22 frets, "McCarty" on truss-rod cover, signature logo on headstock, chrome-plated tuners, ebony tuner buttons.
● Hollow mahogany PRS-shape medium-deep body (1.75"/44mm at rim), spruce top with two f-holes; vintage natural finish and colours.
● Two humbuckers (McCarty Archtop) with nickel-plated covers.
● Two controls (volume and tone) plus three-way toggle pickup selector.
● Nickel-plated PRS Stop-Tail.
Replaced earlier McCarty Hollowbody.
Options include abalone bird inlays; Adjustable PRS Stop-Tail; gold-plated hardware, piezo bridge system.

McCARTY MODEL 1994-current
● One-piece mahogany wide-fat set-neck, rosewood fingerboard, moon inlays, 22 frets, "McCarty" on truss-rod cover, signature logo on headstock; nickel-plated "vintage" tuners.
● Solid mahogany PRS-shape body (slight extra depth) with figured maple top; sunbursts or colours.
● Two humbuckers (Two Dragon Bass with nickel-plated covers until 1995; McCarty Treble and McCarty Bass from 1995).
● Two controls (volume, tone) plus three-way toggle pickup selector (pull-push tone control operates coil-tap from 1995).
● Nickel-plated PRS Stop-Tail.
First 100 signed by Ted McCarty and numbered on rear control cover.
Options include rosewood neck; maple 10-top; PRS vibrato & locking tuners; gold-plated hardware; abalone bird inlays; left-handed version (1999).

McCARTY SOAPBAR 1998-current
● One-piece mahogany wide-fat set-neck, rosewood fingerboard, moon inlays, 22 frets, "McCarty" on truss-rod cover, signature logo on headstock, nickel-plated

"vintage" tuners.
● Solid mahogany PRS-shape body (slight extra depth) with figured maple top (option until 2000); sunbursts or colours.
● Two Seymour Duncan soapbar single-coil pickups.
● Two controls (volume and tone) plus three-way toggle pickup selector
● Nickel-plated PRS Stop-Tail.
Options include rosewood neck (from 2000); figured maple top (until 2000), PRS vibrato and locking tuners (until 2000), gold-plated hardware; abalone bird inlays.

McCARTY SOAPBAR STANDARD 2000-06
● One-piece mahogany wide-fat set-neck, rosewood fingerboard, moon inlays, 22 frets, "McCarty" on truss-rod cover, signature logo on headstock, nickel-plated "vintage" tuners.
● Solid mahogany PRS-shape body (slight extra depth); colours.
● Two Seymour Duncan soapbar single-coil pickups.
● Two controls (volume and tone) plus three-way toggle pickup selector.
● Nickel-plated PRS Stop-Tail.
Options include gold-plated hardware; abalone bird inlays.

McCARTY STANDARD 1994-2006
● One-piece mahogany wide-fat set-neck, rosewood fingerboard, moon inlays, 22 frets, "McCarty" on truss-rod cover, signature logo on headstock; nickel-plated "vintage" tuners.
● Solid mahogany PRS-shape body (slight extra depth). With figured maple top and opaque colour finish (1994-96); colours.
● Two humbuckers (Two Dragon Bass with nickel-plated covers until 1995; McCarty Treble and McCarty Bass from 1995).
● Two controls (volume, tone) plus three-way toggle pickup selector; pull-push tone control operates coil-tap.
● Nickel-plated PRS Stop-Tail.
Options include gold-plated hardware; abalone bird inlays.

METAL 1985-86
● One-piece mahogany regular set-neck, Brazilian rosewood fingerboard, moon inlays, 24 frets, signature logo on headstock; chrome-plated locking tuners.
● Solid mahogany PRS-shape body with custom striped finish (white body/blue stripes; black body/blue stripes; black body purple-orange stripes).
● Two humbuckers (Standard Treble and Standard Bass).
● Two controls (five-way pickup selector, volume) and two-way "sweet switch" tone filter.
● Nickel-plated PRS vibrato.
Options included gold-plated hardware; abalone bird inlays.

MODERN EAGLE 2004-current
● One-piece Brazilian rosewood wide-fat set-neck, Brazilian rosewood fingerboard, ripple abalone bird inlays, 22 frets, Brazilian rosewood headstock overlay with inlaid Modern Eagle, chrome/gold-plated locking grommet tuners.
● Solid mahogany PRS-shape body with highly figured maple top: exclusive Modern Eagle colours (satin nitro-cellulose).
● Two humbuckers (RP Treble and Bass)

with brushed nickel covers and gold-plated polepiece screws.
● Two controls (volume, tone) plus three-way toggle pickup selector; pull-push tone control operates coil-split.
● Gold anodized PRS Stop-Tail.
Options include PRS vibrato.

1980 WEST ST. LTD. 2007-current
● One-piece mahogany wide-fat Santana II set-neck, Brazilian rosewood fingerboard, green heart abalone bird inlays, 24 frets, 24.5" (622mm), inlaid green heart abalone "OM" symbol on Brazilian rosewood truss-rod cover, inlaid green heart abalone eagle on pre-85 Santana-shape sapele veneered headstock; chrome-plated locking tuners with large nickel-plated buttons
● Solid mahogany pre-'85 Santana-shape body with highly figured Artist grade sapele top with small green ripple abalone inlaid dragon; four colours only
● Two "zebra-coil" humbuckers (HFS Treble and ME Bass)
● Two controls (volume, tone) plus three-way toggle pickup selector
● Nickel-plated PRS vibrato
Limited Edition of 250

PRS CUSTOM GUITAR see Custom

PRS GUITAR see Standard

ROSEWOOD LTD. 1996
● One-piece rosewood wide-fat set-neck, Brazilian rosewood fingerboard with tree-of-life inlay, abalone purfling on fingerboard, 22 frets, "Rosewood Ltd." on truss-rod cover, abalone inlaid signature on headstock, tree-of-life inlay on headstock; gold-plated "vintage" tuners.
● Solid mahogany PRS-shape body (slight extra depth) with figured maple top. Colours: black cherry; gray black; purple; violin amber; violin amber sunburst.
● Two humbuckers (McCarty Treble and McCarty Bass) with gold-plated covers.
● Two controls (volume, tone) plus three-way toggle pickup selector; pull-push tone control operates coil-tap.
● Gold-anodised PRS Stop-Tail.
Limited Edition of 100, issued with certificate of authenticity.
Options included gold-plated PRS vibrato & gold-plated locking tuners with walnut burl buttons; semi-hollow body.

SANTANA 1995-98
● One-piece mahogany Santana-shape set-neck, Brazilian rosewood fingerboard, abalone bird inlays, 24 frets, 24.5" (622mm) scale, inlaid "OM" symbol on truss-rod cover, inlaid eagle on pre-85 Santana-shape mahogany-faced headstock; chrome-plated locking tuners.
● Solid mahogany pre-'85 Santana-shape body with figured maple top, paua-shell purfling between pickups and behind bridge. At first available only in Santana yellow; later sunbursts or colours.
● Two "zebra-coil" humbuckers (Santana Treble and Santana Bass).
● Two controls (volume, tone), two pickup-selector mini-switches.
● Nickel-plated PRS vibrato.
"Limited production"; from 1998 available only by special order.

Name changed to Santana II by 1998 – see following entry.

SANTANA II 1998-current
● One-piece mahogany Santana-shape set-neck, Brazilian rosewood fingerboard, abalone bird inlays, 24 frets, 24.5" (622mm) scale, inlaid "OM" symbol on truss-rod cover, inlaid eagle on pre-85 Santana-shape rosewood-faced headstock; chrome-plated locking tuners.
● Solid mahogany pre-'85 Santana-shape body with figured maple top, paua-shell purfling between pickups and behind bridge; sunbursts or colours.
● Two "zebra-coil" humbuckers (Santana Treble and Santana Bass).
● Two controls (volume, tone), three-way toggle pickup selector.
● Nickel-plated PRS vibrato.
Options include gold hardware; PRS Stop-Tail. Previously known as Santana.

SANTANA III 2001-07.
● One-piece mahogany "Santana wide-fat" set-neck, rosewood fingerboard, abalone bird inlays, 24 frets, signature logo on headstock, 24.5" (622mm) scale, pre-'85 "Santana" shape headstock shape; chrome-plated locking tuners.
● Solid mahogany pre-'85 Santana-shape mahogany body with figured maple top; sunbursts or colours.
● Two humbuckers (Santana III treble and bass) with nickel-plated covers.
● Two controls (volume, tone), three-way toggle pickup selector.
● Nickel-plated PRS vibrato.
Options include 10-top maple top; gold-plated hardware.

SANTANA BRAZILIAN 2003
● Brazilian rosewood Santana-shape set-neck, Brazilian rosewood fingerboard, green rippled abalone bird inlays, 24 frets, 24.5" (622mm) scale; inlaid "OM" symbol on truss-rod cover, inlaid eagle on pre-85 Santana-shape rosewood-faced headstock, chrome/gold-plated locking tuners.
● Solid mahogany pre-85 Santana-shape body with 10-top maple top, paua-shell purfling between pickups and behind bridge; sunbursts or colours.
● Two humbuckers (Santana III Treble and Bass) with nickel-plated covers and gold-plated polepiece screws.
● Two controls (volume, tone) plus three-way toggle pickup selector.
● Nickel/gold-plated PRS vibrato.
Options included quilt maple top.
Limited Edition of 200 each with signature (engraved) and numbered backplate.

SC 245 2007-current
● One-piece mahogany wide-fat set-neck, rosewood fingerboard, abalone dot inlays, 22 frets, 24.5" (622mm) scale, signature logo on headstock, "SC 245" on truss-rod cover, nickel-plated "vintage" tuners.
● Solid mahogany single-cutaway PRS-shape body with figured maple top; sunbursts or colours.
● Two humbuckers (245 Treble and Bass).
● Four controls (volume and tone for treble and bass pickups), plus three-way toggle pickup selector.
● Nickel-plated PRS Stop-Tail.

THE PRS MODEL KEY

Options include 10-top maple top (flame or quilt); bird inlays; gold-plated hardware; gold-anodized Stop-Tail.

SC 250 2007-current
● One-piece mahogany wide-fat set-neck, rosewood fingerboard, abalone dot inlays, 22 frets, signature logo on headstock. "SC 250" on truss-rod cover, chrome-plated locking tuners.
● Solid mahogany single-cutaway PRS-shape body with figured maple top; sunbursts or colours.
● Two humbuckers (250 Treble and Bass).
● Four controls (volume and tone for treble and bass pickups), plus three-way toggle pickup selector.
● Nickel-plated PRS Adjustable Stop-Tail.
Options include 10-top maple top (flame or quilt); bird inlays; gold-plated hardware.

SC 250 SATIN 2007-current
● One-piece mahogany wide-fat set-neck, rosewood fingerboard, abalone bird inlays, 22 frets, signature logo on headstock. "SC 250" on truss-rod cover, chrome-plated locking tuners.
● Solid mahogany single-cutaway PRS-shape body with figured maple top; satin nitro-cellulose colours.
● Two humbuckers (250 Treble and Bass).
● Four controls (volume and tone for treble and bass pickups), plus three-way toggle pickup selector.
● Nickel-plated PRS Adjustable Stop-Tail.
Options include 10-top maple top (flame); Artist Package; gold-plated hardware.

SIGNATURE 1987-91
● One-piece mahogany regular set-neck, Brazilian rosewood fingerboard, abalone bird inlays, 24 frets, handsigned signature on headstock; chrome-plated locking tuners.
● Solid mahogany PRS-shape body with "exceptional" maple top; sunbursts or colours.
● Two humbuckers (Standard Bass and Standard Treble).
● Two controls (five-way pickup selector, volume) and two-way "sweet switch" tone filter.
● Nickel-plated PRS vibrato.
Limited Edition of 1,000.
Options included Special Package; gold hardware; multi-tap pickup system; quilted maple top.

SIGNATURE BASS 1987-91
● One-piece maple set-neck, Brazilian rosewood fingerboard (fretted) or ebony fingerboard (fretless), bird inlays, 22 frets (or fretless), 34" (864mm) scale, handsigned signature on headstock; chrome-plated tuners.
● Solid mahogany PRS-bass-shape body with "exceptional" figured maple top; sunbursts or colours.
● Three PRS single-coil pickups, plus hum-cancelling coil in rear of body.
● Four controls (volume, five-way pickup selector, plus "deep" and "clear" EQ) and active circuit switch.
● Nickel-plated PRS bass bridge/tailpiece.
Options included gold hardware; quilted maple top.

SINGLECUT 2000-07
● One-piece mahogany wide-fat set-neck,

rosewood fingerboard, abalone dot inlays, 22 frets, signature logo on headstock, nickel-plated "vintage" tuners.
● Solid mahogany single-cutaway PRS-shape body with figured maple top; sunbursts or colours.
● Two humbuckers (7s) with nickel-plated covers.
● Four controls (volume and tone for treble and bass pickups), plus three-way toggle pickup selector.
● Nickel-plated PRS Stop-Tail.
Options include quilted maple top; 10-top (flame and quilt); abalone bird inlays; gold-plated hardware; Artist Package.

SINGLECUT BRAZILIAN ROSEWOOD 2001
● One-piece Brazilian rosewood wide-fat set-neck, Brazilian rosewood fingerboard, bird inlays, 22 frets, signature logo on headstock, gold-plated "vintage" tuners.
● Solid mahogany single-cutaway PRS-shape body with 10-top figured maple top; sunbursts or colours.
● Two humbuckers (7s) with brushed nickel-plated covers and gold-plated polepiece screws.
● Four controls (volume and tone for treble and bass pickups) plus three-way toggle pickup selector.
● Gold-anodised PRS Stop-Tail.
Limited Edition of 250.

SINGLECUT SATIN 2006-07
● One-piece mahogany wide-fat set-neck, rosewood fingerboard, abalone bird inlays, 22 frets, signature logo on headstock, nickel-plated "vintage" tuners.
● Solid mahogany single-cutaway PRS-shape body with figured maple top; satin nitro-cellulose colours.
● Two humbuckers (7 Treble and Bass) with nickel-plated covers.
● Four controls (volume and tone for treble and bass pickups), plus three-way toggle pickup selector.
● Nickel-plated PRS Stop-Tail.
Options include 10-top maple top; gold-plated hardware; Artist Package.

SINGLECUT STANDARD SATIN 2006-current
● One-piece mahogany wide-fat set-neck, rosewood fingerboard, abalone bird inlays, 22 frets, signature logo on headstock, chrome-plated locking tuners.
● Solid mahogany PRS Singlecut shape body; satin nitro-cellulose colours.
● Two zebra-coiled humbuckers (6 Treble and Bass).
● Two controls (volume, tone) plus three-way toggle pickup selector; pull-push tone control operates coil-split.
● Nickel-plated PRS Stop-Tail.
Options include PRS vibrato; gold-plated hardware.

SINGLECUT STANDARD SOAPBAR SATIN 2006-current
● One-piece mahogany wide-fat set-neck, rosewood fingerboard, abalone bird inlays, 22 frets, signature logo on headstock, chrome-plated locking tuners.
● Solid mahogany PRS Singlecut shape body; satin nitro-cellulose colours.
● Two "specially voiced" Seymour Duncan soapbar single-coils.

● Two controls (volume, tone) plus three-way toggle pickup selector.
● Nickel-plated PRS Stop-Tail.
Options include PRS vibrato; gold-plated hardware.

SINGLECUT TREM 2003-current
● One-piece mahogany wide-fat set-neck, rosewood fingerboard, abalone dot inlays, 22 frets, signature logo on headstock, chrome-plated locking tuners.
● Solid mahogany single-cutaway PRS-shape body with figured maple top; sunbursts or colours.
● Two zebra-coiled humbuckers (6 Treble and Bass).
● Two controls (volume, tone), three-way toggle pickup selector; pull-push tone control operates coil-split.
● Nickel-plated PRS vibrato.
Options include quilted maple top; 10-top (flame and quilt); abalone bird inlays; gold-plated hardware; Artist Package.

SINGLECUT TREM MODERN EAGLE 2006-current
● One-piece Brazilian rosewood wide-fat set-neck, Brazilian rosewood fingerboard, rippled abalone bird inlays, 22 frets, Brazilian rosewood headstock overlay with inlaid Modern Eagle, chrome/gold-plated locking grommet tuners.
● Solid mahogany single-cutaway PRS-shape body with highly figured maple top; exclusive Modern Eagle colours (satin nitro-cellulose).
● Two humbuckers (RP Treble and Bass) with brushed nickel covers and gold-plated polepiece screws.
● Two controls (volume, tone) plus three-way toggle pickup selector; pull-push tone control operates coil-split.
● Nickel/gold-plated PRS Stop-Tail.
No options.

SINGLECUT TREM SATIN 2006-current
● One-piece mahogany wide-fat set-neck, rosewood fingerboard, abalone bird inlays, 22 frets, signature logo on headstock, chrome-plated locking tuners.
● Solid mahogany single-cutaway PRS-shape body with figured maple top; satin nitro-cellulose colours.
● Two zebra-coiled humbuckers (7 Treble and Bass).
● Two controls (volume, tone), three-way toggle pickup selector; pull-push tone control operates coil-split.
● Nickel-plated PRS vibrato.
Options include quilted maple top; 10-top (flame and quilt); abalone bird inlays; gold-plated hardware; Artist Package.

SPECIAL 1987-91
● One-piece mahogany wide-thin set-neck, Brazilian rosewood fingerboard, moon inlays, 24 frets, signature logo on headstock; chrome-plated locking tuners.
● Solid mahogany PRS-shape; colours.
● Two pickups (Single-Coil Bass and HFS Treble humbucker until 1989; Vintage Bass and HFS Treble humbuckers from 1989).
● Three controls (five-way rotary pickup selector, tone, volume).
● Nickel-plated PRS vibrato with up-routing.
Options included abalone bird inlays; gold hardware; multi-tap pickup system.

STANDARD see Standard 24 entry

STANDARD 22 1994-current
● One-piece mahogany wide-fat set-neck, rosewood fingerboard, moon inlays, 22 frets, signature logo on headstock; chrome-plated locking tuners.
● Solid mahogany PRS-shape body; sunbursts or colours.
● Two humbuckers (Dragon Treble and Dragon Bass until 1998; Dragon II Treble and Dragon II Bass from 1998) with nickel-plated covers
● Three controls (five-way rotary pickup selector, tone, volume).
● Nickel-plated PRS Stop-Tail.
Options include McCarty Electronics (two controls [volume, tone] plus three-way toggle pickup selector); PRS vibrato; gold hardware; bird inlays; wide-thin neck.

STANDARD 22 MAPLE TOP 1998-2000
● One-piece mahogany wide-fat set-neck, rosewood fingerboard, moon inlays, 22 frets, signature logo on headstock; chrome-plated locking tuners.
● Solid mahogany PRS-shape body with figured maple top; colours.
● Two humbuckers (Dragon II Treble and Dragon II Bass) with nickel-plated covers.
● Three controls (five -way rotary pickup selector, tone, volume).
● Nickel-plated PRS Stop-Tail.
Options included McCarty Electronics (two controls [volume, tone] plus three-way toggle pickup selector); PRS vibrato; gold hardware; bird inlays; wide-thin neck.

STANDARD 22 SATIN 2006-current
● One-piece mahogany wide-fat set-neck, rosewood fingerboard, abalone bird inlays, 22 frets, signature logo on headstock, chrome-plated locking tuners.
● Solid mahogany PRS-shape body; satin nitro-cellulose colours.
● Two humbuckers (Dragon II Treble and Bass).
● Two controls (volume, tone) plus three-way toggle pickup selector; pull-push tone control operates coil-split.
● Nickel-plated PRS Stop-Tail.
Options include PRS vibrato, three controls (volume, tone and five-way rotary pickup selector switch), gold-plated hardware; wide-thin neck.

STANDARD 24 (aka PRS GUITAR, STANDARD) 1985-current
● One-piece mahogany regular set-neck, rosewood fingerboard (Brazilian until 1991), moon inlays, 24 frets, signature logo on headstock; chrome-plated locking tuners.
● Solid mahogany PRS-shape body; sunbursts or colours.
● Two humbuckers (Standard Bass and Standard Treble until 1991; HFS Treble and Vintage Bass from 1991).
● Two controls (five-way pickup selector, volume) and two-way "sweet switch" tone filter until 1991; three controls (five-way rotary pickup selector, tone, volume) from 1991.
● Nickel-plated PRS vibrato.
Known as PRS Guitar 1985-86; Standard 1987-98; Standard 24 1998-current. New 22-fret version added 1994; see Standard 22.
Options include abalone bird inlays; gold

hardware; PRS Stop-Tail; vibrato up-routing; Studio Package; figured maple top; wide-thin neck; McCarty Electronics (two controls [volume, tone] plus three-way toggle pickup selector).

STANDARD 24 MAPLE TOP 1998-2000
● One-piece mahogany regular set-neck, rosewood fingerboard, moon inlays, 24 frets, signature logo on headstock; chrome-plated locking tuners.
● Solid mahogany PRS-shape body with figured maple top; colours.
● Two humbuckers (HFS Treble and Vintage Bass).
● Three controls (five-way rotary pickup selector, tone, volume).
● Nickel-plated PRS vibrato.
Options included bird inlays; gold hardware; McCarty Electronics (two controls [volume, tone] plus three-way toggle pickup selector); PRS Stop-Tail; wide-thin neck.

STANDARD 24 SATIN 2006-current
● One-piece mahogany regular set-neck, rosewood fingerboard, abalone bird inlays, 24 frets, signature logo on headstock, chrome-plated locking tuners.
● Solid mahogany PRS-shape body; satin nitro-cellulose colours.
● Two humbuckers (HFS Treble and Vintage Bass).
● Two controls (volume, tone) plus three-way toggle pickup selector; pull-push tone control operates coil-split.
● Nickel-plated PRS vibrato.
Options include three controls (volume, tone and five-way rotary pickup selector switch), gold-plated hardware; wide-thin neck.

STUDIO 1988-91
● One-piece mahogany regular set-neck, Brazilian rosewood fingerboard, moon inlays, 24 frets, signature logo on headstock; chrome-plated locking tuners.
● Solid mahogany PRS-shape; colours.
● Three pickups (Hot Vintage Treble humbucker and two PRS single-coils).
● Two controls (five-way pickup selector, volume) and two-way "sweet switch" tone filter.
● Nickel-plated PRS vibrato.
Options included abalone bird inlays, figured maple top (from 1989: Studio Maple Top model from 1990 – see separate listing); tone control replaces sweet switch; Special Package.

STUDIO MAPLE TOP 1990-91
● One-piece mahogany regular set-neck, Brazilian rosewood fingerboard, moon inlays, 24 frets, signature logo on headstock; chrome-plated locking tuners.
● Solid mahogany PRS-shape with figured maple top; sunbursts or colours.
● Three pickups (Hot Vintage Treble humbucker and two PRS single-coils).
● Two controls (five-way pickup selector, volume) and two-way "sweet switch" tone filter.
● Nickel-plated PRS vibrato.
Options included abalone bird inlays, tone control replaces sweet switch; Special Package.

SWAMP ASH SPECIAL 1996-current
● One-piece maple wide-fat bolt-on neck, maple fingerboard, abalone dot inlays, 22

frets, signature logo on headstock; chrome-plated locking tuners.
● Solid swamp ash PRS-shape body; sunbursts or colours.
● Three pickups (McCarty Treble and McCarty Bass humbuckers with nickel-plated covers and one Seymour Duncan Vintage Rails single-coil-size humbucker).
● Two controls (volume, tone) and three-way toggle pickup selector; pull-push tone control operates coil-tap on neck pickup and activates central Vintage Rails pickup.
● Nickel-plated PRS vibrato.
Options include bird inlays; figured maple neck; figured maple fingerboard; PRS Stop-Tail; gold-plated hardware.

10TH ANNIVERSARY 1995
● One-piece mahogany wide-fat (or wide-thin) set-neck, abalone purfling on ebony fingerboard, engraved gold-pearl bird inlays, 22 frets, abalone purfling on truss-rod cover, engraved gold-pearl eagle with "10th Anniversary" inscription on headstock, abalone purfling on headstock; gold-plated locking tuners.
● Solid mahogany PRS-shape body with "exceptional" figured maple top. Colours: amber, dark cherry sunburst, indigo, or teal black.
● Two humbuckers (McCarty Treble and McCarty Bass) with gold-plated covers.
● Two controls (volume, tone) plus three-way toggle pickup selector; pull-push tone control operates coil-tap.
● Gold-plated PRS Stop-Tail.
Limited Edition planned at 200; issued with certificate of authenticity.
Options included semi-hollow body; PRS vibrato; quilted maple top.

TREMONTI MODEL 2001-07
● One-piece mahogany wide-fat set-neck, rosewood fingerboard, mother-of-pearl bird inlays, 22 frets, signature logo on headstock, "Mark Tremonti" inlay at 12th fret, truss-rod cover with mother-of-pearl purfling; chrome-plated locking tuners.
● Solid mahogany single-cutaway PRS-shape body with maple top; black only.
● Two humbuckers (Tremonti treble and bass), bass pickup with nickel plated cover.
● Four controls (volume and tone for treble and bass pickups), three-way toggle pickup selector switch.
● Nickel-plated PRS Adjustable Stop-Tail.
No options on this model.
Platinum offered by 2002.

TREMONTI MODEL second version 2007-current
● One-piece mahogany Tremonti wide-thin set-neck, rosewood fingerboard, mother-of-pearl bird inlays, 22 frets, signature logo on headstock, "Tremonti" on truss-rod cover, chrome-plated locking tuners.
● Solid mahogany single-cutaway PRS-shape body with figured maple top; sunbursts or colours.
● Two humbuckers (Tremonti Treble and Bass).
● Four controls (volume and tone for treble and bass pickups), plus three-way toggle pickup selector.
● Nickel-plated PRS Vibrato (with up rout).
Options include 10-top maple top (flame or quilt).

THE PRS MODEL KEY

THE PRS MODEL KEY

TREMONTI TRIBAL 2004-06

The Tribal has the same specs as the regular Tremonti Model with the exception of the original Tribal artwork designed by Mark's brother. The Tribal pattern is in a pearl white on the body and headstock. There were 100 made, each with a signed (by Mark) and numbered backplate. Production was interrupted in July of 2004 with about 52 or so completed. Production resumed in Sept of 2005 with the last ones being completed in the fall of 2006.

20TH ANNIVERSARY CUSTOM 22 2005-07

● One-piece mahogany wide-fat set-neck, rosewood fingerboard, green ripple abalone 20th Anniversary bird inlays with brown lip mother-of-pearl wisps, 22 frets, signature logo on headstock, black anodized "20th" truss-rod cover, chrome-plated locking tuners.
● Solid mahogany PRS-shape body with figured maple top; sunbursts or colours.
● Two humbuckers (Dragon II Treble and Bass) with nickel-plated covers.
● Three controls (five-way rotary pickup selector, volume, tone).
● Nickel-plated PRS Stop-Tail.
Options included quilt maple top, 10-top maple top (flame or quilt), PRS vibrato; McCarty electronics (two controls [volume, tone] plus three-way toggle pickup selector); gold-plated hardware; Artist Package; wide-thin neck.

20TH ANNIVERSARY CUSTOM 24 2005-07

● One-piece mahogany regular set-neck, rosewood fingerboard, green ripple abalone 20th Anniversary bird inlays with brown lip mother-of-pearl wisps, 24 frets, signature logo on headstock, black anodized "20th" truss-rod cover, chrome-plated locking tuners.
● Solid mahogany PRS-shape body with figured maple top; sunbursts or colours.
● Two humbuckers (HFS Treble and Vintage Bass).
● Three controls (five-way rotary pickup selector, volume, tone).
● Nickel-plated PRS vibrato.
Options included quilt maple top, 10-top maple top (flame or quilt); McCarty electronics (two controls [volume, tone] plus three-way toggle pickup selector); gold-plated hardware; Artist Package; wide-thin neck.

20TH ANNIVERSARY STANDARD 24 2005-06

● One-piece mahogany regular set-neck, rosewood fingerboard, green ripple abalone 20th Anniversary bird inlays with brown lip mother-of-pearl wisps, 24 frets, signature logo on headstock, black anodized "20th" truss-rod cover, chrome-plated locking tuners.
● Solid mahogany PRS-shape body; satin nitro-cellulose colours.
● Two humbuckers (HFS Treble and Vintage Bass).
● Three controls (five-way rotary pickup selector, volume, tone).
● Nickel-plated PRS vibrato.
Options included McCarty electronics (two controls [volume, tone] plus three-way toggle pickup selector); gold-plated hardware; wide-thin neck.

20TH ANNIVERSARY SINGLECUT 2005-07

● One-piece mahogany wide-fat set-neck, rosewood fingerboard, green ripple abalone 20th Anniversary bird inlays with brown lip mother-of-pearl wisps, signature logo on headstock, black anodized "20th" truss-rod cover, chrome-plated locking tuners.
● Solid mahogany single-cutaway PRS-shape body with figured maple top; sunbursts or colours.
● Two humbuckers (7 Treble and Bass) with nickel-plated covers.
● Four controls (volume and tone for treble and bass pickups), plus three-way toggle pickup selector.
● Nickel-plated PRS Stop-tail.
Options included quilted maple top: 10-top (flame and quilt); gold-plated hardware; Artist Package.

20TH ANNIVERSARY SINGLECUT TREM 2005-07

● One-piece mahogany wide-fat set-neck, rosewood fingerboard, green ripple abalone 20th Anniversary bird inlays with brown lip mother-of-pearl wisps, signature logo on headstock, black anodized "20th" truss-rod cover, chrome-plated locking tuners.
● Solid mahogany single-cutaway PRS-shape body with figured maple top; sunbursts or colours.
● Two zebra-coiled humbuckers (6 Treble and Bass).
● Two controls (volume, tone), three-way toggle pickup selector; pull-push tone control operates coil-split.
● Nickel-plated PRS vibrato.
Options include quilted maple top: 10-top (flame and quilt); gold-plated hardware; Artist Package.

20th ANNIVERSARY DRAGON DOUBLE NECK 2005

● Six-string: One piece mahogany wide-fat set-neck, Brazilian rosewood fingerboard with Dragon's tail inlay, black anodized "20th" truss-rod cover, 22 frets, Brazilian rosewood headstock overlay with inlaid signature logo, gold-plated locking tuners with large pearloid buttons.
● 12-string: One piece mahogany regular 12-string set-neck, Brazilian rosewood fingerboard with Dragon's tail inlay, black anodized "20th" truss-rod cover, 22 frets, Brazilian rosewood headstock overlay with inlaid signature logo, gold-plated locking tuners with small pearloid buttons.
● Solid mahogany PRS-double-neck shape body with highly figured maple top and two Dragons fighting inlay; translucent colours.
● Six-string: Two humbuckers (Dragon II Treble and Bass) with scuffed gold-plated covers.
● 12-string: Two humbuckers (12-string Treble and Bass) with scuffed gold-plated covers.
● Three controls (six-string volume, tone and 12-string volume), three switches (pickup selector for each neck: 6/12 selection).
● Six-string: Gold-anodised PRS Stop-Tail.
● 12-string: Gold-anodised PRS 12-string adjustable Stop-Tail.
Limited Edition run of 75.

SE RANGE

The SE range is made entirely in Korea – there are no American parts. Both the PRS Stop-Tail and the PRS vibrato were replicated for these models and although they look very similar to the USA-made parts, they are not made in the USA by Excel but in Korea. The models are easily identified by the headstock logo. Although the first and second version Santana SEs have the same logo, the second version SE is easily identified by numerous differences: a forearm contour, pickguard, fingerboard and headstock binding and uncovered, open-coil humbuckers with black bobbins.

"The Stop-Tail is actually cast aluminium – the USA part is machined – that's how we save the money," says Doug Shive. "To get it machined from a solid block like we do in the US, that would really cost a lot. It does sound a little different – not better or worse, just different. We have put Korean cast bridges on US guitars to hear how they sound and vice versa. We like both, although they're just slightly different. The SE vibrato's top plate is brass, just like the USA part, the saddles are brass too – cast not machined. The vibrato block, rather than being brass, is powdered steel. It does sound a little different, more like an old Fender bridge. We were able to reduce the cost of the bridges dramatically by doing that while maintaining the sound quality that we wanted – Paul was really insistent on that."

COMMON FEATURES

All PRS SE range guitars have the same 25" (635mm) scale as the USA models. Like the USA guitars, all have truss-rod adjustment on the headstock behind the nut. The mahogany and rosewood used for the guitars is a far eastern variant of the South American mahogany and East Indian rosewood used for the USA models. All humbuckers are uncovered – and of the same specification – unless otherwise stated.

SANTANA SE (first version) 2001-02

● One-piece mahogany set-neck, rosewood fingerboard, diagonal-stripe pearloid inlays, 22 frets, "Santana" logo on headstock, chrome-plated tuners.
● Solid mahogany new-Santana SE-shape body; translucent colours.
● Two humbuckers with chrome-plated covers.
● Two controls (volume and tone), three-way toggle pickup selector switch.
● Nickel-plated Korean-made PRS-style Stop-Tail.
Options included Korean-made PRS-style vibrato.

SANTANA SE (second version) 2002-07

● One-piece mahogany set-neck, bound rosewood fingerboard, diagonal-stripe pearloid inlays, 22 frets, "Santana" logo on bound headstock, "PRS" logo on truss-rod cover, chrome-plated tuners.
● Solid mahogany new-Santana SE-shape body with forearm contour; translucent and opaque colours.
● Two humbuckers.
● Two controls (volume and tone), three-way toggle pickup selector switch.

● Plastic pickguard.
● Nickel-plated Korean-made PRS-style Stop-Tail.
Options include Korean-made PRS-style vibrato.

SE SOAPBAR 2004
● One-piece mahogany wide-fat set-neck, rosewood fingerboard, moon inlays, 22 frets, "SE Soapbar" logo on headstock, chrome-plated tuners.
● Solid mahogany single-cut shape body; vintage cherry and black burst.
● Two soapbar single-coils .
● Two controls (volume, tone), three-way toggle pickup selector switch.
● Nickel-plated Korean-made PRS-style Stop-Tail.
No options.

SE EG 2004-current
● One-piece mahogany wide-fat set-neck, rosewood fingerboard, moon inlays, 22 frets, "SE EG" logo on headstock, chrome-plated tuners.
● Solid mahogany new Santana SE-shape body with forearm contour; translucent and opaque colours.
● Three single-coils.
● Two controls (volume, tone), five-way blade pickup selector switch.
● Plastic pickguard (white or tortoiseshell).
● Nickel-plated Korean-made PRS-style Stop-Tail.
Options include Korean-made PRS-style vibrato.
Pickups changed to one bridge humbucker and two single-coils (2005).

SE BILLY MARTIN MODEL 2004-05
● One-piece mahogany wide-fat set-neck, rosewood fingerboard, green plastic dot inlays with "spooky" bat between 11-13th fret, 22 frets, "SE Billy Martin Model" logo on headstock, black-plated tuners.
● Solid mahogany new Santana SE-shape body with forearm contour; flat black only.
● Two humbuckers with black plastic surrounds.
● Two controls (volume, tone), three-way toggle pickup selector switch.
● Black-plated Korean-made PRS-style Stop-Tail.
No options.

SE SOAPBAR II 2004-current
● One-piece mahogany wide-fat set-neck, rosewood fingerboard, moon inlays, 22 frets, "SE Soapbar II" logo on headstock, chrome-plated tuners.
● Solid mahogany new-Santana SE-shape body with forearm contour; sunbursts or colours.
● Two soapbar single-coils.
● Two controls (volume, tone), three-way toggle pickup selector switch.
● Nickel-plated Korean-made PRS-style Stop-Tail.
No options.

SE "CAMO" see SE Standard entry

SE Standard 2005-current
● One-piece mahogany wide-fat set-neck, rosewood fingerboard, moon inlays, 22 frets, "SE Standard" logo on headstock, chrome-plated tuners.

● Solid mahogany new-Santana SE-shape body with forearm contour; satin finish colours.
● Two humbuckers with black surrounds.
● Two controls (volume, tone), three-way toggle pickup selector switch.
● Chrome-plated knurled metal control knobs.
● Nickel-plated Korean-made PRS-style Stop-Tail.
Options include Korean-made PRS-style vibrato.
Originally appeared with same specs, except black hardware, in camouflage satin finish (2005).

SE CUSTOM 2005-current
● One-piece mahogany wide-fat set-neck, rosewood fingerboard, moon inlays, 22 frets, "SE Custom" logo on headstock, chrome-plated tuners.
● Solid mahogany new Santana SE-shape body with flat maple top and flame maple veneer facing; cherry sunburst and gray black both with natural maple edge.
● Two zebra-coiled humbuckers.
● Two controls (volume, tone), three-way toggle pickup selector switch.
● Nickel-plated Korean-made PRS-style Stop-Tail.
Options include Korean-made PRS-style vibrato.

SE SOAPBAR II MAPLE 2005-current
● One-piece mahogany wide-fat set-neck, rosewood fingerboard, moon inlays, 22 frets, "SE Soapbar II Maple" logo on headstock, chrome-plated tuners.
● Solid mahogany new-Santana SE-shape body with forearm contour faced with figured maple veneer; sunbursts or colours.
● Two soapbar single-coils.
● Two controls (volume, tone), three-way toggle pickup selector switch.
● Nickel-plated Korean-made PRS-style Stop-Tail.
No options.

SE SINGLECUT 2006-current
● One-piece mahogany wide-fat set-neck, rosewood fingerboard, moon inlays, 22 frets, SE Singlecut logo on headstock, chrome-plated tuners.
● Solid mahogany single-cut shape body with maple top (opaque colours) and flame maple veneer facing (translucent colours); sunburst and colours with natural maple edge.
● Two humbuckers.
● Two controls (volume, tone), three-way toggle pickup selector switch.
● Nickel-plated Korean-made PRS-style Stop-Tail.
No options.

SE ONE 2007-current
● One-piece mahogany wide-fat set-neck, rosewood fingerboard, moon inlays, 22 frets, "SE Singlecut" logo on headstock, chrome-plated tuners.
● Solid mahogany single-cut shape body.
● One soapbar.
● One control (volume).
● Plastic pickguard.
● Nickel-plated Korean-made PRS-style Stop-Tail.
No options.

SE CUSTOM SEMI HOLLOW 2007-current
● One-piece mahogany wide-fat set-neck, rosewood fingerboard, moon inlays, 22 frets, "SE Custom" logo on headstock, chrome-plated tuners.
● Solid mahogany new-Santana SE-shape body with two tone chambers and one soundhole; flat maple top (opaque colours) plus flame maple veneer facing (translucent colours); natural maple edge.
● Two zebra-coiled humbuckers.
● Two controls (volume, tone), three-way toggle pickup selector switch.
● Plastic pickguard.
● Nickel-plated Korean-made PRS-style Stop-Tail.
No options.

SE PAUL ALLENDER MODEL 2007-current
● One-piece maple wide-thin set-neck, rosewood fingerboard, "bats in flight" inlays, 24 frets, "SE Custom" logo on headstock, gold-plated tuners.
● Solid mahogany new Santana SE-shape body with flat maple top and quilted maple veneer facing; purple "Allender burst" only with natural maple edge.
● Two humbuckers (based on USA HFS Treble and Vintage Bass).
● Two controls (volume, tone), three-way toggle pickup selector switch.
● Gold-plated Korean-made PRS-style vibrato.
No options.

TREMONTI SE 2003-current
● One-piece mahogany wide-fat set-neck, bound rosewood fingerboard, pearloid dot inlays, 22 frets, "Tremonti" logo on bound headstock, chrome-plated tuners.
● Solid mahogany single-cut shape body with bound top edge; black and platinum colours.
● Two humbuckers with black plastic surrounds.
● Two controls (volume, tone), three-way toggle pickup selector switch.
● Nickel-plated Korean-made PRS-style Stop-Tail.
No options; limited run colours offered including white with black binding.

THE PRS MODEL KEY

GUITARS OF THE MONTH

Here are all 12 of the Guitars Of The Month instruments, completed in 1995 and 1996. These were the forerunners of Private Stock. The information comes from PRS's own records. All Guitars Of The Month have an eagle inlay on the headstock.

Key to makers' names: DH Dave Hazel, DN Dean Nitsch, JK Joe Knaggs, N/A information not available, PS Paul Reed Smith, TS Tony Smith, WB Wes Bryant, WK Winn Krozack.

NUMBER	EDITION	SERIAL	DESCRIPTION	MADE BY	COMPLETED
1.	January 1995	4 21037	Turquoise and silver inlay	JK, PS	Jan 11th 95
2.	February 1995	5 21344	Cocobolo neck	JK, PS	Feb 11th 95
3.	March 1995	5 21698	Indian rosewood neck	JK, PS	Mar 29th 95
4.	April 1995	5 22201	Gold inlaid dragon on fingerboard	JK, PS	May 12th 95
5.	May 1995	5 22885	Gold and onyx inlay	JK, PS	Aug 4th 95
6.	June 1995	5 22652	Pinstripe back by car artist Bud Davis	JK, PS	Jul 7th 95
7.	July 1995	5 23053	12-string, gold and coral inlay	JK, PS	Aug 8th 95
8.	August 1995	5 19796	Hand-carved left-handed McCarty Model	TS, JK	Oct 25th 95
9.	September 1995	5 23940	First McCarty Archtop, hand-carved	JK (+WB, DH)	Oct 26th 95
10.	October 1995	5 24167	"Space art" painted body by Enrico Ortega	N/A	Jan 10th 96
11.	November 1995	5 24608	Seven-string baritone/tenor guitar	JK (+DN, DH)	Jan 21st 96
12.	December 1995	6 25205	"Redesigned EG" offset cutaways, 3 pickups	JK, DH, WK, PS	March 3rd 96

PRIVATE STOCK

This inventory details virtually all of the Private Stock (one-off) instruments completed between April 1996 and May 2006, abbreviated from PRS's own records. The completion date noted is either the day on which the instrument was finally assembled or the date on which the instrument's certificate was made (usually but not always the same day or within a few days of each other). On each certificate Smith notes that the woods used are "carefully picked from my private stock for sound and remarkable figure". In the description here, the bird-inlay colour given is more often "flecked" than solid. Almost every Private Stock guitar has an eagle inlaid into the headstock. Some 2005/06 instruments have "20th Anniversary" on the instrument.
(N/A = info not available.)
Serial numbers marked with * do not follow normal PRS serial number format.

No.	SERIAL	DESCRIPTION	COMPLETED
1	6 25741	McCarty Model, "killer" quilted top	Apr 19th 96
2	6 25742	McCarty Model, "killer" quilted top, curly mahogany neck	Apr 18th 96
3	6 27203	Abalone body dragon, "2nd ever made"	Aug 8th 96
4	6 26852	McCarty Model, "killer" tiger-stripe top, curly mahogany neck	Aug 8th 96
5	6 28942	10th Anniversary walnut body, ebony fingerboard, pink pearl inlay	Nov 26th 96
6	6 29518	28"-scale baritone guitar, "Baritone" inlaid on fingerboard	Feb 1st 97
7	6 29160	12-string with ebony fingerboard and head facing "for Jim Jannard"	Dec 19th 96
8	6 29160	McCarty Model 12-string "for Robert Levin"	Dec 14th 96
9	6 28398	Santana with flat "no-radius" fingerboard	Oct 14th 96
10	6 29473	Double-neck "5th ever", vibrato on six-string	Dec 24th 96
11	6 28970	Double-neck "4th ever", shown at NAMM '97	Nov 28th 96
12	6 29332	Swamp Ash Special semi-hollow, one-piece quilted top, "for Robert Wright"	Dec 11th 96
13	6 28940	2nd of 3 McCarty Archtops built 95/96, hand-carved	Nov 15th 96
14	7 29667	3rd of 3 McCarty Archtops built 95/96, hand-carved	Jan 15th 97
15	6 28032	McCarty Model, "killer" tiger-stripe top, curly mahogany neck	Oct 3rd 96
16	6 29125	"Unbelievable" Santana, curly neck, ebony 'board, "for Jim Jannard"	Dec 2nd 96
17	7 31900	Double-neck "6th ever", shown at NAMM Nashville '97	Jul 10th 97
18	7 31884	12-string	Jul 10th 97
19	7 33997	Double-neck "8th ever", semi-hollow body	Nov 19th 97
20	7 33428	Double-neck "7th ever", "for Scott Causey" who named it "The Grail"	Oct 15th 97
21	7 34065	McCarty Model, rosewood neck, red abalone/gold birds	Nov 20th 97
22	7 34304	McCarty Model, rosewood neck, turquoise/gold birds	Jan 7th 98
23	7 33432	McCarty Model, rosewood neck, dark cherry burst, "for Albert Halim"	Oct 15th 97
24	7 34379	McCarty Model, rosewood neck, engraved gold inlay	Jan 7th 98
25	8 36207	Double-neck "9th ever", purple, "unbelievable" top, semi-hollow body	May 13th 98
26	7 32523	McCarty Model, rosewood neck, red coral birds	Aug 12th 97
27	7 32862	McCarty Model, rosewood neck, turquoise/silver birds	Sep 10th 97
28	7 32483	McCarty Model, rosewood neck, red abalone/gold birds	Aug 12th 97
29	8 34429	McCarty Model, rosewood neck, gold/silver birds	Jan 14th 98
30	7 33114	McCarty Model, rosewood neck, silver/gold birds	Sep 29th 97
31	7 33082	McCarty Model, rosewood neck, malachite/gold birds	Sep 22nd 97
32	7 32845	McCarty Model, rosewood neck, malachite/gold birds	Sep 10th 97
33	7 33113	McCarty Model, rosewood neck, engraved silver birds	Sep 30th 97
34	7 34319	McCarty Model, rosewood neck, gold/silver birds	Feb 20th 98
35	7 32839	McCarty Model, rosewood neck, red abalone/gold birds	Oct 9th 97
36	7 33048	McCarty Model, rosewood neck, turquoise/silver birds	Sep 25th 97
37	7 32885	McCarty Model, rosewood neck, red coral/gold birds	Sep 17th 97
38	7 34376	McCarty Model, 2-piece rosewood neck, engraved gold birds	Jan 7th 98
39	8 39196	McCarty Model, rosewood neck, custom gold pheasant inlays	Dec 30th 98
40	7 34305	McCarty Model, 2-piece rosewood neck, 1st natural-finish Private Stock	Dec 17th 97
41	7 34144	McCarty Model, 2-piece rosewood neck, 1st teal blue finish	Dec 9th 97
42	7 33266	McCarty Model, rosewood neck, red abalone/gold birds	Oct 8th 97
43	8 36358	McCarty Model, curly maple neck, turquoise finish, at NAMM '98	Jul 9th 98
44	7 34398	Santana, "Wings of the Heart" logo, "for Brent Broadfoot", amber	Dec 9th 97
45	7 34394	Santana, "Wings of the Heart" logo, "for Brent Broadfoot", turquoise	Dec 9th 97
46	8 35196	Custom 22 semi-hollow, "upside-down left-handed", one f-hole	Apr 6th 98
47	8 34761	12-string, flower inlay headstock, heart/horses inlay truss-rod cover	Feb 10th 98
48	8 34978	McCarty Archtop II 12-string, rosewood neck, at NAMM 98	Jan 23rd 98
49	8 34955	McCarty Hollowbody II, teal blue, specially made for NAMM 98	Jan 23rd 98
50	1998	Prototype 1 Five-string bass specially made for NAMM 98	Jan 28th 98
51	7 34623	McCarty Model, rosewood neck, "for Michael Berman"	Jan 13th 98
52	8 37810	Santana-style double-neck semi-hollow, "for Hal Dalby"	Oct 13th 98
53	8 38594	McCarty Hollowbody II, "one of a kind" dragon fingerboard inlay	Dec 10th 98
54	8 36174	McCarty Model, top from same wood as no 10 & 11	Jul 15th 98
55	8 36276	McCarty Model, rosewood neck, mammoth ivory/maple birds	Jul 9th 98
56	N/A	no information	
57	8 38031	McCarty Archtop II, maple neck, 1-piece maple top, "for Joe Abate"	Nov 19th 98
58	8 38801	Custom 24, Santana electrics, gold birds, "for Bill McDowell"	Dec 22nd 98
59	8 38030	McCarty Model, custom pearl camel inlays, "for Peter Wolf"	Nov 11th 98
60	9 41071	Santana II, "stunning" scarlet red finish, ivory/gold birds	Jul 27th 99
61	7 37700	Custom 24, custom Appenzeler dog inlays, "for Olé Akre"	Oct 5th 98
62	8 38192	McCarty Hollowbody II, "stunning" 1-piece top and back	Nov 11th 98
63	8 38765	McCarty Archtop II, custom dragon inlay, "for Jim Bennett"	Dec 10th 98
64	Prototype #1	Eight-string mandolin, at NAMM '99	Jan 26th 99
65	8 38255	McCarty Model, rosewood neck, 1-piece top, "for Joseph Paul CoCo"	Nov 23rd 98
66	8 38905	Santana, 22-fret, soapbar pickups, "for Paul Buschinger"	Dec 1st 98
67	8 38062	McCarty Model, rosewood neck, "stunning" quilted top	Nov 12th 98
68	9 40701	McCarty Model, ivory/gold birds, "for Al Vontz"	Apr 29th 99
69	8 39062	McCarty Model, curly mahogany neck and back, vintage yellow finish	Dec 30th 98
70	8 39063	McCarty Model, tigerstripe top, scarlet red finish	Dec 30th 98
71	9 41176	Custom 24 12-string, "mountain elk" scene inlay, "for Ole Akre"	May 3rd 99
72	Prototype #1	Large double-cutaway hollow-body, 1st of 2 prototypes	Jan 26th 99
73	9 43297	McCarty Model, push-pull tone knob, 5-way switch, green/gold birds	Oct 18th 99
74	8 39027	McCarty Model, "strange" tigerstripe top, raspberry finish, NAMM 99	Mar 3rd 99
75	Prototype #1	Semi-hollow electric 4-string mandolin, for NAMM 99	Jan 26th 99
76	8 39064	Custom 24, tigerstripe top, "for Ron Stoynoff"	Dec 30th 98
77	N/A	McCarty Hollowbody II, "for Barozzi", no other info	
78	9 40485	Prototype #1 Single-cutaway solidbody 1st prototype, semi-hollow	Mar 30th 99
79	8 39386	McCarty Model, tigerstripe top, figured back, "for Mark Berger"	JDec 30th 98
80	9 404854*	Prototype #2 Single-cutaway solidbody 2nd prototype	Mar 30th 99
81	9 40598	McCarty Model, curly maple neck, ocean turquoise finish	Mar 31st 99
82	8 39237	Santana, original electrics layout, tigerstripe top	Dec 29th 98
83	9 41311	Hollowbody II, piezo & synth pickups, red/gold birds, "for George Famiglio"	May 24th 99
84	9 40419	Archtop II, one of matching pair, red/gold birds, "for Greg Senko"	Mar 30th 99
85	9 40302	Archtop II, one of matching pair, red/gold birds, "for Greg Senko"	Mar 30th 99
86	8 38398	Santana II, marbled neck, tigerstripe top, "for Garry Malone"	Mar 10th 99
87	8 35824	McCarty Hollowbody II, rosewood neck	Dec 30th 98
88	9 41009	Santana II, abalone/gold birds	May 14th 99
89	9 43134	Custom 24, tigerstripe top, semi-hollow, etched birds, "for Jorge Falck"	Sep 28th 99
90	9 42408	Santana II, royal blue finish	Jul 30th 99
91	9 43107	Custom 22, violet finish, gold birds, paua purfling	Sep 24th 99
92	9 42321	McCarty Soapbar, custom electronics, paua purfling, "for Vaughn Cost"	Jun 30th 99
93	9 43381	McCarty Model, custom electronics, red/paua birds, "for Thomas Tucker"	Oct 22nd 99

No.	SERIAL	DESCRIPTION	COMPLETED
94	9 43302	McCarty Hollowbody II, +piezo pickup, initials on truss-rod cover	Oct 28th 99
95	9 42923	Custom 22, blistered maple top, "for Daniele Lotrecchiano"	Dec 8th 99
96	0 44826	11-string, custom neck and body, "for Gonçalo Baptistematos Pereira"	Jan 21st 00
97	9 42344	McCarty Hollowbody II, "for Paul Sanchez"	Jul 30th 99
98	9 43506	Custom 22 Soapbar, hollowed body, custom electronics, "for Terry Mihm"	Oct 30th 99
99	9 41025	McCarty Model, rosewood neck, red birds, "for Giles Massinghan"	Jun 28th 99
100	9 44027	Single-cutaway semi-hollow, "for Garrett Park Guitars"	Nov 29th 99
101	0 44756	Double-neck, "for Scott Causey"	Jan 18th 00
102	9 44451	Single-cutaway semi-hollow, white bound neck/stock, "for Garret/Chris Singh"	Dec 22nd 99
103	9 44028	Single-cutaway semi-hollow, custom sunburst, "for Garrett Park/David Langner"	Nov 29th 99
104	9 44029	Single-cutaway semi-hollow, "for Garrett Park/David Goldsworthy"	Nov 29th 99
105	9 44030	Single-cutaway semi-hollow, "for Garrett Park/Tony Melman"	Nov 29th 99
106	9 44031	Santana, 22 frets, semi-hollow custom body shape, "for Paul Buchinger"	Nov 30th 99
107	9 43797	7-string 24-fret, rosewood neck, "7" inlays, "for Kris Singh"	Oct 26th 00
108	9 44032	Santana II, custom semi-hollow body, "for Joe Coco"	Nov 30th 99
109	9 44512	McCarty Model, rosewood neck, paua/gold birds, "for Chuck Walters"	Dec 27th 99
110	0 45892	McCarty Model, rosewood neck, red/gold birds, chambered body	Mar 15th 00
111	0 45703	McCarty Model, custom semi-hollow, +piezo pickup, "for Steven Bienkowski"	Feb 29th 00
112	0 45499	Custom 22 Soapbar, orange-red birds, "for David Goldsworthy"	Feb 29th 00
113	0 45077	7-string, at NAMM '00	Feb 2nd 00
114	0 45059	Single-cutaway, hollowed-out back	Feb 1st 00
115	0EB 00011	Electric Bass Maple Top, at NAMM '00	Feb 1st 00
116	0 45498	McCarty Soapbar, vintage natural sunburst, rosewood neck	Feb 29th 00
117	3 73585	Singlecut Hollowbody, enlarged body, custom headstock, tree-of-life inlay	Feb 26th 03
118	0 46186	Santana, orange, 2-piece rosewood neck, repro *Supernatural*-CD guitar	Mar 22nd 00
119	0 46187	Santana, orange, 2-piece rosewood neck, repro *Supernatural*-CD guitar	Mar 22nd 00
120	0 46434	McCarty Model, chambered body, two-piece rosewood neck	Apr 14th 00
121	0 49675	McCarty Hollowbody II, +piezo pickup, custom inlays, "for Jim Wald"	Sep 22nd 00
122	0 49676	McCarty Archtop II, +piezo pickup, custom inlays, "for Jim Wald"	Sep 22nd 00
123	0 49677	Custom 24, custom electronics/inlays, "for Jim Wald"	Sep 22nd 00
124	0 49678	Custom 24, tortoiseshell finish, custom inlays, "for Jim Wald"	Dec 6th 00
125	1 54692	12-string, chambered body	Mar 28th 01
126	1 54421	McCarty Hollowbody II, curly redwood top, +piezo pickup	Mar 28th 01
127	0 51563	McCarty Model, custom inlays, "for Jim Wald"	Jan 15th 01
128	0 47834	Santana II, deep chambered body, angel inlay	JJun 26th 00
129	0 49679	Santana II, custom inlays, "for Max Miranucci"	Sep 22nd 00
130	0 46550	Santana, custom inlay and electronics	Apr 24th 00
131	0 46188	Santana, orange, 2-piece rosewood neck, repro *Supernatural*-CD guitar	Mar 22nd 00
133	0 49756	McCarty Model, rosewood neck, etched birds, "for Richard Carrier"	Sep 18th 00
134	0 48162	McCarty-style single-cutaway, rosewood neck, "for Kris Singh"	Jul 25th 00
135	0 47372	Custom 22, maple neck	May 26th 00
136	0 47818	Singlecut, maple neck	Jun 26th 00
137	0 48386	Singlecut, rosewood board/stock veneers	Aug 9th 00
138	0 47210	McCarty Hollowbody II, red/gold birds	May 20th 00
139	0 47182	McCarty Model, red/gold birds	May 26th 00
140	0 47371	McCarty Model, gold birds and side dots, "for Mr Machann"	Jun 14th 00
141	0 47910	Singlecut, gold birds and side dots, "for Mr Machann"	Jun 26th 00
142	0 47211	Custom 22, gold birds and side dots, "for Mr Machann"	Jun 26th 00
143	0 49680	Singlecut, nitro-cellulose finish, "for David Langner"	Sep 22nd 00
144	0 49380	Singlecut, custom thickness, rosewood neck, "for David Goldsworthy"	Sep 7th 00
145	0 47778	Custom 22, black/silver birds	Aug 9th 00
146	0 47092	Custom 22, chambered body	May 15th 00
147	0 48388	McCarty Model, maple neck, gold birds, ebony fingerboard	Jul 28th 00
148	0 47369	Custom 24, one-piece maple body	May 26th 00
149	0 48973	Singlecut, paua birds, "Marilyn" on headstock, "for Mike Anderson"	Aug 18th 00
150	0 47186	McCarty 22, rosewood neck, ivory/gold birds, "for Toyo Shimano"	May 19th 00
151	0 51279	Singlecut, ribbon-striped mahogany body, violin amber sunburst	Nov 21st 00
152	0 47185	McCarty 22, custom electronics, chambered body, red/gold birds	May 18th 00
153	0 47464	McCarty Hollowbody II, maple neck, +piezo pickup	Jun 30th 00
154	0 47208	McCarty Model, custom neck, abalone birds	May 31st 00
155	0 49681	Double-neck, scarlet finish, red birds, "for Lindsey Kris Roland"	Oct 6th 00
156	0 47403	McCarty Model, rosewood neck, ivory/gold birds	May 25th 00
157	0 467821*	Santana II, green birds	Jun 26th 00
158	0 48156	Santana, orange, 2-piece rosewood neck, repro *Supernatural*-CD guitar	Jul 12th 00
159	0 48158	McCarty Model, pearl/gold birds	Jul 18th 00
160	0 48385	Singlecut, tiger eye finish	Jul 27th 00
161	0 48500	McCarty Model, left-hander, one-piece figured top/back, "for Dave Gookin"	Jul 31st 00
162	0 50399	McCarty Model, chambered body, "for Dave Gookin"	Dec 15th 00
163	1 53073	Custom 22, left-hander, eagle inlay on heel, "for Dave Gookin"	Jan 30th 01
164	0 48298	McCarty Soapbar, violin amber sunburst, paua purfling	Jul 19th 00
165	0 50715	McCarty Soapbar, three P-90s, custom scale length, "for Joe Sacco"	Oct 31st 00
166	0 49681	McCarty Model, rosewood neck, ivory/gold birds	Sep 22nd 00
167	N/A	no information	
168	0 47414	McCarty Model, rosewood neck, ivory inlays	Aug 18th 00
169	0 50414	Custom 24, custom electronics, chambered body, ivory/gold birds	Oct 23rd 00

No.	SERIAL	DESCRIPTION	COMPLETED
170	0 51066	Santana, rosewood neck, knobs, truss cover	Nov 28th 00
171	0 51461	Singlecut, rosewood neck, tree-of-life inlay	Nov 28th 00
172	0 49683	McCarty Model, chambered body, custom electronics	Sep 25th 00
173	0 49684	Singlecut, chambered body, maple neck	Sep 26th 00
174	1 56138	7-string, chambered body, maple neck	May 31st 01
175	0EB 00082	Electric Bass Maple Top, pearl/gold birds	Nov 30th 00
176	0 50737	McCarty Hollowbody II, +piezo pickup	Oct 30th 00
177	0 50816	Santana, custom electronics & scale length, "for Wendell Crusenberry"	Oct 30th 00
178	0 49685	Custom 22, maple neck	Sep 26th 00
179	0 51005	Singlecut, maple neck, pearl/gold birds	Nov 7th 00
180	0 51565	Custom 22, custom neck radius, frets & tuners, "for Brian Eberhardt"	Dec 4th 00
181	0 49447	McCarty Hollowbody II, +piezo pickup, maple neck	Sep 14th 00
182	0 49686	McCarty Model, custom electronics & inlays, "for Dave Wessell"	Sep 26th 00
183	1 52683	McCarty Hollowbody II, +piezo pickup, paua purfling	Jan 18th 01
184	1 57902	Custom 24, slate blue, maple board with waterfall inlay, "for Ole Akre"	Aug 17th 01
185	1 57068	Custom 24, maple board, agoya inlays & purfling	Jul 20th 01
187	0 51552	Singlecut, rosewood neck, chambered body, etched birds	Nov 30th 00
188	0 52013	McCarty Model, rosewood neck, pearl/gold birds	Dec 19th 00
189	0 51267	Custom 22, semi-hollow with one f-hole, "for John Plummer"	Nov 22nd 00
190	0 52229	McCarty Hollowbody II, one-piece top, +piezo pickup, "for Albert Vonts III"	Dec 29th 00
191	0 52190	Custom 24, one-piece body, etched birds	Dec 29th 00
192	1 55307	Custom 24, one-piece flame maple body, etched birds	Apr 23rd 01
193	0 49082	Custom 22, etched pink birds	Aug 29th 00
194	0 50138	Singlecut, red/gold birds	Oct 9th 00
195	0 52203	McCarty Model, semi-hollow with one f-hole, "for Jim Varnier"	Dec 29th 00
196	0 49687	McCarty Model, 1 of 3 auctioned to benefit Johns Hopkins Oncology Center	Sep 21st 00
197	0 49688	McCarty Model, 1 of 3 auctioned to benefit Johns Hopkins Oncology Center	Sep 21st 00
198	0 49689	McCarty Model, 1 of 3 auctioned to benefit Johns Hopkins Oncology Center	Sep 21st 00
199	1EB 00089	Electric Bass Maple Top, ash back, black/gold birds	Feb 28th 01
200	1 50000	Santana II, chambered body, rosewood neck, red abalone birds	Jan 31st 01
201	0 52014	Singlecut, beige finish, rosewood neck	Dec 29th 00
202	1 53516	Singlecut, rosewood neck, etched birds	Feb 22nd 01
203	0 52242	Santana II, rosewood fingerboard, red/gold birds	Dec 29th 00
204	1 52655	Santana, orange finish, rosewood neck	Jan 15th 01
205	0 52248	Santana, orange finish, rosewood neck	Dec 29th 00
206	1 53798	Santana II, gold birds	Feb 27th 01
207	1 54691	McCarty Model, baseball inlays, "for Bobby Bonilla"	Apr 6th 01
208	1 53048	Custom, maple neck, etched gold birds	Jan 31st 01
209	1 56131	Santana II, korina back/neck, paua birds, "Private Stock" on headstock	Jun 29th 01
210	1 56134	Santana II, thicker korina body with custom tremolo cavity	May 31st 01
211	1 54353	Santana II, tiger eye finish	Mar 19th 01
212	1 55456	Santana II, etched gold birds	May 31st 01
213	0 51460	McCarty Model, rosewood neck, red/gold birds	Nov 28th 00
214	0 51436	Custom 22, maple neck	Nov 29th 00
215	0 52128	Custom 24, etched gold birds	Dec 29th 00
216	0 51469	McCarty Model, rosewood neck, red/gold birds	Nov 28th 00
217	1 53609	Singlecut, red/gold birds	Feb 28th 01
218	1 53348	Singlecut, turquoise finish/inlays	Feb 20th 01
219	1 53608	Singlecut, black/gold birds	Feb 22nd 01
220	1 54140	Singlecut, pearl/gold birds	Mar 19th 01
221	1 52556	McCarty Model, rosewood neck, turquoise finish/inlays	Jan 9th 01
222	1 54558	McCarty Model, black/gold birds	Mar 28th 01
223	1 54403	Custom 24, rosewood neck, pearl/gold birds	Mar 19th 01
224	1 56880	Custom 24, rosewood neck, red finish, ivory/gold birds	Jun 25th 01
225	1 56879	Custom 22, rosewood neck, ivory/gold birds	Jun 26th 01
226	1 55197	Singlecut, ebony board, etched gold birds	Jun 23rd 01
227	1 53517	Custom 22, rosewood neck, black/gold birds	Feb 23rd 01
228	0 50256	Custom 22, rosewood neck, one-piece top, red/gold birds	Oct 11th 00
229	0 50245	Santana II, rosewood neck, etched gold birds	Oct 10th 00
230	0 49761	Singlecut, rosewood neck, red/silver birds	Sep 30th 00
231	1 52924	McCarty Hollowbody II, soapbar pickups	Jan 30th 01
232	1 53007	Singlecut, custom electronics	Jan 29th 01
233	0 52142	McCarty Model, rosewood neck, green birds, "for Tom Jensen"	Dec 29th 00
234	0 52224	McCarty Hollowbody II, +piezo pickup, "for James Mintzer"	Dec 29th 00
235	1 54642	McCarty Model, rosewood neck, etched ivory birds, chambered body	Apr 2nd 01
236	1 55152	McCarty Model, maple neck, red/gold birds	Apr 24th 01
237	1 60453	Santana II, one-piece top with f-holes, rosewood neck	Dec 14th 01
238	1 53351	McCarty Model, maple neck, paua/gold birds	Feb 12th 01
239	1 53491	McCarty Hollowbody II, maple neck, etched gold birds	Feb 20th 01
240	0 51435	McCarty Hollowbody II, one-piece top, +piezo pickup, red sunburst	Nov 28th 00
241	1 53340	McCarty Hollowbody II, rosewood neck, green/gold birds, +piezo pickup	Feb 20th 01
242	1 54690	Santana II, "Rastafarian tri-color" finish, paua birds	Mar 30th 01
243	1 52364	Santana II, rosewood neck, red/gold birds, red finish	Jan 10th 01
244	1 52363	Singlecut, red finish, rosewood neck, red/gold birds, at NAMM '01	Jan 5th 01
245	1EB 00083	Electric Bass Maple Top, +piezo pickup, at NAMM '01	Jan 15th 01

No.	SERIAL	DESCRIPTION	COMPLETED
246	1 53893	McCarty Model, ivory/gold birds, "for Supap Puranitee"	Mar 7th 01
247	2 63312	Singlecut, maple neck, swamp ash back, +piezo pickup, tree of life inlay	Feb 12th 02
248	1 60268	Singlecut, aquamarine finish, rockfish inlay, +piezo pickup	Oct 31st 01
249	1 61292	Custom 22, chambered body, maple neck, +piezo pickup	Dec 13th 01
250	1 58688	Santana, rosewood neck, green birds	Sep 10th 01
251	1 56081	Santana, rosewood neck, green birds	May 31st 01
252	1 56080	Singlecut, rosewood neck, paua birds/purfling	Jun 11th 01
253	1 56695	McCarty Hollowbody II, one-piece top, turquoise finish	Jun 25th 01
254	1 54576	McCarty Hollowbody II, maple neck, +piezo pickup	Mar 29th 01
255	1 56109	McCarty Model, left-hander, rosewood neck, red/gold birds	May 31st 01
256	1 56082	Santana II, rosewood neck, pearl inlays, ivoroid binding	May 31st 01
257	1 57542	Singlecut, rosewood neck, paua birds/purfling	July 20th 01
258	1 61143	Singlecut, rosewood neck, etched gold birds, agoya purfling	Nov 28th 01
259	1 56782	Singlecut, rosewood neck, red/gold birds	Jun 21st 01
260	1 55504	Custom 22, rosewood neck, paua/gold birds	Apr 30th 01
261	1 58499	Custom 22, etched tree-of-life inlay	Aug 28th 01
262	1 55491	McCarty Model, rosewood neck, paua/gold birds	Apr 23rd 01
263	1 56234	Singlecut, rosewood neck, paua/gold birds	May 30th 01
264	1 57113	Custom 22, red finish, maple neck, red/gold birds	Jun 28th 01
265	1 56265	McCarty Hollowbody II, +piezo pickup, pearl/gold birds	Jun 7th 01
266	1 55447	McCarty Model, one-piece top, ivory/gold birds	Apr 30th 01
267	2 68255	Santana I semi-hollow double-neck 6/12, rosewood necks, red birds	Aug 26th 02
268	1 55459	McCarty Hollowbody II, +piezo pickup, black/gold birds	May 4th 01
269	1 59701	McCarty Model, rosewood neck, pearl/gold birds	Oct 11th 01
270	1 58392	McCarty Model, maple neck, ivory/gold birds	Aug 27th 01
271	1 56103	Singlecut, rosewood neck, etched gold birds	May 31st 01
272	1 57898	McCarty Model, rosewood neck, pearl/gold birds	Jul 22nd 01
273	1 56783	Custom 22, rosewood neck, green/gold birds	Jun 21st 01
274	1 55468	12-string, teal sunburst, etched silver birds	May 8th 01
275	1 57728	McCarty Model, rosewood neck, red/gold birds	Jul 31st 01
276	1 56707	McCarty Model, rosewood neck, paua/gold birds, paua purfling	Jun 15th 01
277	1 57294	McCarty Hollowbody II, one-piece top/back, ivory/gold birds	Jul 22nd 01
278	1 56333	Santana II, ivory/gold birds	Jun 8th 01
279	1 56137	Singlecut, burled top, chambered body, green/gold birds	Jun 26th 01
280	1 55456	Singlecut, chambered body, one-piece top, red/gold birds	May 4th 01
281	1 58587	Santana II, turquoise finish/birds/purfling, rosewood neck	Aug 29th 01
282	1 54559	Singlecut, blue finish, red/gold birds	Mar 28th 01
283	1 55198	Custom 22, etched gold birds	Apr 19th 01
284	1 56366	Singlecut, tree-of-life inlay, rosewood neck	Aug 28th 01
285	1 56366	Singlecut, rosewood neck, ivory/gold birds	May 31st 01
286	1 58094	McCarty Model, ash back, copperhead sunburst, snakewood/gold birds	Aug 17th 01
287	1 57651	Santana II, beige, rosewood neck, green/gold birds	Jul 31st 01
288	1 59442	Santana, rosewood neck, green birds	Oct 3rd 01
289	1 56705	Custom 24, rosewood neck, red/gold birds	Jun 15th 01
290	1 54686	Custom 22, rosewood neck, paua/gold birds	Mar 29th 01
291	1 57404	McCarty Hollowbody II, one-piece top/back, maple neck, black/gold birds	Jul 31st 01
292	1 59470	Santana, orange, rosewood neck, etched gold birds	Oct 3rd 01
293	2 65428	Baritone Hollowbody, 28-inch scale, lapis/gold birds	Apr 10th 02
294	1 558370*	Santana II, etched gold birds	Aug 27th 01
295	1 583561*	Santana II, etched gold birds	Aug 28th 01
296	1 54686	Custom 22, paua/silver birds	Jun 28th 01
297	2 62521	Custom 22, left-hander, rosewood neck, chambered body, pink pearl birds	Feb 14th 02
298	1 57819	Custom 22, beige, etched gold birds	Sep 26th 01
299	N/A	no information	
300	1 57473	McCarty Model, maple neck, red/gold birds, paua purfling	Jul 27th 01
301	1 58250	Singlecut, charcoal sunburst, rosewood neck, pearl/silver birds	Aug 28th 01
302	1 60380	Singlecut, aquamarine finish, turquoise/gold birds, +piezo pickup	Oct 30th 01
303	1 58804	Singlecut, red finish, maple neck, ivory/gold birds	Sep 18th 01
304	1 59336	McCarty Model, maple neck, red/gold birds	Sep 27th 01
305	1 61485	Custom 24, one-piece top, custom electronics, paua birds	Dec 17th 01
306	1 57805	Santana, paua birds/purfling, custom electronics	Jul 31st 01
307	1 59479	Custom 22, amber, custom electronics, paua birds	Oct 8th 01
308	1 56783	McCarty Model, rosewood neck, red/gold birds	Jun 26th 01
309	1 58959	Custom 22, paua/gold birds	Sep 24th 01
310	1 60366	Santana II, rosewood neck, green/silver birds	Oct 31st 01
311	1 59067	McCarty Hollowbody II, maple back, gold birds	Sep 20th 01
312	1 61870	Singlecut, snakewood/gold birds, at NAMM '02	Jan 3rd 02
313	1 62179	McCarty Hollowbody I, snakewood/gold birds, +piezo pickup, at NAMM '02	Jan 2nd 02
314	1 61708	12-string, snakewood/gold birds, +piezo pickup, at NAMM '02	Dec 15th 01
315	1 59895	Santana II, rosewood neck, ivory/gold birds	Oct 24th 01
316	1 60348	Santana II, copperhead finish, rosewood neck, ivory/gold birds	Oct 31st 01
317	1 58738	Singlecut, rosewood neck, pearl/gold birds	Sep 28th 01
318	1 60298	Singlecut, beige, rosewood neck, snakehead/gold birds	Oct 30th 01
319	1 50977	Singlecut, beige, rosewood neck, ivory/gold birds	Sep 20th 01
320	2 66373	Custom 22, rosewood neck, pearl dolphin inlays	May 23rd 02
321	1 58862	Singlecut, rosewood neck, pearl/gold birds	Sep 12th 01
322	1 60284	McCarty Hollowbody II, +piezo pickup, black/gold birds	Oct 29th 01
323	2 64819	McCarty Model, rosewood neck, red/gold birds	Mar 15th 02
324	1 60949	Custom 22, rosewood neck, black/gold birds	Nov 19th 01
325	2 63077	Singlecut, rosewood neck, pearl/gold birds	Jan 31st 02
326	1 61891	McCarty Model, rosewood neck, red finish, gold/gold birds	Dec 31st 01
327	1 60340	McCarty Archtop II, all-maple body, +piezo pickup, black/gold birds	Oct 30th 01
328	1 59762	Singlecut, Microsoft logo on body and inlays	Oct 11th 01
329	2 63642	McCarty Hollowbody II, +piezo/synth pickups, "for George Famiglio"	Feb 14th 02
330	2 66372	Santana II, semi-hollow, rosewood neck, etched ivory inlays	May 23rd 02
331	1 60263	McCarty Hollowbody II, all-maple body, ivory/gold birds	Oct 29th 01
332	2 66459	McCarty Soapbar/Custom 22, semi-hollow, rosewood neck, tree-of-life inlay	Jun 6th 02
333	1 62022	Santana II, rosewood neck, maple-cap back, ivory birds	Jan 28th 02
334	1 61981	McCarty Model, rosewood neck, black/gold birds	Jan 11th 02
335	2 63106	McCarty Hollowbody II, maple neck/back, gold/gold birds	Jan 31st 02
336	1 61238	Singlecut, charcoal sunburst, +piezo pickup, black/silver birds	Nov 29th 01
337	2 71453	Santana II, semi-hollow, rosewood neck, green inlays with angel	Nov 12th 02
338	2 65484	Santana I, rosewood neck, paua birds	Apr 29th 02
339	1 61271	McCarty Hollowbody II, maple neck, +piezo pickup, ivory/gold birds	Nov 30th 01
340	1 60205	McCarty Model, red, rosewood neck, pearl/gold birds	Oct 29th 01
341	2 63021	McCarty Model, aquamarine, rosewood neck, turquoise/gold birds	Feb 14th 02
342	2 63019	Custom 22, rosewood neck, etched gold birds	Jan 30th 02
343	2 63132	McCarty Model, rosewood neck, ebony board, gold/gold birds	Jul 30th 02
344	1 62133	Custom 22, aquamarine, rosewood neck, turquoise/gold birds	Dec 31st 01
345	2 64828	Custom 24, rosewood neck, ebony board, red/gold birds	Mar 15th 02
346	2 65482	Custom 22, rosewood neck, black/gold birds	Apr 29th 02
347	2 66347	Singlecut, rosewood neck, black/silver birds	May 31st 02
348	2 64818	Singlecut, rosewood neck, green/gold birds	Mar 15th 02
349	2 65322	Custom 22, rosewood neck, ebony board, snakewood/gold birds	Apr 12th 02
350	2 65233	McCarty Model, rosewood neck, ebony board, ivory/gold birds	Apr 10th 02
351	2 65340	Custom 22, rosewood neck, ivory/gold birds	Apr 28th 02
352	2 65407	McCarty Model, rosewood neck, red/gold birds	Apr 16th 02
353	2 66460	Singlecut, rosewood neck, gold/gold birds	May 29th 02
354	2 66371	Custom 22, rosewood neck, green/gold birds	May 23rd 02
355	N/A	no information	
356	1 61240	Santana, aquamarine finish, maple neck, etched gold birds	Nov 29th 01
357	1 61247	Santana, etched gold birds	Nov 30th 01
358	1 61257	Santana, red, etched gold birds	Nov 29th 01
359	1 61246	Singlecut, maple neck, red/gold birds	Dec 5th 01
360	2 65967	Singlecut, rosewood neck, green ripple birds	May 23rd 02
361	2 62904	Custom 22, maple neck, black/gold birds	Jan 30th 02
362	1 62051	McCarty Model, rosewood neck, black/silver birds, chambered body	Dec 31st 01
363	1 61032	Santana II, rosewood neck, paua/gold birds	Nov 21st 01
364	2 62872	McCarty Model, rosewood neck, red/gold birds	Jan 30th 02
365	2 64388	Custom 22, rosewood neck, hum-single-hum with 5-way, paua/gold birds	Mar 15th 02
366	1 68876	McCarty Model, maple neck, chambered body, etched gold birds	Jan 28th 02
367	4 84839	Hollowbody II double-neck, pearl/gold birds, piezo	Apr 28th 04
368	2 62372	Custom 22, rosewood neck, pearl/gold birds, signature inlay on headstock	Jan 31st 02
369	1 60271	McCarty Hollowbody II, maple neck, pearl/gold birds	Oct 29th 01
370	1 60389	McCarty Hollowbody II, charcoal finish, +piezo pickup	Oct 30th 01
371	2 65321	McCarty Model, rosewood neck, etched gold/gold birds	Apr 12th 02
372	N/A	no information	
373	2 71855	Singlecut, tree-of-life and various custom inlays	Dec 10th 02
374	2 70618	Custom 24, paua birds, stained quilted maple board	Nov 25th 02
375	2 66400	Singlecut, maple neck, red/gold birds	May 23rd 02
376	2 66824	McCarty Model, rosewood neck, etched ivory birds	Jun 11th 02
377	2 64763	Singlecut, maple neck, red/gold birds	Mar 15th 02
378	1 61046	McCarty Model, aquamarine finish, rosewood neck, gold birds	Nov 29th 01
379	2 69254	Singlecut, ivory/silver birds, custom routed vibrato	Sep 19th 02
380	2 64812	Singlecut, rosewood neck, eagle body inlay, green/gold birds	Mar 15th 02
381	2 67516	Santana II, rosewood neck, eagle heel inlay, green/gold birds	Jul 24th 02
382	2 67186	Santana II, rosewood neck, green/gold birds	Jun 24th 02
383	2 64813	Singlecut, rosewood neck, eagle body inlay, green/gold birds	Mar 15th 02
384	2 63089	McCarty Model, ivory/gold birds	Jan 31st 02
385	2 66417	Archtop II, maple features, eagle rear headstock inlay, black/silver birds	Jun 11th 02
386	1 61933	McCarty Hollowbody II, purple finish, "Art Nouveau" inlays, +piezo pickup	Dec 19th 01
387	2 67517	McCarty Model, rosewood/gold birds	Feb 14th 02
388	3 75318	McCarty Model, rosewood neck, eagle heel inlay, paua/gold birds	Apr 28th 03
389	1 68845	Santana II, rosewood neck, quilted maple back, eagle heel inlay, ivory/gold birds	Apr 28th 02
390	2 66838	McCarty Model, pearl/abalone moon inlays	Jun 20th 02
391	N/A	no information	
392	2 67917	Santana III, rosewood neck, etched gold inlays	Jul 30th 02
393	2 67849	Santana I, rosewood neck, green ripple inlays, "Motoko Hosoya" 12th fret inlay	Jul 24th 02
394	2 63898	Singlecut, paua/gold birds (eagle 1st fret)	Jan 28th 02
395	1 62178	Santana II, rosewood neck, etched ivory birds, chambered body	Dec 31st 01

No.	SERIAL	DESCRIPTION	COMPLETED
396	2 63891	Custom 22, rosewood neck, malachite birds	Jan 28th 02
397	2 63459	McCarty Model, rosewood neck, gold/gold birds	Feb 14th 02
398	2 70616	Custom 24, maple neck, snakewood board, black/gold birds	Oct 21st 02
399	1 66978	Hollowbody I, snakewood board, snakewood/gold birds	Jun 21st 02
400	2 67919	McCarty 12-string, snakewood/gold birds	Jul 24th 02
401	1 67138	Singlecut, snakewood board, snakewood/gold birds	Jun 21st 02
402	2 66467	Custom 22, snakewood board, gold/gold birds	May 31st 02
403	2 66668	Hollowbody I, snakewood board, gold birds	Jun 14th 02
404	2 68284	Santana I, rosewood neck, green ripple/gold birds	Aug 8th 02
405	2 69477	Custom 24, rosewood neck, etched gold birds	Jan 2nd 03
406	2 70027	Santana I, rosewood neck, green ripple birds	Oct 18th 02
407	2 67606	Singlecut, etched ivory birds	Jul 25th 02
408	2 69224	Hollowbody, custom headstock inlay, paua/gold birds, piezo	Sep 26th 02
409	2 70778	Santana II, semi-hollow with f-hole, paua/gold birds	Oct 21st 02
410	3 80006	Hollowbody II, maple neck, cherub inlays	Oct 13th 03
411	2 70707	Singlecut, rosewood neck, turquoise/gold birds	Oct 21st 02
412	3 77801	Santana II, rosewood neck, flat body, custom scale, ivory birds	Oct 2nd 03
413	2 67918	Hollowbody II, maple neck, paua/gold birds, piezo	Jul 24th 02
414	2 71442	McCarty Model 12-string, turquoise/gold birds	Nov 22nd 02
415	2 70026	Hollowbody I, tree-of-life inlay, piezo	Oct 21st 02
416	2 68844	Santana I, maple neck, black/gold birds	Aug 23rd 02
417	1 68846	Santana II, rosewood neck, etched gold birds	Aug 23rd 02
418	2 70796	Singlecut, ivory inlays, Fralin single-coils, piezo	Nov 14th 02
419	2 65483	Singlecut, rosewood neck, paua/gold birds	Apr 29th 02
420	2 67231	Custom 22, maple neck, paua/gold birds	Jun 24th 02
421	2 67751	Custom 24, Santana tri-color finish, paua/gold birds	Jun 24th 02
422	2 67212	Custom 24, 1-piece maple top/back, paua/gold birds	Jun 24th 02
423	2 65488	12-string, green/gold birds	Apr 29th 02
424	2 64814	Singlecut, rosewood neck, gold/gold birds	Mar 28th 02
425	2 71382	Santana, rosewood neck, Smith signature body inlay	Jun 22nd 04
426	2 67211	Custom 24, 1-piece maple top/back, maple neck, abalone/gold birds	Jun 24th 02
427	2 65521	Archtop II, 1-piece maple top/back, abalone/gold birds, piezo	Apr 29th 02
428	2 68009	Hollowbody I, rosewood neck, green/gold birds	Jul 30th 02
429	2 68065	Singlecut, rosewood neck, green/gold birds	Jul 30th 02
430	2 69759	Archtop II, gold/gold birds, piezo	Sep 26th 02
431	2 66782	Santana I, green birds	Jun 20th 02
432	2 67822	Custom 24, maple neck, abalone/gold birds	Jul 24th 02
433	2 69687	Custom 22, etched silver birds	Sep 24th 02
434	2 69692	McCarty Model, 'smoked' finish, red/gold birds, Fralin pickups, custom switching	Sep 24th 02
435	2 68137	Custom 24, maple neck, lefty controls, gold birds	Jul 24th 02
436	2 67210	Custom 22, maple neck, pearl/gold birds	Jun 24th 02
437	2 66190	Custom 22, maple neck, etched gold birds	May 23rd 02
438	2 67789	Santana II, rosewood neck, paua birds	Jul 24th 02
439	2 68956	Santana II, rosewood neck, eagle heel inlay, red birds	Sep 18th 02
440	2 68462	Archtop II, 'smoked' finish, black/gold birds	Aug 19th 02
441	2 68062	McCarty Model, maple neck, turquoise/gold birds	Jul 30th 02
442	4 EB00480	4-string custom bass, rosewood neck, turquoise/gold birds, "for 04 NAMM show"	Feb 17th 04
443	4 EB00479	4-string fretless custom bass, rosewood neck, snakewood/gold birds, "for 04 NAMM"	Feb 17th 04
444	4 90538	Hollowbody II, eagle heel inlay, etched gold birds, piezo	Oct 19th 04
445	4 87850	Hollowbody II, abalone eagle	May 17th 05
446	3 82063	513, turquoise birds, "for 04 NAMM show"	Jan 23rd 04
447	3 73640	Custom 24, rosewood neck, eagle first-fret inlay, paua/gold birds	Feb 21st 03
448	2 69689	Santana I, rosewood neck, bird between-pickups inlay, green birds	Sep 24th 02
449	2 67607	Hollowbody I, etched gold birds, piezo	Jul 25th 02
450	2 72513	Custom 24, rosewood neck, paua/gold birds	Jan 15th 03
451	2 69560	Singlecut, red/gold birds, maple leaf rear-headstock inlay, piezo	Oct 7th 02
452	2 69876	Santana II, bird heel inlay, turquoise birds	Oct 18th 02
453	2 70617	Custom 22, 1-piece maple top/back, eagle heel inlay, etched gold birds	Oct 21st 02
454	3 77241	Hollowbody II baritone, lapis birds, piezo	Jul 8th 03
455	3 73258	Archtop 12-string, red/purple finish, abalone birds	Feb 27th 03
456	2 72187	Custom 22, maple neck, black/gold birds	Dec 24th 02
457	3 72998	Singlecut, rosewood neck, turquoise/silver birds	Jan 29th 03
458	3 72623	McCarty Model, rosewood neck, paua/gold birds	Jan 28th 03
459	3 74296	Archtop II, eagle heel inlay, ebony knobs, etched silver birds	Mar 24th 03
460	3 73541	Hollowbody II, maple neck, abalone/gold birds, piezo	Feb 27th 03
461	2 72474	Singlecut, eagle rear-body inlay, turquoise/gold birds	Jan 9th 03
462	3 72622	Custom 22, rosewood neck, etched pearl birds	Jan 15th 03
463	3 74065	Custom 24, rosewood neck, etched ivory birds	Mar 14th 03
464	2 69686	Santana I, 'smoked' finish, green/gold birds	Sep 25th 02
465	2 69142	Custom 22, 'smoked' finish, ivory/gold birds	Oct 4th 02
466	3 72955	Singlecut, rosewood neck, paua/gold birds and snakewood bird at 12th fret	Jan 28th 03
467	3 74289	Hollowbody I, rosewood neck, turquoise birds and 'Tone' 12th fret inlay, piezo	Mar 18th 03
468	2 68843	Custom 22, rosewood neck, turquoise/gold birds	Aug 27th 02
469	3 76213	Singlecut Trem, 25.5-inch scale, ivory/gold birds	May 23rd 03
470	2 72186	McCarty Model, rosewood neck, abalone birds	Dec 24th 02
471	2 69688	McCarty Model, rosewood neck, pearl/gold birds	Sep 24th 02
472	2 69877	Custom 22, pearl/gold birds	Oct 21st 02
473	2 69767	Custom 22, maple neck, abalone/gold birds	Sep 24th 02
474	2 69690	Custom 22, maple neck, abalone/gold birds	Sep 24th 02
475	2 69760	Hollowbody II, pearl/gold birds, piezo	Sep 25th 02
476	2 69691	McCarty Model, paua/gold birds	Sep 25th 02
477	3 73257	McCarty Model, pearl/gold birds	Feb 18th 03
478	3 72623	McCarty Model, rosewood neck, etched gold birds	Jan 17th 03
479	3 72910	McCarty Model, maple neck, etched gold birds	Jan 28th 03
480	3 72909	Santana II, rosewood neck, paua birds	Jan 28th 03
481	3 77531	Santana II, ivory birds	Jul 15th 03
482	2 71276	Santana II, rosewood neck, eagle heel inlay, ivory/gold birds	Nov 14th 02
483	2 70028	Santana I, rosewood neck, paua/gold birds	Oct 21st 02
484	2 72514	Singlecut, rosewood neck, pearl/silver birds	Jan 15th 03
485	3 75898	Custom 24, tri-color finish, maple neck, paua/gold birds	May 13th 03
486	3 75006	Hollowbody II, maple neck, "MJF" heel inlay, pearl/gold birds, piezo	Apr 22nd 03
487	2 71432	Hollowbody II, lapis/gold birds, piezo	Nov 25th 02
488	2 71807	Hollowbody II, ivory/gold birds, piezo	Dec 11th 02
489	2 71441	McCarty Model, pearl/gold birds	Nov 25th 02
490	3 72676	Santana II, green birds	Jan 17th 03
491	3 79857	McCarty Model, maple neck, tiger inlays, black/gold eagle	Oct 13th 03
492	3 79881	McCarty Model, rosewood neck, phoenix inlays, pearl/gold eagle	Oct 16th 03
493	3 76622	Custom 22 12-string, eagle 1st-fret inlay, paua birds	Jun 24th 03
494	3 74977	Singlecut, etched silver birds	Apr 22nd 03
495	3 72674	Santana II, etched gold birds	Jan 20th 03
496	3 75157	Custom 24, maple neck, paua/gold birds	Apr 22nd 03
497	3 76210	Tremonti Model, 'Dragon violin carve', rosewood neck, gold birds	May 23rd 03
498	3 74932	Santana I, rosewood neck, etched gold birds	Apr 22nd 03
499	3 79017	Santana II, rosewood neck, ivory "OM" truss-rod-cover inlay, ivory/gold birds	Sep 11th, 03
500	3 79995	Hollowbody II, reversed ivory/gold 12th-fret eagle, awabi "OM" truss-rod-cover inlay	Oct 14th 03
501	2 71098	McCarty Model, rosewood neck, red/gold birds	Nov 11th 02
502	3 73259	McCarty Soapbar, rosewood neck, black/gold birds	Feb 18th 03
503	2 71293	Hollowbody II, maple neck, gold/gold birds, piezo	Nov 14th 02
504	3 75451	Archtop, smokey blonde finish, maple body and neck, black/gold birds, piezo	Apr 28th 03
505	2 71725	Swamp Ash Special, black/gold birds	Dec 10th 02
506	n/a	Custom 24, rosewood neck, gold/gold birds	Dec 10th 02
507	2 71384	Hollowbody I, malachite/gold birds, piezo	Nov 15th 02
508	2 71186	Custom 22, snakewood fingerboard, pearl/gold birds	Nov 11th 02
509	3 72794	Custom 22, maple neck, etched ivory birds	Jan 20th 03
510	2 71726	Hollowbody I, snakewood fingerboard, black/gold birds	Dec 10th 02
511	3 75005	Archtop, pearl/gold birds, piezo	Apr 22nd 03
512	2 71723	Santana II, rosewood neck, etched gold birds	Dec 20th 02
513	2 71385	McCarty Model, rosewood neck, ivory/gold birds	Nov 11th 02
514	3 78563	Santana II, stoptail, gold "OM" truss-rod-cover inlay, f-holes, etched gold birds	Aug 15th 03
515	5 93219	Santana II double-neck 6/12, rosewood necks, etched gold birds	Feb 18th 05
516	2 71187	Singlecut, rosewood neck, red/gold birds	Nov 11th 02
517	3 73256	Santana I, rosewood neck, ebony body inlays, turquoise/gold birds	Feb 21st 03
518	3 72675	Custom 24, maple neck, turquoise/gold birds	Jan 17th 03
519	3 72990	Santana I, maple neck, gold/gold birds	Jan 29th 03
520	3 74023	Singlecut, semi-hollow, maple neck, turquoise/pearl birds	Mar 18th 03
521	4 85905	Custom 24, bonsai tree inlays, green eagle, "for Ole Akre"	May 10th 04
522	3 78250	McCarty Model, abalone birds	Mar 18th, 03
523	3 74979	Singlecut Trem, paua birds	Apr 22nd 03
524	3 78559	Santana II, green "OM" truss-rod-cover inlay, green birds	Aug 15th 03
525	3 75155	Archtop II, gold signature 12th fret, paua birds, piezo	Apr 28th 03
526	3 74064	Hollowbody II, malachite/gold birds, piezo	Mar 14th 03
527	3 74066	Hollowbody II, pearl/gold birds, piezo	Mar 19th 03
528	3 74297	Singlecut Trem, orange/gold birds	Mar 14th 03
529	3 73551	Custom 22, rosewood neck, paua/gold birds	Feb 21st 03
530	3 76703	Custom 22, rosewood neck, paua/gold birds	Jun 24th 03
531	3 73552	Custom 22, agoya/gold birds	Feb 21st 03
532	3 74468	Singlecut Trem, pearl/gold birds	Mar 27th 03
533	3 74251	Singlecut Trem, black/gold birds	Mar 14th 03
534	3 77119	Hollowbody I, rosewood neck, pearl/gold birds, piezo	Jun 30th 03
535	3 75667	Singlecut Trem, lapis/gold birds	May 16th 03
536	3 75156	Hollowbody II, maple neck, red/gold birds, piezo	Apr 22nd 03
537	3 76212	Custom 22, rosewood neck, etched gold birds	May 23rd 03
538	3 79382	McCarty, semi-hollow, Santana neck carve, etched ivory birds	Sep 22nd 03
539	3 78093	Custom 22, semi-hollow, tree-of-life inlays	Aug 27th 03
540	3 74895	'Santana Original', green birds	Apr 22nd 03
541	3 81163	Singlecut Trem, paua/gold birds	Nov 19th 03
542	3 76264	Custom 24, rosewood neck, paua bird 12th fret, paua dots	May 23rd 03
543	4 82463	Singlecut Jumbo Archtop, maple neck, tree-of-life inlays, "for 04 NAMM show"	Sep 28th 05
544	4 88892	Santana I, rosewood neck, Chicago inlays, pearl "OM" truss-rod-cover inlay	Aug 20th 04
545	4 89719	Santana II, rosewood neck, red/gold birds	Sep 21st 04

No.	SERIAL	DESCRIPTION	COMPLETED	No.	SERIAL	DESCRIPTION	COMPLETED
546	3 75158	Hollowbody II, rosewood neck, pearl/gold birds	May 16th 03	621	4 84549	Santana II, ivory/gold birds	Mar 23rd 04
547	3 75913	Santana, rosewood neck, abalone birds, "for June 03 Tokyo Guitar Show"	May 13th 03	622	4 84397	Santana II, maple neck, pearl/gold birds	Mar 29th 04
548	3 75908	Santana, rosewood neck, abalone birds, "for June 03 Tokyo Guitar Show"	May 13th 03	623	4 84160	Archtop II baritone, maple neck, abalone/gold birds, piezo	Mar 11th 04
549	3 75909	Santana, rosewood neck, abalone birds, "for June 03 Tokyo Guitar Show"	May 13th 03	624	3 81098	Singlecut Trem, pearl/gold birds, "for 04 Winter NAMM trade show"	Feb 17th 04
550	3 75910	Santana, rosewood neck, abalone birds, "for June 03 Tokyo Guitar Show"	May 13th 03	625	4 82329	Singlecut Hollowbody II, pearl birds, piezo, "for NAMM 04 show"	Feb 17th 04
551	3 75907	Santana, rosewood neck, abalone birds, "for June 03 Tokyo Guitar Show"	May 13th 03	626	3 n/a	5-string Bass, rosewood neck, pearl/gold birds, "for 04 NAMM show"	Jan 22nd 04
552	4 86614	Custom 22 double-neck, gold/gold birds, piezo	Jun 2nd 04	627	4 82387	Singlecut Hollowbody II, rosewood neck, paua/gold birds, piezo, "for NAMM 04"	Jan 22nd 04
553	3 77529	McCarty Model, maple neck, etched gold birds	Jul 15th 03	628	3 81982	Hollowbody II 12-string, maple neck, pearl/gold birds, "for NAMM 04 show"	Feb 23rd 04
554	3 77530	McCarty Model, maple neck, green/gold birds	Jul 15th 03	629	3 81981	513, maple neck, pearl birds, "for 04 Winter NAMM show"	Feb 17th 04
555	3 79345	Hollowbody II, brown-lip/gold birds, piezo	Sep 22nd 03	630	3 81137	Hollowbody II, agova/gold birds, piezo	Nov 18th 03
556	3 76211	Hollowbody II, ivory birds, piezo	May 27th 03	631	4 84967	McCarty 24, rosewood neck, abalone/gold birds	Apr 13th 04
557	3 77197	Custom 22, pearl/gold birds, "for Guitarist magazine 03 Guitar Giveaway"	Jul 8th 03	632	3 81059	McCarty Model, rosewood neck, abalone/gold birds	Nov 26th 03
558	3 76625	Custom 22, maple neck, lapis/gold birds	Jun 24th 03	633	3 81293	Singlecut Trem, etched gold birds	Nov 26th 03
559	3 76695	Custom 24, red/gold birds, "for 03 Nashville NAMM show"	Jun 24th 03	634	3 78995	Archtop, abalone/gold birds, piezo	Sep 11th 03
560	3 76795	Hollowbody II, agova/gold birds	Jun 24th 03	635	3 80234	Hollowbody II, agova/gold birds, piezo	Oct 20th 03
561	3 76697	McCarty Model, rosewood neck, red/gold birds	Jun 24th 03	636	4 83425	Singlecut Trem, maple neck, pearl/gold birds	Feb 17th 04
562	3 76797	Hollowbody II, agova/gold birds, piezo, "for 03 Nashville NAMM show"	Jun 24th 03	637	3 82137	Singlecut Trem, rosewood neck, paua/gold birds	Dec 30th 03
563	3 77023	Singlecut Trem, paua/gold birds	Jun 24th 03	638	4 86804	Hollowbody II, rosewood neck, pearl/gold birds, piezo	Jun 21st 04
564	3 77398	Custom 22, maple neck, awabi/gold birds	Jul 15th 03	640	4 86072	Singlecut Trem, rosewood neck, turquoise birds	May 17th 04
565	3 77528	Custom 22, maple neck, awabi/gold birds	Jul 15th 03	639	3 79410	Hollowbody II, maple neck, paua/gold birds, piezo	Sep 25th 03
566	3 77458	Custom 22, rosewood neck, awabi/gold birds	Jul 15th 03	641	3 80941	Singlecut, rosewood neck, paua birds	Nov 18th 03
567	3 78966	Custom 22, pearl dolphin inlays	Sep 11th 03	642	6 105317	Santana "pre-factory", rosewood neck, abalone bird 12th-fret inlay, dragon top inlay	May 15th 06
568	3 77567	Custom 24, white gold birds	Jul 18th 03	643	4 89563	Custom 24, paua birds, paua body strips, "custom neck scale"	Sep 21st 04
569	3 77533	Custom 24, black onyx/silver birds	Jul 15th 03	644	3 81083	Custom 24, tri-color finish, agova birds	Nov 19th 03
570	3 77568	Custom 24, rosewood neck, ivory/gold birds	Jul 18th 03	645	4 89124	Santana I, tri-color finish, maple neck, etched ivory birds, ivory "OM" inlay	Aug 25th 04
571	3 78620	Custom 22 12-string, rosewood neck, black onyx/silver birds	Aug 26th 03	646	4 89728	Santana I, maple neck, etched ivory birds, ivory "OM" inlay	Sep 21st 04
572	3 78618	Custom 24, maple neck, pearl/gold birds	Aug 26th 03	647	4 83186	McCarty Model, maple neck, paua/gold birds	Feb 12th 04
573	3 79380	Custom 24, ivory eagle 12th fret inlay	Sep 17th 03	648	3 80983	Custom 22, no inlay	Nov 18th 03
574	3 79124	Custom 24, pearl/silver birds	Sep 11th 03	649	5 93195	Custom 24 double-neck 6/12, rosewood necks, agova birds	Mar 17th 05
575	3 78286	McCarty Model, rosewood neck, brown-lip/gold birds	Aug 27th 03	650	3 79635	McCarty Model, onyx/gold birds	Oct 13th 03
576	3 78447	Singlecut, gold/gold birds	Aug 27th 03	651	3 79997	Custom 24, pearl/gold birds	Oct 13th 03
577	3 78403	Hollowbody II, maple neck, ivory/silver birds, piezo	Aug 27th 03	652	3 79883	Singlecut Trem, paua/gold birds	Oct 13th 03
578	3 78446	Santana II, paua/gold birds, paua "OM" symbol	Aug 27th 03	653	3 80165	McCarty Model, rosewood neck, abalone birds	Oct 20th 03
579	3 78404	McCarty Model left-hander, rosewood neck, paua birds	Aug 27th 03	654	4 84589	Hollowbody II, maple neck, etched ivory birds, piezo	Mar 23rd 04
580	n/a	Custom 24 7-string, awabi/gold birds	Aug 20th 03	655	3 79937	Hollowbody II, maple neck, ivory/gold birds, piezo	Oct 13th 03
581	3 78407	Hollowbody II, abalone birds	Aug 27th 03	656	4 n/a	Custom 22 12-string, maple neck, abalone moons	Mar 10th 04
582	3 78476	McCarty Model, abalone/gold birds	Aug 15th 03	657	4 85385	Custom 24, pearl/gold birds	Apr 27th 04
583	3 78298	McCarty Model, abalone birds	Aug 27th 03	658	3 80345	Custom 24, abalone birds	Oct 28th 03
584	3 78406	Hollowbody II, paua birds	Aug 27th 03	659	3 26679	CE 24 Maple Top, rosewood neck, paua birds, "second Private Stock CE 24 made"	Oct 29th 03
585	3 76702	Singlecut Trem, pearl/gold birds	Jun 24th 03	660	3 80128	Singlecut Trem, snakewood/gold birds, "for 04 Winter NAMM trade show"	Feb 23rd 04
586	3 76700	Singlecut Trem, mahogany neck, pearl/gold birds	Jun 24th 03	661	3 26455	CE 24 Maple Top, rosewood neck, ivory/gold birds, "third Private Stock CE 24"	Oct 28th 03
587	3 76796	Singlecut, black onyx/gold birds	Jun 24th 03	662	3 80931	Hollowbody II, agova/gold birds, piezo	Nov 18th 03
588	4 86198	Santana II, rosewood neck, pearl/gold birds, mandolin eagle heel inlay	Jun 1st 04	663	3 80344	Custom 22, maple neck, onyx/gold birds	Oct 28th 03
589	3 77534	Custom 22, rosewood neck, paua birds	Jul 15th 03	664	3 80930	Singlecut, pearl/gold birds, "for 04 Winter NAMM show"	Feb 23rd 04
590	4 84107	Custom 24 7-string, abalone birds, Duncan pickups	Mar 10th 04	665	3 80932	Singlecut Trem, pearl/gold birds	Nov 18th 03
591	3 77659	Custom 22, maple neck, etched gold birds	Jul 23rd 03	666	4 83761	Custom 24, maple neck, etched gold birds	Mar 8th 04
592	3 81167	Custom 22, dolphin inlays, dolphin body inlays	Nov 19th 03	667	4 90932	Custom 22, maple neck, pearl/gold birds	Nov 18th 04
593	3 78173	Singlecut, turquoise/gold birds	Aug 15th 03	668	4 92022	Hollowbody II, maple neck, pearl/gold birds, piezo	Dec 21st 04
594	3 80046	Custom 22 7-string, maple neck, abalone birds	Oct 14th 03	669	4 87868	Hollowbody II, maple neck, paua birds, piezo	Jul 15th 04
595	4 85301	McCarty Soapbar, rosewood neck, abalone moons	Apr 22nd 04	670	4 85379	Custom 24, rosewood neck, etched silver birds	Apr 27th 04
596	3 76947	Custom 22, maple neck, ivory/gold birds	Jun 24th 03	671	4 83700	Hollowbody II, pearl/gold birds, piezo	Mar 8th 04
597	3 77566	Custom 22 12-string, lapis/gold birds	Jul 18th 03	672	4 84120	Singlecut Trem, rosewood neck, pearl/gold birds	Mar 8th 04
598	3 77625	Singlecut, etched silver birds	Jul 22nd 03	673	4 84452	Hollowbody II, maple neck, ivory/gold birds, piezo	Mar 29th 04
599	3 77626	Hollowbody II, maple neck, etched gold birds, piezo	Jul 22nd 03	674	4 85028	Singlecut Trem, rosewood neck, ivory/gold birds	Apr 27th 04
600	4 82968	Singlecut, rosewood neck, rosewood top, abalone/gold birds	Jan 30th 04	675	4 85620	Custom 22, rosewood neck, maple-cap back, etched silver birds	Apr 27th 04
601	4 90326	Custom 22, rosewood neck, abalone/gold birds	Oct 14th 04	676	4 87138	McCarty Model, rosewood neck, turquoise/silver birds	Jun 21st 04
602	4 82502	Hollowbody II, etched ivory birds, "for NAMM 04 trade show"	Feb 12th 04	677	4 84198	Hollowbody II, pearl/gold birds, piezo	Mar 11th 04
603	3 79771	McCarty Model, pearl/gold birds	Oct 13th 03	678	4 84113	Singlecut Trem, rosewood neck, etched silver/gold birds	Mar 8th 04
604	3 80928	Custom 24, pearl/gold birds	Nov 19th 03	679	4 85436	Santana, rosewood neck, paua birds	Apr 23rd 04
605	3 79788	Santana, abalone birds	Oct 9th 03	680	5 96595	McCarty Model, pearl headstock signature, abalone birds	Aug 31st 05
606	3 80929	Singlecut Trem, mahogany neck, lapis/gold birds	Nov 26th 03	681	4 84940	Hollowbody II, maple neck, paua birds, etched ivory eagle, piezo	Apr 14th 04
607	3 26678	CE 24 Maple Top, mandolin eagle 12th-fret inlay, "first Private Stock CE 24"	Oct 28th 03	682	5 100716	Singlecut Trem, rosewood neck, "Private Stock #682" anniversary head inlay	Oct 12th 05
608	4 84477	Hollowbody II, maple neck, ebony/gold birds, piezo	Mar 23rd 04	683	5 90326	Custom 22, rosewood neck, abalone/gold birds	Mar 17th 05
609	3 78478	Hollowbody II, paua/gold birds, piezo	Aug 15th 03	684	4 84349	Singlecut Trem, etched ivory birds	Mar 29th 04
610	3 80684	Hollowbody II, maple neck, etched ivory birds, piezo	Dec 17th 03	685	4 84106	Singlecut Soapbar, etched ivory birds	Mar 8th 04
611	3 80984	Custom 22, maple neck, etched gold birds	Nov 18th 03	686	4 83011	McCarty Model, pearl/gold birds, "for Scott Lawson"	Feb 12th 04
612	3 79628	Hollowbody II, abalone/gold birds, piezo	Oct 9th 03	687	4 83279	McCarty Model, paua/gold birds	Feb 12th 04
613	3 82159	McCarty Model, maple neck, etched gold birds, "displayed at 04 NAMM show"	Jan 23rd 04	688	4 82499	Custom 22, rosewood neck with lam maple strip, pearl/gold birds, "for NAMM 04"	Feb 17th 04
614	n/a	n/a	n/a	689	4 82896	McCarty Model, rosewood neck, abalone/gold birds	Jan 23rd 04
615	4 82335	Singlecut Jumbo, turquoise/gold birds, "for NAMM 04 trade show"	Jan 22nd 04	690	4 89729	Custom 22 12-string, rosewood neck, paua/gold birds	Sep 21st 04
616	4 82412	Singlecut Jumbo, pearl/gold birds, "displayed NAMM 04", "for Tom Kaney"	Jan 22nd 04	691	4 88630	Santana II, rosewood neck, onyx/silver birds	Aug 17th 04
617	3 82156	Singlecut Hollowbody II, pearl/gold birds, piezo, "for NAMM 04 show"	Jan 23rd 04	692	4 83291	Custom 22, rosewood neck, agova/gold birds	Mar 3rd 04
618	4 82500	8-string mandolin, mandolin eagle fingerboard inlay, "for NAMM 04 show"	Jan 22nd 04	693	4 83567	Custom 22, rosewood neck, etched gold birds	Mar 8th 04
619	n/a	n/a	n/a	694	4 83226	Singlecut Trem, pearl/gold birds	Feb 12th 04
620	4 87976	Santana II, etched silver birds	Jul 20th 04	695	4 83426	Custom 24, red/gold birds	Feb 17th 04

No.	SERIAL	DESCRIPTION	COMPLETED
696	5 93196	513 Rosewood, ivory birds	Jan 24th 05
697	4 90675	Santana II, rosewood neck, turquoise birds, bat heel inlay	Nov 15th 04
698	4 88067	McCarty Model, rosewood neck, red/gold birds	Jul 27th 04
699	4 83324	McCarty Model, maple neck, pearl/gold birds	Feb 17th 04
700	4 84114	McCarty Model, pearl/gold birds	Mar 8th 04
701	4 86204	Custom 24, pearl/gold birds	Jun 1st 04
702	4 87760	Santana, abalone birds, abalone "OM"	Jul 15th 04
703	4 87759	Santana, abalone birds, abalone "OM"	Jul 15th 04
704	4 86871	Custom 24, gold birds, "for Miles Hardenstein"	Jun 21st 04
705	4 87860	Custom 22, rosewood neck, pearl/gold birds	Oct 14th 04
706	4 87157	McCarty Model, maple neck, etched gold birds	Jun 21st 04
707	4 85717	Singlecut Trem, snakewood/gold birds	May 11th 04
708	4 88590	Archtop II, rosewood neck, ivory/gold birds, piezo	Aug 17th 04
709	4 88875	Custom 22, pearl spiral inlays, pearl signature	Aug 20th 04
710	4 89978	Hollowbody II, gold/gold birds, piezo	Oct 14th 04
711	4 90554	Hollowbody II, maple neck, pearl/gold birds, piezo	Oct 19th 04
712	4 88243	Hollowbody II, maple neck, etched ivory birds, piezo	Jul 27th 04
713	4 87913	McCarty Model, rosewood neck, paua/gold birds	Jul 27th 04
714	4 88242	Santana II, rosewood neck, etched gold birds	Jul 27th 04
715	4 88241	Custom 22, maple neck, pearl/gold birds	Jul 30th 04
716	5 92711	Santana II, maple neck, paua birds, piezo, "for 05 NAMM trade show"	Jan 24th 05
717	4 88163	Santana I, rosewood neck, red abalone birds	Jul 27th 04
718	4 87960	Hollowbody II, maple neck, etched gold birds, piezo	Jul 20th 04
719	4 88908	McCarty Model, rosewood neck, etched ivory birds	Aug 25th 04
720	5 95022	Custom 24, maple neck, turquoise/gold birds	Apr 21st 05
721	4 85504	Custom 24, abalone birds, "for 04 Tokyo trade show"	Apr 27th 04
722	5 93823	Santana II, gold/silver birds, ebony body strips	Feb 17th 05
723	4 87162	Singlecut, rosewood neck, ivory/gold birds	Jun 21st 04
724	4 87987	Custom 22, maple neck, pearl/gold birds	Jul 27th 04
725	4 88909	Custom 24, turquoise/silver birds	Aug 20th 04
726	4 92430	Hollowbody II, maple neck, silver/gold birds, piezo	Nov 15th 04
727	4 92372	Hollowbody II, maple neck, pearl/gold birds, piezo	Dec 21st 04
728	4 87139	McCarty Model, maple neck, pearl/gold birds	Jun 21st 04
729	4 90628	Hollowbody II, maple neck, tiger and cobra inlays, piezo	Oct 19th 04
730	4 89293	Custom 24, rosewood neck, snakewood/gold birds	Sep 21st 04
731	4 87137	McCarty Model, maple neck, abalone/gold birds	Jun 21st 04
732	4 88076	Santana II, rosewood neck, paua/silver birds, silver "OM"	Jul 27th 04
733	4 86073	Singlecut, rosewood neck, paua birds	Jun 1st 04
734	4 83275	Singlecut Trem, rosewood neck, turquoise birds	Mar 2nd 04
735	4 92218	Santana I, rosewood neck, "for Koichi Hanada", "Midori" and wedding inlays	Dec 21st 04
736	5 95869	Hollowbody II, maple neck, onyx/gold birds, piezo	Apr 26th 05
737	4 90670	Hollowbody II, pearl birds	Nov 15th 04
738	4 90495	Hollowbody II, pearl birds	Oct 19th 04
739	4 88205	Santana III, rosewood neck, pearl/silver dot inlays	Jul 27th 04
740	4 89734	Santana II, rosewood neck, paua birds	Sep 21st 04
741	4 89087	Santana II, rosewood neck, abalone birds	Aug 23rd 04
742	5 100429	Hollowbody II, ivory/gold birds, piezo	Oct 6th 05
743	4 89720	Santana I, rosewood neck, paua birds	Sep 21st 04
744	4 92092	McCarty Model, rosewood neck, paua/gold birds	Dec 21st 04
745	4 89489	McCarty Model, maple neck, etched gold birds	Sep 14th 04
746	4 86570	McCarty Model, rosewood neck, agoya/gold birds, "for 04 Summer NAMM show"	Jun 21st 04
747	5 92375	Custom 22 12-string, maple neck, abalone birds	Jan 24th 05
748	4 86574	Singlecut Trem, abalone/gold birds	Jun 21st 04
749	4 86573	Singlecut, pearl/gold birds, "for Eric Clapton Crossroads Guitar Festival"	Jun 2nd 04
750	4 86957	Hollowbody II, pearl/gold birds, piezo	Jun 30th 04
751	4 86795	Custom 22, rosewood neck, agoya/gold birds	Jun 21st 04
752	4 86571	Custom 24, agoya/gold birds, "for Eric Clapton Crossroads Guitar Festival"	Jun 2nd 04
753	4 87004	Custom 24, pearl/gold birds	Jul 15th 04
754	4 89487	McCarty Model, maple neck, etched gold birds	Sep 15th 04
755	4 88953	Hollowbody I, turquoise/gold birds, hummingbirds 12th-fret inlay, piezo	Oct 14th 04
756	5 94224	Custom 22, maple neck, onyx/turquoise/silver birds, "for Joey Boyer"	Mar 17th 05
757	4 87952	Custom 22, abalone/gold birds	Jul 27th 04
758	4 88244	Hollowbody II, red/gold birds, piezo	Jul 27th 04
759	4 89530	Santana I, rosewood neck, etched silver birds	Sep 21st 04
760	4 88637	McCarty Model, maple neck, pearl/gold birds	Aug 17th 04
761	5 94561	Custom 24, rosewood neck, paua/gold birds, rosewood knobs	Mar 17th 05
762	5 CE27728	CE 24 Maple Top, rosewood neck, gold/silver dot inlays	Feb 17th 05
763	4 CE27255	CE 24 Maple Top, maple neck, etched gold birds	Jul 27th 04
764	4 91521	Hollowbody II, maple neck, etched gold birds, piezo	Dec 21st 04
765	5 93204	Hollowbody II, abalone birds, piezo	Jan 24th 05
766	5 101132	Singlecut, paua/gold birds	Oct 24th 05
767	5 93821	McCarty Model, rosewood neck, tree of life inlays	Feb 17th 05
768	4 89737	Modern Eagle	Sep 21st 04
769	4 88736	Hollowbody II, rosewood neck, red/gold birds, piezo	Aug 20th 04
770	4 90490	513 Rosewood, pearl birds	Oct 27th 04
771	n/a	n/a	n/a
772	4 90489	Custom 22, maple neck, paua birds, abalone side dots, paua truss-rod-cover inlay	Oct 19th 04
773	5 96592	McCarty Soapbar, korina neck/top/back, ebony/silver birds	May 19th 05
774	5 93198	Hollowbody II, fly-fishing inlay, piezo	Jan 24th 05
775	5 96534	Archtop II, maple neck, paua/gold eagle inlay between 10th/13th frets, piezo	Feb 17th 05
776	4 88638	McCarty Model, maple neck, etched silver birds	Aug 17th 04
777	6 107160	Singlecut, rosewood neck, onyx/gold birds, mandolin eagle back-body inlay	May 22nd 06
778	4 89562	Custom 22, paua/gold birds	Sep 21st 04
779	4 90673	Hollowbody II, maple neck, pearl/gold birds, piezo	Oct 19th 04
780	5 93822	McCarty Model, pearl/gold birds	Feb 17th 05
781	5 93740	Custom 22, rosewood neck, paua/gold birds	Feb 17th 05
782	5 93589	Santana II, etched gold birds, gold "OM"	Feb 17th 05
783	4 91517	McCarty Soapbar, rosewood neck, pearl/gold birds	Nov 15th 04
784	4 92020	Hollowbody II, pearl/gold birds, piezo	Dec 21st 04
785	4 90494	Custom 24, maple neck, snakewood/gold birds	Oct 19th 04
786	4 91419	Custom 22, pearl/gold birds	Nov 15th 04
787	4 90668	Custom 24, maple neck, pearl/gold birds	Oct 19th 04
788	4 91215	McCarty Model, rosewood neck, red/gold birds	Nov 15th 04
789	5 96871	513, maple neck, ash back, ebony fret, 2 dots at 12th fret	Jun 20th 05
790	5 96879	513 Rosewood, ash back, silver birds	Jun 20th 05
791	4 89735	Hollowbody II, turquoise/gold birds, piezo	Sep 21st 04
792	4 89528	McCarty Soapbar, rosewood neck, pearl/gold birds	Sep 21st 04
793	4 89529	Custom 24, rosewood neck, abalone/gold birds	Sep 21st 04
794	4 90976	Santana II, pearl birds and "OM"	Nov 15th 04
795	5 97723	Santana, rosewood neck, paua birds, hummingbirds heel inlay, gold side dots	Jul 13th 05
796	5 93825	Santana II, abalone/gold birds, gold "OM"	Feb 17th 05
797	5 96405	Santana I, rosewood neck, red birds	May 17th 05
798	4 91516	Custom 24, onyx/silver birds	Nov 15th 04
799	4 91519	Custom 22, paua birds	Nov 18th 04
800	5 93295	McCarty Model, pearl/gold birds	Feb 18th 05
801	5 98594	Santana II, maple neck, paua/gold birds, paua "OM", piezo	Aug 11th 05
802	5 98764	Hollowbody II, maple neck, etched ivory birds, piezo	Aug 17th 05
803	5 95505	Custom 24, maple neck, etched silver birds	Apr 21st 05
804	5 93199	Custom 22, rosewood neck, paua birds	Jan 24th 05
805	5 95510	Custom 22, maple neck, etched gold birds	Apr 20th 05
806	5 93802	McCarty Model, rosewood neck, pearl/gold birds	Feb 17th 05
807	4 90493	Custom 24, pink abalone birds	Nov 5th 04
808	4 90492	Custom 24, pink abalone birds	Oct 19th 04
809	4 90577	Custom 24, pink abalone birds	Oct 19th 04
810	4 90720	Custom 24, pink abalone birds	Nov 5th 04
811	4 91187	Custom 24, pink abalone birds	Nov 15th 04
812	4 91081	Custom 24, pink abalone birds	Nov 15th 04
813	4 91190	Custom 24, pink abalone birds	Nov 15th 04
814	4 90934	Custom 24, pink abalone birds	Nov 15th 04
815	4 90933	Custom 24, pink abalone birds	Nov 15th 04
816	4 90975	Custom 24, pink abalone birds	Nov 15th 04
817	4 91325	Custom 24, pink abalone birds	Nov 15th 04
818	4 91477	Custom 24, pink abalone birds	Nov 15th 04
819	4 91520	Custom 24, pink abalone birds	Nov 18th 04
820	4 92021	Custom 24, pink abalone birds	Dec 20th 04
821	4 91944	Custom 24, pink abalone birds	Dec 20th 04
822	4 92157	Custom 24, pink abalone birds	Dec 20th 04
823	4 92249	Custom 24, pink abalone birds	Dec 20th 04
824	4 92131	Custom 24, pink abalone birds	Dec 20th 04
825	4 92132	Custom 24, pink abalone birds	Dec 20th 04
826	4 92281	Custom 24, pink abalone birds	Dec 20th 04
827	4 92373	Custom 24, pink abalone birds	Dec 20th 04
828	5 92555	Custom 24, pink abalone birds	Jan 23rd 05
829	5 93207	Custom 24, pink abalone birds	Jan 23rd 05
830	5 93197	Custom 24, pink abalone birds	Jan 23rd 05
831	5 93801	Custom 24, pink abalone birds	Feb 17th 05
832	5 93355	Custom 24, pink abalone birds	Feb 14th 05
833	5 93762	Custom 24, pink abalone birds	Feb 17th 05
834	5 94587	Custom 24, pink abalone birds	Mar 17th 05
835	5 95507	Custom 24, pink abalone birds	Apr 21st 05
836	5 95440	Custom 24, pink abalone birds	Apr 20th 05
837	5 97755	Santana II, maple neck, alder back, ivory/gold birds, ivory "OM"	Jul 18th 05
838	5 96518	Santana II, rosewood neck, pearl/gold birds	May 17th 05
839	5 101118	Santana II, maple neck, etched silver birds, silver "OM"	Oct 24th 05
840	5 93200	McCarty Soapbar, rosewood neck, snakewood/gold birds, custom bird 12th-fret inlay	Jan 24th 05
841	5 93202	McCarty Model, rosewood neck, snakewood/gold birds, custom bird 12th-fret inlay	Jan 24th 05
842	5 94575	Custom 24, maple neck, etched gold birds	Mar 17th 05
843	4 90576	Custom 24, red/gold birds	Oct 19th 04
844	5 94714	Hollowbody II, maple neck, pearl/gold birds, piezo	Mar 17th 05
845	5 94362	Santana II, red/gold birds, red "OM"	Mar 17th 05

No.	SERIAL	DESCRIPTION	COMPLETED	No.	SERIAL	DESCRIPTION	COMPLETED
846	5 93593	Custom 22 12-string, abalone/gold birds	Feb 17th 05	921	5 98770	McCarty Soapbar, rosewood neck, onyx/gold birds	Aug 11th 05
847	5 93358	Hollowbody II, turquoise/gold birds, hummingbird 12th-fret inlay, piezo	Feb 18th 05	922	6 106791	McCarty Soapbar, rosewood neck, onyx/gold birds	May 24th 06
848	5 95508	McCarty Soapbar, rosewood neck, etched ivory birds	Apr 21st 05	923	6 105284	Custom 24 chambered body, maple neck, etched gold birds	Mar 13th 06
849	5 97348	McCarty Model, maple neck, etched gold birds, gold "OM"	Jun 20th 05	924	6 105122	Custom 22, maple neck, pearl/gold birds	Mar 13th 06
850	5 94900	McCarty Model, maple neck, abalone/gold birds, signed on head	Mar 22nd 05	925	5 101967	Hollowbody II, tri-color burst, maple neck, abalone/gold birds, piezo	Dec 8th 05
851	5 94058	Santana II, etched ivory birds, ivory "OM"	Mar 17th 05	926	6 104332	Hollowbody II, maple neck, pearl/gold birds, piezo	Feb 13th 06
852	4 92369	Hollowbody II, etched gold birds, piezo	Dec 20th 04	927	6 104716	Hollowbody II, maple neck, pearl/gold birds, piezo	Feb 28th 06
853	4 92302	Santana II, etched gold birds, gold "OM"	Dec 20th 04	928	5 100462	Hollowbody II, maple neck, pearl/gold birds, piezo	Oct 6th 05
854	5 94615	Santana II, ivory/gold birds, ivory "OM"	Mar 17th 05	929	5 100664	McCarty Model, rosewood neck, abalone/gold birds	Oct 12th 05
855	5 93717	Custom 24, rosewood neck, abalone/gold birds	Feb 17th 05	930	5 101039	Custom 22, maple neck, paua/gold birds	Oct 24th 05
856	5 95509	McCarty Model, paua birds	May 27th 05	931	6 105401	Hollowbody II, maple neck, etched ivory birds	Mar 21st 06
857	5 93203	McCarty Soapbar, rosewood neck, onyx/gold birds	Jan 24th 05	932	6 106225	Hollowbody II, maple neck, etched ivory birds	Apr 24th 06
858	5 102562	Custom 24, pearl inlays, "tiger scratch" truss-rod-cover inlays	Dec 19th 05	933	5 103000	513, maple neck, pearl birds	Dec 29th 05
859	5 97501	513 Rosewood, pearl birds	Jun 21st 05	934	6 104766	513 Rosewood, coral birds	Mar 13th 06
860	5 92910	Custom 22, rosewood neck, paua birds	Jan 24th 05	935	n/a	n/a	n/a
861	5 94766	Hollowbody II, pearl/gold birds, piezo	Mar 30th 05	936	5 100608	Custom 24, maple neck, lapis/gold birds	Oct 13th 05
862	5 95941	McCarty Model, rosewood neck, etched gold birds, Custom 22 neck carve	May 17th 05	937	6 105202	Hollowbody II, maple neck, gold/silver birds, maple pickup rings	Mar 15th 06
863	5 97391	McCarty Model, maple neck, etched gold birds, Custom 22 neck carve	Jun 20th 05	938	6 105205	Hollowbody II, maple neck, ivory/gold birds	Mar 13th 06
864	5 92895	Custom 24, etched pearl birds, "for 05 NAMM trade show"	Jan 24th 05	939	5 102349	Custom 24, rosewood neck, ivory/gold birds	Dec 7th 05
865	5 92926	Custom 22, abalone birds, falcon carving on body	Feb 7th 05	940	5 101715	Santana I, maple neck, etched gold birds	Nov 10th 05
866	5 94672	Custom 22, maple neck, etched ivory birds	Mar 17th 05	941	5 100461	McCarty Model, maple neck, etched gold birds	Oct 4th 05
867	5 97841	McCarty Model, maple neck, abalone birds	Jul 13th 05	942	6 106056	Santana I, maple neck, onyx/silver birds, silver "OM"	Apr 19th 06
868	5 102786	McCarty Model, rosewood neck, etched ivory birds	Dec 21st 05	943	6 106147	McCarty Model, maple neck, etched silver birds	Apr 19th 06
869	5 98674	Custom 22, maple neck, etched gold birds	Aug 17th 05	944	5 94973	Custom 22, rosewood neck, abalone/gold birds	Mar 31st 05
870	5 98765	Hollowbody II, maple neck, gold birds	Sep 21st 05	945	6 106066	Santana II, abalone cat inlays	Apr 19th 06
871	5 98188	Custom 24, maple neck, pearl/gold birds	Jul 18th 05	946	6 105123	McCarty model, "Z06" fingerboard inlay, Corvette crossed-flags body inlay	Mar 13th 06
872	5 97417	Hollowbody II, maple neck, abalone birds, piezo	Jun 20th 05	947	5 100653	Custom 24, maple neck, ash back, pearl/gold birds	Oct 12th 05
873	6 106063	Santana Hollowbody II, maple neck, pearl/gold birds, pearl "OM", piezo	Apr 19th 06	948	5 98769	Custom 24, rosewood neck, abalone/gold birds	Aug 11th 05
874	5 102354	Hollowbody II, maple neck, abalone/gold birds, piezo	Dec 8th 05	949	6 103166	513 Rosewood semi-hollow, paua birds	Jan 6th 06
875	5 97404	McCarty Model, rosewood neck, lapis/silver birds	Jun 20th 05	950	5 101644	Custom 24, maple neck, orange spiney birds	Nov 10th 05
876	5 97355	McCarty Model, rosewood neck, ivory eagle at 11th-13th frets, Custom 22 neck carve	Jun 20th 05	951	n/a	n/a	n/a
877	6 105935	Hollowbody II, abalone/pearl birds	Apr 13th 06	952	5 101845	McCarty Model, maple neck, paua/gold birds	Nov 17th 05
878	5 96872	Modern Eagle, etched ivory birds, Santana neck carve	Jun 20th 05	953	5 98625	McCarty Model, korina neck, korina back, etched gold birds	Aug 17th 05
879	5 96594	Custom 24, rosewood neck, maple back, paua birds, violin carve to back horns	May 19th 05	954	6 106928	Custom 24 semi-hollow, maple neck, maple back, etched gold birds	May 22nd 06
880	5 97451	Hollowbody Spruce, paua birds, abalone side dots, piezo	Jun 23rd 05	955	5 100950	Custom 22, onyx/silver birds, ebony pickups rings/knobs/switch-tip	Oct 24th 05
881	5 99910	513, maple neck, ebony birds	Sep 21st 05	956	6 105499	Custom 24, pearl/gold birds	Apr 5th 06
882	5 99911	513, maple neck, ebony birds, 2 dots at 12th fret	Sep 21st 05	957	5 99021	Custom 24, pearl/gold birds	Aug 18th 05
883	5 100423	513, maple neck, pearl birds	Oct 13th 05	958	5 101047	Hollowbody II, pearl/gold birds, piezo	Oct 24th 05
884	5 97352	Custom 22, rosewood neck, pearl birds	Jun 20th 05	959	5 101704	Custom 24, maple neck, turquoise/silver birds	Nov 10th 05
885	5 98767	Santana II, etched gold birds	Aug 17th 05	960	5 100954	McCarty Model, rosewood neck, pearl/gold birds	Oct 24th 05
886	5 98124	513 Rosewood, pearl birds, "for Tim Lulliette"	Jul 18th 05	961	6 106792	Custom 22, maple neck, abalone/gold birds	May 15th 06
887	5 97772	Custom 24, rhodonite/silver birds	Jul 13th 05	962	6 105432	Archtop II, onyx/gold birds	Mar 21st 06
888	6 105242	McCarty baritone, rosewood neck, onyx/silver birds, black eagle heel inlay	Mar 15th 06	963	5 102255	McCarty Model, korina neck, korina back, pearl/gold birds	Dec 5th 05
889	5 98114	Custom 24, rosewood neck, onyx/gold moons, scripted truss-rod cover	Jul 18th 05	964	5 96036	Hollowbody II, mahogany back, ivory/gold birds, piezo	May 17th 05
890	5 98187	Santana, abalone birds, abalone "OM"	Jul 18th 05	965	5 96406	Hollowbody II, mahogany back, paua/gold birds, piezo	May 17th 05
891	5 100265	Custom 24, rosewood neck, silver birds, 2 dots 12th fret, Custom 22 neck carve	Sep 27th 05	966	n/a	n/a	n/a
892	n/a	n/a	n/a	967	5 96519	McCarty Model, rosewood neck, pearl/gold birds	May 17th 05
893	5 98001	Custom 22, maple neck, onyx/silver birds, Custom 24 neck carve	Jul 18th 05	968	5 100243	Custom 22, rosewood neck, pearl/gold inlay	Sep 27th 05
894	5 102774	Custom 22, maple neck, etched gold birds	Dec 19th 05	969	5 95763	McCarty Model, abalone/gold birds	May 26th 05
895	5 97450	McCarty Model, pearl/gold birds, Custom 22 neck carve	Jun 20th 05	970	5 95506	Custom 24, lapis/gold birds	Apr 21st 05
896	6 105891	McCarty Model, maple neck, pearl/gold birds	Apr 3rd 06	971	5 95714	Custom 24, pearl/gold birds	Apr 21st 05
897	5 97847	McCarty Model, onyx/silver birds, Custom 22 neck carve	Jul 13th 05	972	5 101956	Custom 22, rosewood neck, paua/gold birds	Nov 17th 05
898	5 98768	Hollowbody II, gold/silver birds, piezo	Aug 17th 05	973	5 97335	McCarty Soapbar, pearl/gold birds	Jun 20th 05
899	5 100009	McCarty Model, maple neck, pearl/gold birds	Sep 16th 05	974	5 96616	Custom 24, abalone/gold birds	May 18th 05
900	5 97810	McCarty Model, rosewood neck, ornate eagle plus phoenix inlay	Jul 13th 05	975	5 97351	Custom 24, paua/gold birds	Jun 20th 05
901	5 99058	McCarty Model left-hander, maple neck, etched gold birds	Aug 17th 05	976	5 97418	Custom 24, pearl/gold birds	Jun 20th 05
902	5 100463	Custom 24, maple neck, malachite/gold birds	Oct 4th 05	977	5 96619	McCarty Soapbar, abalone/gold birds	May 18th 05
903	5 101076	Santana II, rosewood neck, San Francisco skyline inlay	Oct 28th 05	978	5 97876	Custom 24, abalone/gold birds	Jul 14th 05
904	5 97420	McCarty Soapbar, rosewood neck, onyx/gold birds	Jun 22nd 05	979	5 98222	Custom 24, pearl/gold birds, "hand carving by Joseph Knaggs at 05 Tokyo show"	Jul 28th 05
905	5 105416	Custom 24 "85 reproduction", faded-look stain, original neck carve and hardware	Apr 3rd 06	980	5 98186	Custom 24, ivory/gold birds, "hand carving by Joseph Knaggs at 05 Tokyo show"	Jul 18th 05
906	5 105417	Custom 24 "85 reproduction", faded-look stain, original neck carve and hardware	Mar 22nd 06	981	5 97787	Custom 24, abalone/gold birds	Jul 13th 05
907	5 105418	Custom 24 "85 reproduction", faded-look stain, original neck carve and hardware	Apr 3rd 06	982	5 97406	Hollowbody II, pearl/gold birds	Jun 20th 05
908	5 105419	Custom 24 "85 reproduction", faded-look stain, original neck carve and hardware	Mar 22nd 06	983	5 98130	Hollowbody II, paua/gold birds, piezo	Jul 14th 05
909	5 105420	Custom 24 "85 reproduction", faded-look stain, original neck carve and hardware	Apr 3rd 06	984	6 n/a	513 Rosewood semi-hollow, ivory/silver birds, mandolin eagle back-cover inlay	May 10th 06
910	5 105421	Custom 24 "85 reproduction", faded-look stain, original neck carve and hardware	Apr 3rd 06	985	6 106149	513 semi-hollow, alder body maple neck, onyx birds, mandolin eagle back-cover inlay	May 15th 06
911	5 105422	Custom 24 "85 reproduction", faded-look stain, original neck carve and hardware	Mar 27th 06	986	6 n/a	513 semi-hollow, ash back/top, maple neck, mandolin eagle back-cover inlay	May 10th 06
912	5 105423	Custom 24 "85 reproduction", faded-look stain, original neck carve and hardware	Apr 3rd 06	987	5 98772	Hollowbody II, pearl/gold birds, piezo	Aug 17th 05
913	5 105424	Custom 24 "85 reproduction", faded-look stain, original neck carve and hardware	Apr 3rd 06	988	5 101970	Custom 24, maple neck, pearl/gold birds	Nov 17th 05
914	5 105425	Custom 24 "85 reproduction", faded-look stain, original neck carve and hardware	Mar 27th 06	989	6 105890	Hollowbody II, maple neck, pearl/gold birds, piezo	Apr 3rd 06
915	5 101737	Hollowbody II, tri-color burst, maple neck, pearl/gold birds, piezo	Dec 8th 05	990	5 101968	Custom 22, paua/gold birds	Nov 28th 05
916	6 104445	Hollowbody II, maple neck, etched ivory birds, piezo	Feb 16th 06	991	6 104818	513 Rosewood, gold birds	Mar 13th 06
917	5 101648	McCarty Model, rosewood neck, paua/gold birds	Dec 8th 05	992	5 100847	Custom 22, maple back, ivory/gold birds	Oct 19th 05
918	6 103949	Hollowbody II, maple neck, pearl/gold birds, piezo	Feb 10th 06	993	6 106242	Hollowbody II, maple neck, turquoise/gold birds, piezo	Apr 19th 06
919	5 100385	Santana II, rosewood neck, gold birds, gold "OM"	Oct 10th 05	994	6 106976	513, maple neck, abalone birds	May 15th 06
920	5 101969	Custom 22, maple neck, pearl/gold birds	Dec 8th 05	995	6 107002	Hollowbody II, maple neck, pearl/gold birds, piezo	May 15th 06

No.	SERIAL	DESCRIPTION	COMPLETED
996	5 100994	Custom 24, maple back, onyx/silver birds	Oct 24th 05
997	6 105983	513, maple neck, ivory birds	Apr 19th 06
998	5 102205	513 Rosewood, pearl birds	Dec 5th 05
999	5 101256	Custom 24, etched gold birds	Oct 28th 05
1000	6 103103	Custom 22 10th Anniversary 1st/only prototype, rosewood neck, custom inlays	Jan 13th 06
1001	n/a	n/a	n/a
1002	6 105521	McCarty Model, rosewood neck, pearl/gold birds	Mar 22nd 06
1003	5 102570	Custom 22, "Z06" fingerboard inlay	Dec 28th 05
1004	5 102571	Custom 22, "Z06" fingerboard inlay	Dec 19th 05
1005	6 106065	Custom 22, "Z06" fingerboard inlay, Corvette crossed-flags body inlay	Apr 19th 06
1006	6 106316	Custom 22, "Z06" fingerboard inlay, Corvette crossed-flags body inlay	Apr 24th 06
1007	6 104819	Hollowbody II, maple neck, paua/gold birds, piezo	Mar 14th 06
1008	5 96348	Santana II, maple neck, etched silver birds	May 17th 05
1009	6 105965	513, maple neck, silver birds	Apr 19th 06
1010	6 105964	513, maple neck, ivory birds	Apr 19th 06
1011	6 106051	Hollowbody II, maple neck, pearl/gold birds, piezo	Apr 19th 06
1012	6 105204	Custom 24, rosewood neck, abalone/gold birds, "for Bryan Saleeba"	Mar 14th 06
1013	5 97353	Custom 22, rosewood neck, pearl/gold birds	Jun 20th 05
1014	5 96522	Custom 22, pearl/gold birds	May 17th 05
1015	5 97916	Hollowbody II, pearl birds, piezo	Jul 18th 05
1016	6 105129	513 Rosewood, silver birds, "for DOI"	Mar 14th 06
1017	6 105451	Custom 22, rosewood neck, abalone birds	Mar 21st 06
1018	6 104259	Custom 24, maple neck, red/gold birds	Feb 27th 06
1019	6 105934	McCarty Model chambered body, maple neck, paua/gold birds	Apr 19th 06
1020	6 107497	Santana Hollowbody II, maple neck, etched gold/pearl birds, gold "OM"	May 30th 06
1021	5 102523	Custom 22, rosewood neck, onyx/silver birds	Dec 19th 05
1022	5 102524	Custom 24, rosewood neck, onyx/silver birds	Dec 19th 05
1023	6 100421	Santana II, "Rasta colored stripes", rosewood neck, etched gold birds, gold "OM"	Apr 20th 06
1024	5 102328	Custom 22, pearl/gold birds, rosewood knobs/pickup rings	Dec 15th 05
1025	6 103012	Custom 24, rosewood neck, paua/gold birds, paua side dots	Jan 12th 06
1026	n/a	n/a	n/a
1027	6 106793	Custom 22 Soapbar, maple neck, white gold/gold birds	May 23rd 06
1028–1030		n/a	n/a
1031	5 98033	McCarty Model, maple neck, abalone birds, Santana neck carve	Jul 18th 05
1032–1033		n/a	n/a
1034	6 107444	Custom 22 12-string, paua birds, snakewood tuner buttons	May 31st 06
1035	5 97727	Custom 22, maple neck, abalone/gold birds, rosewood heel cap	Jul 13th 05
1036	5 99737	Custom 24, maple neck, ivory birds, 2 side dots 12th fret, "for Nagase Special"	May 15th 06
1037	5 99855	McCarty Model, abalone/rosewood birds, 2 dots at 12th fret	Sep 16th 05
1038	5 99686	Custom 24, abalone birds, 2 dots at 12th fret	Sep 16th 05
1039	5 100420	McCarty Model, maple neck, abalone birds, 2 dots at 12th fret	Oct 3rd 05
1040	6 106815	Hollowbody II, maple neck, pearl/rosewood/silver birds	May 15th 06
1041	5 99600	Custom 24, gold/silver birds	Sep 26th 05
1042–1051		n/a	n/a
1052	6 106808	Custom 22, maple neck, abalone/gold birds	May 15th 06
1053	6 106401	Santana II, rosewood neck, onyx/silver birds, silver "OM"	Apr 20th 06
1054	6 105360	Hollowbody II, pearl/gold birds, piezo	Mar 20th 06
1055	6 105077	Custom 24, pearl/gold birds	Mar 13th 06
1056	5 98397	Custom 24, pearl/gold birds	Jul 28th 05
1057	5 99001	Custom 24, gold eagle/dot markers/side dots	Aug 17th 05
1058	5 98675	Custom 22, gold eagle/dot markers/side dots	Aug 11th 05
1059	5 98785	McCarty Soapbar, pearl/gold birds	Aug 17th 05
1060	5 98523	Custom 24, pearl/gold birds	Aug 11th 05
1061	5 98803	Hollowbody II, lapis/gold birds	Aug 22nd 05
1062	5 98626	Custom 22, ebony/silver birds	Aug 11th 05
1063	5 98783	Hollowbody II, abalone/gold birds, gold fretwire, piezo	Aug 17th 05
1064	5 98802	McCarty Model, pearl/gold birds	Aug 17th 05
1065–1066		n/a	n/a
1067	6 103176	McCarty Model, rosewood neck, abalone birds, maple pickup rings	Jan 9th 06
1068–1070		n/a	n/a
1071	6 107138	513, maple neck, alder back, ebony birds, black side dots	May 31st 06
1072	n/a	n/a	n/a
1073	6 105203	Artist III, paua/gold birds	Mar 13th 06
1074	6 107198	Swamp Ash Special, maple top, rosewood fingerboard, glued-in neck	May 23rd 06
1075	6 104336	Custom 24, rosewood neck, turquoise/gold birds	Feb 13th 06
1076	n/a	n/a	n/a
1077	6 107193	Hollowbody II, maple neck, ivory/gold birds, piezo	May 23rd 06
1078	n/a	n/a	n/a
1079	6 107449	Hollowbody II, maple neck, paua/silver birds, piezo, custom strap buttons	May 30th 06
1080–1082		n/a	n/a
1083	6 106810	513 Rosewood, abalone birds	May 15th 06
1084	6 107201	Custom 22, gold "20th" (anniversary) on truss-rod cover, abalone/gold birds	May 23rd 06
1085	n/a	n/a	n/a
1086	6 106814	Custom 22, maple neck, paua/gold birds	May 15th 06
1087	6 107415	McCarty Model, rosewood neck, ivory/gold birds	May 23rd 06

No.	SERIAL	DESCRIPTION	COMPLETED
1088–1090		n/a	n/a
1091	6 107316	Custom 22, maple neck, abalone birds	May 23rd 06
1092–1095		n/a	n/a
1096	6 103424	Gary Grainger Bass, maple neck, abalone/gold birds	Jan 13th 06
1097–1099		n/a	n/a
1100–1101		n/a	n/a
1102	6 107499	Modern Eagle 24-fret	May 30th 06
1103–1106		n/a	n/a
1107	5 101367	Modern Eagle	Oct 31st 05
1108–1112		n/a	n/a
1113	6 106910	McCarty Model, snakewood/gold birds, Custom 22 neck carve	May 22nd 06
1114	6 107348	Custom 22 Soapbar, rosewood neck, ash back, paua/gold birds	May 23rd 06
1115	n/a	n/a	n/a
1116	6 107380	McCarty Model, lapis/gold birds, Custom 22 neck carve	May 30th 06
1117–1118		n/a	n/a
1119	6 107162	McCarty Model, abalone/gold birds, Custom 22 neck carve	May 22nd 06
1120	6 105666	Standard 24, ebony fingerboard, pearl eagle and side dots	Apr 5th 06
1121	6 107203	McCarty Model, rosewood neck, abalone birds, Custom 22 neck carve	May 17th 06
1122–1123		n/a	n/a
1124	6 107161	Hollowbody I, koa top, pearl/gold birds, piezo	May 22nd 06
1125–1128		n/a	n/a
1129	5 100396	Singlecut Trem, pearl/gold birds	Oct 6th 05
1130–1143		n/a	n/a
1144	5 100125	Custom 24, pearl eagle and 12th-fret bird	Oct 13th 05
1145	5 102769	Singlecut, gold/silver birds	Dec 21st 05
1146	5 102814	Singlecut, etched gold/silver birds	Dec 28th 05
1147	5 102770	Singlecut Trem, pearl/gold birds	Dec 21st 05
1148–1151		n/a	n/a
1152	5 101957	Custom 22, maple neck, pearl/gold birds	Nov 28th 05
1153–1207		n/a	n/a
1208	6 107494	McCarty Model 12-string, maple neck, abalone birds, wide-thin Santana neck carve	May 31st 06
1209–1210		n/a	n/a
1211	6 106790	Custom 22, maple neck, tree-of-life inlays	May 15th 06
1212–1226		n/a	n/a
1227	6 106146	513 Rosewood, ivory/gold eagle 11th-13th frets, "for Martin Barre from Jethro Tull"	Apr 19th 06
1228	6 103404	Custom 24 10th Anniversary 1st/only prototype, rosewood neck, multiple-inlay	Jan 31st 06
1229	6 103412	Singlecut Trem 10th Anniversary 1st/only prototype, rosewood neck, multi-inlay	Jan 13th 06
1230	6 103402	Custom 22 10th Anniversary, rosewood neck, multiple inlay	Jan 13th 06
1231	6 103403	Singlecut Jumbo Thinline, "for NAMM 06 trade show"	Jan 13th 06
1232	6 100776	Singlecut Jumbo Archtop	Jan 9th 06
1233	5 102965	Singlecut, cedar back, paua birds	Dec 29th 05
1234	6 107347	513, maple neck, alder back, ebony birds	May 23rd 06
1235–1238		n/a	n/a
1239	6 103167	McCarty Model, Schultz red-tail-hawk top inlay, "for Private Stock 10th anniversary"	Jan 13th 06
1240–1244		n/a	n/a
1245	6 104258	Custom 24 left-hander, pearl/gold birds	Feb 13th 06
1246–1281		n/a	n/a
1282	6 104331	Custom 24, gold/silver birds	Feb 24th 06
1283	6 106788	Santana I, maple neck, ivory/gold birds, ivory "OM"	May 15th 06

DATING INFORMATION

The serial number on each instrument provides the most reliable method for determining its age. Details of the systems used are given here, along with date-related spec changes.

SERIAL NUMBERS

The serial number that appears on virtually every PRS production instrument can be used as a reasonably accurate guide to the year in which it was produced.

SET-NECK SERIALS

The present system at PRS is that each guitar is assigned its sequential number (currently five digits) when the body and neck have been sanded, and before the guitar enters the finish area. On solidbody instruments this is written in the rear pickup cavity. The full number – with single-digit year prefix added to the sequential number – is painted on to the back of the headstock, after the guitar has received its colour coat finish and before it receives its top coat finish.

That single-digit prefix is a good guide to the date of production of a PRS guitar, although there are some problems with this method. Here are the prefixes and relevant years:

SERIAL NUMBER PREFIX DIGIT: YEAR CODES

Prefix Number	Year
0	1990, 2000
1	1991, 2001
2	1992, 2002
3	1993, 2003
4	1994, 2004
5	1985, 1995, 2005
6	1986, 1996, 2006
7	1987, 1997, 2007
8	1988, 1998
9	1989, 1999

As you can see, some of the prefixes apply to instruments from two or three different years decades apart. In most cases when the decade of the production of a guitar is in question, it can be determined by other factors, most of which are dealt with in the Model Key. But we have also calculated for your assistance a rough guide to the sequential numbers used for each year. These have been determined by a combination of information from PRS's own records, as well as logging the numbers of several hundred PRS guitars and wielding a calculator and a bottle of Lagavulin. Please note that we've arrived at estimates only, and that it is quite likely that numbers will be seen that fall beyond the allocated years, especially in the early part of the list. Note also that these numbers apply only to set-neck guitars. Basses and bolt-on-neck guitars have separate sequences, noted nearby. This help-list for set-neck guitars is intended primarily to provide general guidance with the "which decade" question.

SET-NECK GUITARS: SEQUENTIAL NUMBERS

Approximate Numbers	Year
0001-0400	1985
0401-1700	1986
1701-3500	1987
3501-5400	1988
5401-7600	1989
7601-10100	1990
10101-12600	1991
12601-15000	1992
15001-17900	1993
17901-20900	1994
20901-24600	1995
24601-29500	1996
29501-34600	1997
34601-39100	1998
39101-44499	1999
44500-52199	2000
52200-62199	2001
62200-72353	2002
72354-82254	2003
82255-92555	2004
92556-103103	2005
103104-114940	2006
114941-	2007

The final start number was the only information available for 2007 at the time of writing. Here's a few examples to show how the numbers combine. A serial number reading 5 0155 indicates a guitar from 1985. That first 5 could make it an '85, '95 or 2005: the sequential number 0155 confirms 1985. The number 9 6038 indicates a guitar from 1989. The first 9 could be on an '89 or a '99 guitar, but the sequential number 6038 confirms 1989.

The serial number 3 17512 on a guitar indicates that it was produced in 1993. The first 3 confirms that, as does the sequential number 17512. And a serial number reading 8 35895 indicates a guitar from 1998. The first 8 could make it an '88 or a '98: the sequential number 35895 confirms 1998.

BASSES AND BOLT-ON-NECK GUITARS

The early PRS bass guitars (set-neck and bolt-on models) and the bolt-on-neck guitars (the various CE, EG and Swamp Ash Special models) have serial number systems separate from the set-neck guitars already covered.

BASS SERIALS

Bolt-on basses have a serial number that starts with a single-digit year prefix (see Prefix: Year Codes table, left). The year prefix is followed by a 4, the code number to denote a bolt-on-neck bass. After the year digit and the 4 is a four-digit sequential number. For example, 1 40188 would indicate a 1991 (the first 1) bolt-on-neck bass (the opening 4) sequential number 0188. Approximate sequential numbers from PRS's records are as follows:

SET-NECK GUITARS: BOLT-ON-NECK BASSES: SEQUENTIAL NUMBERS

Approximate Numbers	Year
0001-0030	1989
0031-0140	1990
0141-0200	1991

Set-neck basses have a serial number that starts with a single-digit year prefix (see Prefix: Year Codes table, left). The year prefix is followed by a 9, the code number to denote a set-neck bass. After the year digit and the 9 is a four-digit sequential number. For example, 7 90168 would indicate a 1987 (the first 7) set-neck bass (the opening 9) sequential number 0168. Approximate sequential numbers from PRS's records are as follows:

SET-NECK BASSES: SEQUENTIAL NUMBERS

Approximate Numbers	Year
0001-0230	1986/87
0231-0350	1988
0351-0680	1989
0681-0730	1990
0731-0800	1991

A new bass model appeared in 2000, the Electric Bass (plus Maple Top variant). Serial numbers for these are prefixed with the letters EB. Approximate sequential numbers from PRS's records are as follows:

ELECTRIC BASS: SEQUENTIAL NUMBERS

Approximate Numbers	Year
00007-00072	2000
00073-00199	2001
00200-00422	2002
00423-00501	2003
00502-00632	2004
00633-00642	2005

According to PRS's records just 439 Electric Basses were shipped during the production period. Just nine basses shipped in 2005 fulfilling existing orders taken the previous year.

CE SERIALS

The various CE models have a serial number that usually appears on the neckplate (the square-shape plate on the back of the body that reinforces the neck/body joining screws). The serial numbers for CEs start with a single-digit year prefix (see Prefix: Year Codes table, above left). The year prefix is followed by a 7 or CE, the code number or letters that denote a CE model. After the year digit and the 7 or CE is a four- or five-digit sequential number. For example, 0 72737 would indicate a 1990 (the first 0) CE model (the opening 7) sequential number 2737. Or, 8 CE19249 would indicate a 1998 (the first 8) CE model (the opening CE) sequential number 19249. During 1998 the this confused picture was cleared up when all CE serials were given a "CE" prefix instead of a 7. For example, a CE Maple Top model completed in January 2002 was numbered 2 CE23319 on the neck plate. This indicated 2002 (the opening 2) CE model (the CE prefix) and sequential number 23319. Approximate sequential numbers from PRS's records are:

CE MODELS: SEQUENTIAL NUMBERS

Approximate Numbers	Year
0001-0270	1988
0271-1830	1989
1831-3200	1990
3201-4540	1991
4541-7090	1992
7091-8820	1993
8821-10700	1994
10701-13000	1995
13001-14680	1996
14681-17130	1997
17131-19580	1998
19581-20749	1999
20750-21599	2000
21600-23199	2001
23200-25389	2002
25390-26399	2003
26400-27900	2004
27901-29200	2005
29201-31800	2006
31801-	2007

EG SERIALS

The various EG models have a serial number that usually appears on the neckplate (the square-shape plate on the back of the body that reinforces the neck/body joining screws). The serial numbers for EGs start with a single-digit year prefix (see Prefix: Year Codes table, far left). The year prefix is followed by a 5, the code number to denote an EG model. After the year digit and the 5 is a four-digit sequential number. For example, 1 51224 would indicate a 1991 (the first 1) EG model (the opening 5) sequential number 1224. Approximate sequential numbers from PRS's records are as follows:

EG MODELS: SEQUENTIAL NUMBERS

Approximate Numbers	Year
0001-0920	1990
0921-1290	1991
1291-2070	1992
2071-2870	1993
2871-3190	1994
3191-3300	1995

SE SERIALS

The Korean-made PRS range has a single serial-number decal on the back of the headstock.

Prefix Letter	Year
A	2000
B	2001
C	2002
D	2003
E	2004
F	2005
G	2006
H	2007

During the first year of production (2001) a five-digit sequential number was prefixed by the letter B. This was due to change in 2002 to a letter C prefix. First-version Santana SEs therefore have a B prefix, while second-version models produced late in 2001 retain the same prefix despite the spec changes on the guitar. For example, a second-version SE made late in 2001 and displayed at the winter NAMM show in January 2002 had the serial number B10179.

SWAMP ASH SPECIAL SERIALS

The Swamp Ash Special has a serial number that usually appears on the neckplate (the square-shape plate on the back of the body that reinforces the neck/body joining screws). The first 200 Swamp Ash Specials made from January 1996 to June 1997 were allocated CE-style serial numbers. After that, a separate sequence was started for Swamp Ash Specials. These appear to start with 7, 7 SA, or 8 (to denote a Swamp Ash Special) and then a five-digit sequential number. During 1998 the confusion was cleared up when all SA serials were given an "SA" prefix instead of an 8. For example, a Swamp Ash Special model with a completion date in June 2001 was numbered 1 SA01309 on the neck plate. This indicated 2001 (the opening 1) SA model (the SA prefix) and sequential number 01309. Approximate sequential numbers from PRS's records are as follows:

SWAMP ASH SPECIAL: SEQUENTIAL NUMBERS

Approximate Numbers	Year
00001-00410	1997
00411-00760	1998
00761-00969	1999
00970-01179	2000
01180-01399	2001
01400-01899	2002
01900-02099	2003
02100-02287	2004
02288-02700	2005
02701-02800	2006
02801-	2007

GENERAL SPEC CHANGES

Although the serial number charts (here) and the other information contained in the Model Key should enable you to date your PRS guitar, the various changes made to the guitars over the years can also be usefully noted.

BODY THICKNESS

As more models have been added to the PRS line, the number of body thicknesses has changed accordingly.

Customs, Standards, and CEs (two horns/non-Singlecut shape): 1.929" (49mm)
McCartys: 2.054" (52.2mm)
Singlecut Tremolos, Singlecut Standard Satin and Singlecut Standard Soapbar Satin: 2.098" (53.3mm)
Singlecuts (thick body with four knobs and upper switch): 2.29" (58.2mm)
Santanas: 2.093" (53.2mm)
Hollowbodies: 2.796" (71mm)

Dimensions are from the back surface to the thickest part of the top surface of the body. Just keep in mind that sanding and finish will slightly change these dimensions.

HEADSTOCK LOGO

Up to the start of 1995, the Paul Reed Smith "signature" logo on the headstock of the main production guitars consisted of a gold decal (transfer) under the finish. Very early 1985 guitars had no logo at all. From 1995 the signature was changed to a raised, gold-plated metal logo placed on top of the finish.

Paul Reed Smith's handsigned signatures on the headstock indicate the Signature and Limited Edition guitars, although these have also been used on occasional one-off models.

The handmade pre-factory guitars used an eagle inlay on the headstock. This returned for the Guitars Of The Month and Private Stock instruments (and was also occasionally used on special one-offs). Private Stock instruments always use the single large eagle inlay on an un-purfled rosewood headstock facing. Further levels of headstock decoration indicate one of the Artist Series models or the various limited-edition instruments.

During 2000 and 2001 certain Electric Bass, Swamp Ash Special and Custom 22 Soapbar models were fitted with a raised black chromed-plastic signature logo on the headstock, dependent upon model and colour. PRS says it decided not to proceed with this type of logo.

NUTS, NUT WIDTHS AND HEELS

The standard nut on all PRS guitars is made from a friction-reducing black plastic. From the late nineties Rytan, a harder nut material (also slightly greyer in colour), is used for certain instruments. Late pre-factory and very early factory production samples have a slightly yellow-tinged plastic nut, but this material proved too slippery to cut.

Three main neck profiles are offered by PRS. The "regular" neck is 1 21/32" (42mm) wide at the nut. The "wide-thin" neck has a nut width of 1 11/16" (42.9mm). The "wide-fat" neck has the same nut-width as the wide-thin, but with a bigger cross-section, similar to the regular neck. The wide-fat neck is invariably identified by its longer heel. The shorter regular neck heel is quite rounded, while the wide-thin's heel is smaller and a little flatter.

The Santana features a 1 21/32" (42mm) nut width, the same as the regular, but Smith describes the shape as "a little fuller and slightly rounder. It's thicker front to back, the thickest we make." The "513 neck carve is very close to that of the wide-fat profile", says PRS, "but the nut width is in between our wide-fat and regular at about 1 43/64"" (42.5mm). Unsurprisingly, the Custom 22/12 has the widest nut width at 1 47/64" (44mm).

PICKUPS & ELECTRICS

The primary pickup and electronics changes are documented on pages 80-81, and the pickups themselves are listed on the follwing page. Apart from various minor component changes over the years, a major visual difference occurred in June 1995 when the new PCB-mounted five-way rotary switch replaced the older "open-style" switch. (To see this, you need to have the rear electrics cover plate removed.)

The original wiring of the Swamp Ash Special (see page 81) changed in mid 2003. The pull-push switch now splits the bridge pickup (instead of the neck pickup) to single-coil and activates the centre pickup.

SCALE LENGTH & FINGERBOARD RADIUS

PRS's standard scale length is 25" (635mm). The Santana is shorter at 24.5" (622mm) and this scale has been adopted for the 2007 SC 245. The 513 has the longest scale length at 25.25" (641mm). The fingerboard radius of PRS guitars is 10" (254mm) with the exception of the Santana and the Custom 22/12 where it's flatter at 11.5" (292mm)

SIDE DOTS

Late in 1999 PRS changed the side-dot material from nickel-silver to Delrin plastic. The reason, cited on the ECN implemented 1st Dec, was that the new material was "more visible for the player". For nearly 20 years, all PRS guitars, unusually, featured just one side dot at the 12th fret whereas virtually all other brands feature two. The first PRS guitar to feature two side dots was the 513 Rosewood. According to an ECN implemented 12th January 2005, double dots would be now be added to all 25" scale necks.

STOP-TAIL

Made of machined aluminium and always engineered by Excel, the Stop-Tail bridge/tailpiece is primarily gold-or nickel-plated. (Anodised Stop-Tails, both gold-and chrome-coloured, have appeared on various one-offs.) The Adjustable Stop-Tail first appeared on the McCarty Archtop in 1998, though earlier one-offs and some artist-intended guitars featured this bridge before that date.

TRUSS-ROD

In 1992 the truss-rod in PRS necks was changed from a single-action rod to a dual-action type. This is easily identified: the single-action rod has a brass-coloured adjustment nut with a collar: the dual-action has a steel-coloured nut without a collar. The truss-rod cover is plain black plastic on the majority of production guitars.

TUNERS

Very early Virginia-Avenue guitars used Schaller-made large-bodied tuners with chrome-winged locking collars instead of the standard black collars. All tuners were changed to 14:1 ratio "low mass" mini-Schaller types by February 1st 1998. Tuner buttons on all McCarty Hollowbody and Archtop models are ebony; standard models retained large chrome buttons until 1999 when these were changed to "ebonized" black plastic buttons.

The McCarty Model marked the introduction on the production guitars of non-locking Kluson-style "vintage" tuners. Earlier, the first-series EG models came as standard with non-locking Schaller M6 tuners, while today's Hollowbody and Archtop models use non-locking low-mass Schaller tuners.

New locking tuners were fitted from January 2002 on all models specified with "low mass locking tuners". They are a new PRS design also made by Schaller. Instead of the top-mounting cam-locking collar, a ribbed black locking bolt sits on top of the string post with a coin slot that allows firm locking or unlocking of the string within the post. Also, the plastic ebony-look buttons were changed back to standard chrome (Schaller mini size) at the same time, with the exception of the proper ebony buttons on the McCarty Hollowbody and Archtop guitars.

VIBRATO

From 1985 to the early 1990s the PRS vibrato was made by John Mann's company, Mann Made USA. The top-plate and block are a one-piece brass casting, either nickel-or gold-plated. Excel (see page 51) began making the PRS vibrato in the early 1990s. Originally they made it as a two-piece machined brass item, easily identified by the visible bolts on the top-plate (below the saddles). For a short period in 1992-93 Excel made a polished stainless-steel-topped bridge with, initially, brass and then an aluminium block. Excel believe they made around 2,000 of these bridges before they reverted to the two-piece brass design during 1993. (No doubt the actual units appeared on later-date PRS Guitars – for example, the stainless-steel bridge, according to PRS's Sales Guide, appeared on guitars made during 1993-94.) In February 1997 the stainless-steel saddle-screws for height and intonation adjustment were changed to nickel-plated brass.

PRS-RELATED PATENTS

US Patent No 4,295,404: Compensated Nut for a Lute-Type Instrument.
Inventor: Paul Reed Smith
Assignee: DiMarzio Musical Instrument Pickups (later reassigned to PRS Guitars)
Filed: March 14th 1980
Granted: October 20th 1981
Relates to: A nut design to improve tuning accuracy. All Paul Reed Smith/PRS guitars made since 1980 use a nut that's placed closer (compensated) to the first fret position.

US Patent No 4,453,443: Pitch Stabilized String Suspension System for Musical Instruments.
Inventor: Paul Reed Smith
Assignee: PRS Guitars
Filed: April 13th 1982
Granted: June 12th 1984
Relates to: The PRS vibrato and various other bridges, nut-end termination designs, roller nut, roller bridge and string ball-end attachment.

US Patent No 4,589,321: String Attachment Means for a Tuning Machine.
Inventor: Eric K. Pritchard
Assignee: PRS Guitars
Filed: June 25th 1984; Granted: May 20th 1986
Relates to: The original PRS locking-tuner design.

A patent for the piezo circuitry relating to PRS's piezo bridge system is applied for but not yet granted.

PRS PICKUPS

Here we list the various PRS pickups, and compile a collection of what the company said about them through the years – with some more recent comments from Paul Reed Smith thrown in for good measure.

ARTIST BASS *

"Driven by vintage alnico, this neck pickup has a unique and beautiful tone. The winding is a little hotter than our Vintage Bass. A favourite of Paul's. [Suitable for] blues, rock and jazz."

ARTIST TREBLE *

"Sounds clear and full with tons of tone," said PRS at the time of the pickup's launch. "This bridge pickup is built similarly to the Artist Bass, with extra turns for added warmth. [Suitable for] blues, rock, jazz."

CHAINSAW

"Dark low-end, Chainsaw high-end. "Basically," Smith says, "these were Deep Dishes with stainless-steel slug polepieces on both sides. It was a very powerful mid-heavy pickup. I hardly remember it." It was used on early Classic Electrics in the bridge position, before the twin-Vintage layout was settled on for that model. "We changed pretty quickly, if I remember correctly," says Smith. "You know why we called it a Chainsaw? It sounded like one!"

DAVID GRISSOM

"It was based on an original and favourite Standard Treble pickup that David really liked," Smith recalls now. PRS said: "David gets a tone all his own. This pickup combines alnico magnet types for a big Texas sound. With a vintage Marshall and a 4 x 12 cab and the gain on six... look out!"

DEEP DISH

"Fat, woody tone." Smith smiles when he says that the name came from deep-dish pizzas. "Our bobbins are a little deeper than Gibson's, for example," he explains. "Ours are about 40-thousandths of an inch deeper, so that we could get more turns around them. The idea was to get them to sound like a P-90. We must have wound 30 or 40, and I'd be playing in a band every night with a new version on my guitar. Then I found one I really liked, and that became the Deep Dish pickup. I used that for ages, it's still in the guitar [his rosewood-neck amber Dragon: see page 71]. Then we changed the magnet to an alnico II type – they have less bass – and that's where the Deep Dish II came from. It replaced the Deep Dish."

DEEP DISH II

"Fat, warm humbucker with single-coil tonal characteristics," said PRS. "The Alnico-driven coils of this pickup are wound deeper and with more turns than a vintage humbucking, similar in sound to an old P-90 single-coil: big and warm with a clear high-end. The Deep Dish II is the perfect bridge pickup for fattening up the tone without losing clarity or adding unwanted grind and harshness."

DH TREBLE

"I don't really remember what this was... sort of a Deep Dish monster," laughs Smith. PRS said at the time: "DH stands for Dan Huff, studio guitarist from the band Giant. Dan's tone is 'Giant'. A wide, modern sound, grinding and powerful, while retaining the clarity and audibility of each note. Hot alnico for modern rock."

DRAGON BASS *

"Designed for the neck position. The tone is perfect. This lower-output pickup has a combination of rich, warm bass with 'angelic' high-end. Beautiful for solos. The Dragon is also our best jazz pickup. Vintage alnico and vintage winding. [Suitable for] all types of music."

DRAGON TREBLE *

"Paul's personal favourite," said PRS. "Sounds great clean or high-gain. Fat, fat, fat with zero loss of clarity. The Dragon Treble uses a powerful ceramic magnet combined with our highest number of turns. [Suitable for] blues, rock, metal."

DRAGON II TREBLE * and BASS *

"We're changing some of the pickups, adding covers and changing the tone. They won't be as powerful," said Smith back in 1997, just before these covered pickups were announced. "The PRS sound is very clear and powerful with no harsh high-end. It's not as rhythm-guitary as a Fender in some ways, but it's also not as dark as some Gibson stuff... it's powerful and clear. The new pickups are not as powerful: they're more woody-sounding, with more tone. Not that they didn't sound that way before, but I think there's a move to a more natural tone." Carlos Santana is now using these pickups.

513 *

The completely new-design pickups that were conceived for this guitar are patent-pending. They are only available on this guitar and immediately recognisable by their domed plastic covers (see page 118-119).

HFS TREBLE *

"Hot, fat and screams. A kick-butt lead tone." First appeared as the bridge pickup on the Special. In 1993 it was described as "PRS's most popular pickup. The HFS is wound hot with a ceramic magnet for power. Wound to sound a little dark when clean, the HFS comes alive when cranked up through a hot amp. The single-coil sounds are also real nice. There is a trick to making a ceramic magnet pickup musical and not harsh; the HFS incorporates this specialised winding. [Suitable for] rock".

HFS II

"Powerful humbucker with 'metal' bass, solid mids and smooth highs," said PRS. Appeared on some early EG models.

HIGH INDUCTANCE PASSIVE BASS

These passive single-coil pickups are stock items on the Electric Bass and Electric Bass Maple Top models. "The inductance of the pickups is increased by the amount of metal that's in the pickup," explains Winn Krozack. "Basically there's one big slug, or core, with an alnico magnet underneath." Krozack says that, compared to a Fender Jazz Bass pickup, it should help to create a thicker-sounding note and increase the lower end, primarily the lower-midrange. "We tried to give it a classic sound character, although our pickups are a bit stronger in output than vintage pickups."

The top of these pickups have a radius that matches the string curve, and incorporate we a thumb rest. "We thought it would be convenient to have a thumb rest," says Krozack. "Without some protection, we figured a player might rest their thumb on the pickup and, over time, damage the coils."

HOT VINTAGE TREBLE

"Hot and sweet." This one was standard in the bridge position on the Studio model, partnered by two PRS single-coils.

JH TREBLE * AND BASS *

Described by PRS, the JH Treble is "a cross between a clear McCarty treble pickup and an over-wound 'Country Style' single-coil. Johnny [Hiland] is able to get an enormous amount of versatility with this pickup which allows him to play almost any style of music." Apparently the pickup is based on a new David Grissom pickup that should surface in 2007. "The JH Bass is a powerful and clear pickup with lively vintage characteristics. It complements the JH Treble pickup perfectly."

PRS MODEL

(see McCarty Treble)

McCARTY ARCHTOP TREBLE * and BASS *

Developed for the '98 launch of the McCarty Archtop and Hollowbody. These covered humbuckers use the same wire and alnico magnets as the McCarty Treble and Bass but with fewer turns and a lower output. A third pair of McCarty series pickups, the 5000T and 5000B, sit spec-wise halfway between these Archtop pickups and the standard McCarty pickups; they have been used for artist-intended guitars but have not appeared on any production instruments.

McCARTY TREBLE * and BASS *

"Dragon bass pickups are essentially the same as McCarty pickups," explains Smith. PRS use nickel silver covers – the original McCarty pickups used nickel-plated brass covers. "The Dragon Bass evolved into the McCarty with a few teeny changes," continues Smith. "We never announced it. But it makes me think that the market has been subjected to a tremendous amount of my experimenting. However, I like to experiment. Even now we still do it. It turns out we never made that pickup on my guitar [the rosewood-neck amber Dragon on page 71] which I love so much. So there may be some more changes. Is that bad?" Obviously not. These pickups, which replicate those on Paul's amber Dragon, appeared as "PRS Model" humbuckers on the Dragon 2000.

PRS NUMBERS *

PRS has named many of its new pickups with numbers – like the Singlecut 7s and the Singlecut Trem 6s. There are also 8s, 9s and 10s but at the time of writing these are not available on standard PRS models, although they are used for artist guitars and as the basis of new designs. The 8 Treble and Bass are what Paul Reed Smith has in his own Dragon guitar (see page 71) and he refers to them as "reproductions of the original McCarty prototype pickups," though both are slightly hotter than the standard-spec McCartys. The 9 Treble and Bass are PAF-style vintage-spec humbuckers – probably the basis for the SC 245 pickups – and the 10 Treble and Bass are again quite vintage-like but more powerful.

RP TREBLE * AND BASS *

Currently used on the Modern Eagle guitars. RP pickups (named after Ralph Perucci) are close to those on Paul Reed Smith's own Dragon (see page 71). "There are a few more turns on the treble pickup compared to my Dragon; the bass pickup has got a couple of turns less. They were originally built for Ralph: the bass pickup's a little clearer and the treble pickup's got a teeny bit more... it's not quite as clear. I really like it." Also known as Modern Eagle.

SANTANA SE first version

These alnico-loaded humbuckers with nickel-plated covers are made in China and designed by EMG's Rob Turner. "Rob is one of the few people to really crack the problem of Korean pickups sounding weak," observed Doug Chandler. Unlike many Far Eastern designs, these pickups have polepiece spacing that matches the relevant string spacing at the neck and bridge positions. "They have a big Carlos-like tone," reckons Smith. "Actually, Carlos really liked the way they sound. He played the Santana SE and asked me if it was the Santana III model. I said no!"

SANTANA SE second version

This updated guitar uses two alnico-loaded, uncovered, open-coiled humbuckers with black bobbins. Unlike the covered pickups of the first version, these new pickups are Korean-made and, despite appearances, are not based on any specific US-made PRS pickup.

SANTANA TREBLE * and BASS *

(see page 82-83)

SANTANA III TREBLE * and BASS *

Originally called New Santana pickups, this pair are stock items on the Santana III model. According to Smith they're actually a Dragon II Treble, with the old-style Gibson-type hook-up wire, and a Santana Bass with a cover "which changes it completely". He says these are the pickups that Carlos Santana is now ordering from PRS.

SE HUMBUCKERS *

"We developed them here," explains Doug Shive, "when we knew we'd be making mainly mahogany guitars and Paul had an idea of what it should sound like. So we went to the pickup winders here and got them to make some pickups and we tested them." The original 2001 Santana SE had featured covered humbuckers that the tone-hounds at PRS weren't 100 per cent happy with. "So we put the new pickups into one of those original SE's until we found a new one we liked. We sent those pickups over to a Korean pickup manufacturer, we changed after the first year of SE production, and we told them the wire gauge, magnets, number of turns... all the important aspects. They matched our pickups and sent 'em back. They sounded exactly like the ones we'd made here so we went for it. It's a good middle ground pickup, like a McCarty pickup is – you can dirty it up but it sounds good clean."

2007's Paul Allender model saw the addition of a new Korean-made humbucking pair to the SE range. "They'll have the same specs as the USA made HFS and Vintage Bass. No covers, black bobbins," says Shive.

6 TREBLE * AND BASS *

Designed for the Singlecut Trem, "the new [6] pickups lie somewhere between the Singlecut's 7 pickups and Dragon IIs", said Paul Reed Smith at the launch of the guitar in 2003. "They are powerful like a 7 but sweeter like a Dragon II – that was our intention. Pickup covers warm up the pickup's sound – no question. It's like in the old days with PAFs, people would take off the covers and think they'd look cooler but the sound was brighter. We use covers to sweeten pickups. So, if you're using an uncovered pickup you have to make them different so it actually sounds like a covered pickup."

"The treble pickup is not the same pickup at all," Smith said in late 2005 of the Singlecut Trem's bridge humbucker. "The Singlecut has a little more open sounding pickup, a little more bass and treble. The Singlecut Trem has a little bit more midrange." And presumably these pickups are different from those you use on the double-cut guitars? "Yes, you have to voice the pickups quite differently with single or double-cut guitars."

7 TREBLE * and BASS *

(see pages 102-103)

SINGLE-COIL BASS

"A single-coil (not humbucking) pickup," emphasised PRS, "in a humbucking frame,

for guitars already routed for humbuckers. A terrific Strat-sound neck position pickup." This unit appeared only on the Special model.

STANDARD BASS

"The Standard in the bass [neck] position offers the smooth rich clarity of a classic humbucker, with extra high-end bite." Partnered the Standard Treble on the Signature, Custom and Standard models.

STANDARD TREBLE

"The classic Paul Reed Smith sound. This pickup offers the smooth, rich clarity of a classic humbucker, with extra high-end bite, while still sounding warm on the high E-and B-strings." Before 1987 the Standard Treble appeared without this "warming" modification (see pickups and electrics page 80).

TREMONTI TREBLE * and BASS *

(see pages 104-105)

12-STRING TREBLE * AND BASS *

Used exclusively on the Custom 22/12, "they're based on West St. prototypes from 25 years ago", says Paul Reed Smith, "and John Ingram had a lot to do with the design. Output is about normal, but they're very clear". The centre Fralin single-coil on the 22/12 is, "the Blues Special", confirms Joe Knaggs. "It's a wonderful, traditional single-coil pickup with a slight bit more output than an old Strat pickup."

245 TREBLE * AND BASS *

These covered alnico-loaded humbuckers are designed to sound like old PAFs and are used exclusively on the 2007 SC 245.

250 TREBLE * AND BASS *

According to Paul Reed Smith these are basically the Tremonti Treble and Bass pickups and are used on the 2007 SC 250; the 250 Treble is used in bridge position of the Chris Henderson signature model.

VINTAGE TREBLE and BASS *

Originally PRS suggested these sounded "as close to the famous Patent Applied For [PAF] humbuckers as you can get", a statement Paul Reed Smith today disagrees with. "The Vintage Treble and Bass pickups offer a warm high-mid sound that's excellent for rock or jazz." This pair first appeared on the Classic Electric model. The Vintage Bass was also featured on the Special model by 1989, and the pair then cropped up on the Limited Edition guitar.

*Please note that a * next to an entry indicates pickups that are still in production.*
"Bass" refers to a neck-position pickup;
"Treble" refers to a bridge-position pickup.

DATING INFORMATION CONTINUED

INDEX

Page numbers in bold type refer to illustrations

OWNERS' CREDITS
Guitars photographed came from the following individuals' collections, and we are most grateful for their help. The owners are listed here in the alphabetical order of the code used to identify their guitars in the Key To Guitar Photographs below.

AM Adam Malone; **BS** Barbara Smith; **BZ** Bryan Zajchowski; **CB** Colin Barker; **CS** Carlos Santana; **DB** Dave Burrluck; **DG** David Grissom; **FS** Floyd Scholz; **GA** Garrett Park Guitars; **GAM** Gareth Malone; **GM** Garry Malone; **JC** Julian Carter; **JJ** Jim Jannard; **JJO** Joe Johnson; **JK** Joe Knaggs; **JR** Jim Rosenthal; **JTU** Jesse Toliver Urie; **LS** Larry Sifel; **MQ** Marc Quigley; **PA** PRS Guitars archive collection; **PD** Paul Day; **PP** PRS Guitars production; **PRS** Paul Reed Smith; **PW** Peter Wolf; **RLP** Ralph Perucci; **RM** Robert Malone; **RNP** Randy Perry; **SLS** Sarah Laine Smith; **SM** Sharon Malone; **SRS** Samuel Reed Smith; **TB** Tom Bayster; **TH** Tony Hicks; **WA** Washburn Uk; **WWS** William Warren Smith.

KEY TO GUITAR PHOTOGRAPHS
The following key is designed to identify who owned which guitars at the time they were photographed for the various editions of this book. After the relevant page number (*in italic type*) we list: the model and where necessary other identifier, followed by the owner's initials in **bold type** (see Owners' Credits above). For example, "*11/12/13* Frampton guitar **PA**" means that the Frampton guitar shown across pages 11, 12 and 13 was owned by the PRS Guitars archive.
Jacket front: main guitar McCarty Model **GAM**; smaller guitars left to right: Dragon II **BS**; Santana **PA**; Hollowbody **PP**. *Jacket front flap:* Custom **PA**. *Rear of jacket:* rear of Private Stock #13 **PA**. *8/9/10* first guitar **PA**. *9/10* first instrument **PA**. *10* second guitar **PA**. *11/12/13* Frampton guitar **PA**. *14/15* first dragon-inlay guitar **PA**. *16/17* double-neck **PA**. *18/19* mahogany guitar **PA**. *20/21* Santana guitar **CS**. *22/23* Santana double-neck **CS**. *24/25* Sorcerer's Apprentice **PA**. *26/27* PRS Guitar **PA**. *30/31* Custom **RLP**. *31/32* Custom **RLP**. *33/34/35* Custom **PA**. *36/37* Custom **PA**. *37* Custom 22 **DB**. *38* Custom 22 **PP**; Custom Soapbar **SM**. *38/39* Custom 22 lefty **WA**. *39* Custom 22 **PP**; Custom 24 **GM**. *40/41* Curly Bass-4 **TB**, employee guitar **TB**. *41* Bass-4 **PA**. *42/43* Metal **TH**. Standard 24 **PP**. *43* PRS Guitar **GA**. Standard 22 **PP**. *44/45* Standard **DG**. *45* Studio Maple Top **JC**. *46/47* Signature **SRS**, one-off **GM**. *47* Limited Edition **SLS**. *49* Three body fronts, left to right: Hollowbody **PA**; Swamp Ash **PP**; Standard 24 **PP**. Body back: Santana **PA**. *53/54* Private Stock #62 **JJ**, four burst-sequence shots **PP**. *54* Signature **SRS**. *55* Santana **TH**, Hollowbody II **GM**, detail Custom 22 **GM**. *56* Archtop Artist **GM**. Archtop II **GM**, detail **GM**. *57* Artist IV **GM**. Custom 22 **PP**, detail Artist I **WWS**. *58/59* CE 24 **PP**. Classic Electric **DB**. *60/61* CE 22 Maple Top **PP**. *61* EG 4 **JJO**. EG 3 **PD**. EG II proto **PA**. EG II lefty **JJO**. EG II **PA**. *62/63* Artist I **WWS**. Artist I proto **PA**. *64/65* Artist Limited **CB**. Artist II **BZ**. *65* Custom **JTU**. *69* HG-70 head/412 cabinet **GM**. HG-212 combo **GM**. *70/71* Dragon I proto **PRS**. *71* Dragon I **AM**. PRS Original **PRS**. *72* Dragon fingerboards, top to bottom: I proto **PRS**; I proto pearl wings **LS**; II proto **BS**; III proto **PA**. *72/73* Dragon II **GM**, Dragon III **PA**. *74/75* Dragon 2000 **GM**. *74/75/76* Dragon III lefty **RNP**. *77/78* McCarty Model **GAM**. *78/79* McCarty Model proto **PA**. *82* pre-factory Schon guitar **PA**. *82/83* Santana **PA**. *83* 10th Anniversary **PA**. *84* detail **MQ**. *84/85* Bryant employee guitar **GM**. *85* Machinehead **GM**. Rausch employee guitar **GM**. *88/89* Swamp Ash **PA**. *89* Swamp Ash proto **RLP**. Rosewood Ltd **PA**. *90* Private Stock #59 **PW**. *90/91* Private Stock #86 **GM**. *91* Private Stock #13 **PA**. Golden Eagle **RM**. *92/93* Artist III **PA**. *93* Artist IV **PA**. *94/95* McCarty Standard **PP**. *95* McCarty Model **RLP**. McCarty Soapbar **WA**. *96* Archtop proto **GM**. *96/97* Archtop II proto **JK**. *97/98* Archtop Artist **FS**. *98* Archtop II natural **PP**. Archtop II red **JR**. *99/100/101* Hollowbody II **PP**. *100/101* Hollowbody **PA**. *102/103* turquoise Singlecut **PP**. *103* Singlecut proto **GM**. *104-145* all **PP**.

Principal guitar photography was by Miki Slingsby, with the exception of the EG 3 on page 61 which was by Garth Blore. Miki Slingsby also photographed the various factory scenes on pages 48, 51, 52, 76, 91, 106-111, and the Hard Rock Café shot on page 79. The section break photographs on pages 6, 28, 86, 104 and 112, the photographs of the three Guitars Of The Month instruments on page 85 and of the guitars on pages 102 to 117 were all supplied by PRS. The section break photo on page 124, the guitars (basses and amps) featured on pages 116-145, the shot of Paul Reed Smith on page 118 were all taken by Marc Quigley. The wood blocks on pages 49 and 50 were supplied by Sid Poole and photographed by Miki Slingsby. The Guitarist Magazine cover on page 131 was conceived by Phil Millard and Matt Ward and shot by Future Publishing's in-house photography studio. The shots of Joe Knaggs on page 97, the dismembered Archtop on page 98, Paul Reed Smith and Ted McCarty on page 101, the Private Stock team and workshop on page 139, Gary Grainger/Peter Wolf on page 141, Paul Reed Smith and Doug Shive on page 144 were taken by Dave Burrluck.

MEMORABILIA and stuff illustrated in this book, including advertisements, brochures, catalogues, hardware and photographs (in fact anything that isn't a whole gee-tar), came from the collections of Tony Bacon, Dave Burrluck, Joe Johnson & Randy Perry (Excel), Howard Leese, PRS Guitars, Larry Sifel (Pearl Works), and Paul Reed Smith. These astonishing visual treats were seen through the eye of a lens by Miki Slingsby.

PRICES The prices for new instruments past and present quoted throughout the book are full US domestic list-prices in US dollars. Prices outside the US will vary. TRADEMARKS A number of non-PRS guitar products are identified in this book by their trade names (Les Paul, Stratocaster, PAF and so on), many of which are claimed as legally protected trademarks by the companies that manufacture and/or market these products. Rather than clutter the book with ™ symbols, we state here that we are simply referring to the trade names in an editorial fashion, primarily to offer comparisons of sound and design, and that in doing so we do not intend to infringe any trademark.

THE AUTHOR would like especially to thank: Georgia, Lauren, Lucy, Roxanne and Sacha, Joan and Jim and cousin Pam – I couldn't have done this without you guys.

All the staff at PRS Guitars (past and present) who have always been welcoming and supportive and have put up with all my questions, especially Bonnie Lloyd, John Ingram, Mike Deely, Laura Rausch, Rob Martin, Clay Evans, Greg Pope, Jim Cullen, Dave Hazel, Winn Krozak, Jeff Lanahan, The Dragons, Church, Rebecca Eaddy, Tina Benson, Bill Oertel, and the people of Annapolis.

Extra special thanks must go to Paul Reed Smith, Joe Knaggs, Marc Quigley, Larry Urie, Doug Shive, Peter Wolf and Jack Higginbotham.

This book would have been impossible without: Tony (lists, humour, original Model Key and Index, organisation and more lists); Nigel (he knows royalty, you know); Sally (tea and biscuits, oh, and fab design); Paul Cooper (more fab design); Phil (he boldly goes...); Miki (stories, drinks, pig-tail, driving and incredible photography); Marc (more incredible photography); Pete Chrisp (eagle eyes and Index update); Doug & Tina Chandler (inspiration, hospitality, T-shirts, Dragons and tour guides); Sid Poole, who not only provided technical and emotional support for the original book but still keeps an eye on progress; Ted McCarty, whose guiding light has been an inspiration to us all; and the Presidents of Barking. Additional thanks to Tom Wheeler for this book's foreword and for setting the standards that I've tried to follow.

And thanks to: All the staff – past and present – at Guitarist (UK), especially Neville Marten, Michael Leonard, Mark Thomas, Phil Millard, Matt Ward, and Katherine Raderecht. The Guitar & Bass Magazine (UK); Paul Day (faith, EGs, and original model chronology).

Gavin, Sue, Mark and Nick (Headline Music), Gary Sharpe (Sounds Great), David Dyke (wood info), Charlie Chandler, Jeff Pumfret and Jason Ward (Machinehead Music), Geoff Whitehorn, Phil Hilborne, Sylvie and Damian Wolf, Johnny Hiland.

And thanks to: All the staff (past and present) at Guitar Player magazine especially Andy Ellis, Tom Wheeler and Dan Erlewine for all their intelligent writing over the years. Let's not forget Larry Sifel and Pearl Works, and Joe 'n' Randy at Excel for sharing their craft. And to J.D. Considine, Stanley Hall, Rick Turner and Barnard Collier for spreading the word and the new writers, editors and photographers that continue their work.

The source material for this book was gathered primarily from the author's interviews with Paul Reed Smith and other key staff at PRS Guitars over the past years (for International Musician & Recording World, The Guitar Magazine, Guitarist, Music Business, Play and Reverb). Additional material came from Paul Reed Smith's scrapbooks. Magazines consulted for research material include Guitar For The Practising Musician, The Guitar Magazine, Guitar Player, Guitar World, Guitar Shop, Guitarist, Musician, and Vintage Guitar.

This third edition of The PRS Guitar Book is dedicated to the memory of inlay master Larry Sifel who translated the dreams of Paul Reed Smith and PRS Guitars into some of the most fantastic inlays ever seen.

PAUL REED SMITH writes: "I would like to express my debt of gratitude to those people who have supported PRS Guitars, believed in the dream and worked tirelessly to help us become what we are today. I would like to specifically thank Ted McCarty who gave his name, his knowledge and his many years of experience, and Carlos Santana, without whose support we may never have had the credibility we needed to launch this inspiring enterprise. To everyone associated with PRS Guitars, thank you for your faith and dedication."

THE PUBLISHERS would like to thank: Colin Barker; Tom Bayster; Julie Bowie; Dave Burrluck; Mario Campa & John DeSilva (Toys From The Attic); Julian Carter; Doug and Tina Chandler (Guitar XS); Pete Chrisp; Paul Cooper; Paul Day; Mike Deely; Max Fiddes; Paula Fiddes; Jack Gretz (Magdon Music); David Grissom; Heath (Brockton Music); Tony Hicks; Rick Hogue (Garrett Park Guitars); Jim Jannard; Joe Johnson (Excel); Joe Knaggs; Mike Koontz; Garry Malone; James Morgan; Gavin Mortimer (Headline Music); Music Services Inc; Randy Perry (Excel); Ralph Perucci; Jeff Pumfret (Machinehead); Laura Rausch; Phil Richardson; Jim Roberts; Ed Roman (World Class Guitars); Jim Rosenthal; Bruce Sandler (Guitar Exchange); Carlos Santana; Jorge Santana; Paul Schein (Washington Music Center); Floyd Scholz; Larry Sifel (Pearl Works); Miki Slingsby; Sally Stockwell; Larry Urie; Tom Wheeler; Peter Wolf; Michael Wright; Bryan Zajchowski (Ron's Guitars); and everyone at Anorak Magnet Holdings (2007) plc.

Special thanks to everyone at the PRS factory. We could not have wished for a more friendly and helpful reaction from everyone we met during our visit. The co-operation and team spirit that goes into producing such great guitars was a joy to behold. And multo extra special thanks to: Greg Pope for dusty numerical assistance; Scott Shirley for ensuring that the burst sequence on pages 53/54 happened on time; Marc Quigley for sending just that one last CD (and quite a few more) and for showing us the way to the clipping path; and Paul Reed Smith... for doing it.

*"This very remarkable man
Commands a most practical plan:
You can do what you want
If you don't think you can't,
So don't think you can't think you can."
Charles Inge. 1928.*